CLARISSA McNAIR was born in Mississippi, graduated from Briarcliff College in New York, and had many jobs before becoming a journalist. In Toronto, she worked as a researcher for CBC-TV's award-winning documentary on organized crime, *Connections*. In Rome, she was a news writer, newscaster, and producer of documentaries for Vatican Radio. In Los Angeles, she worked in film.

McNair has published several novels, a memoir, and has written about true crime.

Her firm, Green Star Investigations, handles all sorts of cases including missing persons, intellectual property, stolen art recovery and homicide. She has worked undercover with the Joint Terrorist Task Force, the Organized Crime Intelligence Division of the NYPD, the Federal Marshals, and the F.B.I.

McNair's show, *Basic Black*, broadcast on World Radio Paris, is vignettes of French crime, scandal, and death.

Clarissa McNair, also known as Cici, is a private detective living in Paris.

BOOKS BY CICI MCNAIR

Detectives Don't Wear Seat Belts
Never Flirt with a Femme Fatale
Kiss the Risk

BOOKS BY CLARISSA MCNAIR

Garden of Tigers
A Flash of Diamonds
Dancing With Thieves
The Hole in the Edge

Detectives Don't Wear Seat Belts:

"A wonderful, wonderful read, an amazing true story told in the voice of a born storyteller . . . she's funny, she's honest and completely fascinating . . . This is a memoir written by someone who made her own life into an adventure story, and who knows exactly how to grab your hand and pull you along."

—Perri Klass, author of *The Mercy Rule*

"This improper Southern belle's memoir as a private detective combines the immediate impact of a newspaper column with the ironic detachment of a fine novel. McNair's crafted vignettes of low-rent detectives are like chocolate truffles: dark, bittersweet and addictive."

—Bruce Schimmel, founder and columnist, *Philadelphia City Paper*

"Detectives may not wear seat belts, but you definitely should hang on to your seat when you read Cici McNair's saucy, smart memoir about a hot female P.I. from the South. I always knew Cici was a pistol, but she really blew me away with this one!"

—Lewis Burke Frumkes,
author of *How to Raise Your I.Q. by Eating Gifted Children*

"Cici McNair is the most glammapuss lady detective since Nora Charles . . ."

—Phoebe Eaton, novelist and screenwriter

Never Flirt with a Femme Fatale:

"A classic from the hands of a pro . . . what makes this book work so well is that the author is part of the drama. Besides being a fine and skilled writer, she is a Private Investigator."

—John W. Bowers, associate professor, Columbia University,
and author of *Love in Tennessee*

"Real life drama told with a master storyteller's touch. If you like Dominick Dunne then you will love *Never Flirt with a Femme Fatale*."

—Donna Huston Murray,
author of The Ginger Barnes Main Line Murder mysteries

THE DEMONS OF CORAL GABLES

*the true story of a detective,
a psychic and an exorcist*

THE DEMONS OF CORAL GABLES

*the true story of a detective,
a psychic and an exorcist*

CLARISSA McNAIR

FEDORA PRESS

Copyright © 2014 by Clarissa McNair

All rights reserved. Except as permitted under the U.S. Copyright Act of 1976, no part of this publication may be reproduced, distributed or transmitted in any form or by any means, or stored in a database or retrieval system, without the prior written permission of the publisher. This is a work of fiction; any character's resemblance to any living person is coincidental.

First edition May 2014

Library of Congress Cataloging-in-Publication Data
McNair, Clarissa
THE DEMONS OF CORAL GABLES

ISBN: 978-1-936712-07-6

This book is dedicated to the psychic and the exorcist who wish to remain anonymous, to the seven psychics of Virginia plus one little girl who gave up Halloween. You saved me and I will be forever grateful.

This book is also dedicated to the truest of friends in the darkest of times: David M. Anderson, John Doty, Lisa Romanello-Johnson, Renwick Matthews, Baroness Bronwen von-Goetze Claren, and Baroness Doreen von Karger. You gave me courage and you made me laugh.

JANUARY, 2014

Today is my birthday and it's nearly midnight so I have only a few minutes left to officially celebrate. I consider it a great privilege to be alive and a tremendous stroke of luck to feel strong and to be happy. I am writing this in Paris, in my apartment on rue Elzevir, far away from a place called Coral Gables.

I lived in that wealthy suburb of Miami, Florida, for three years. It was in the summer of 2006, when the unusual events began in my penthouse though the psychic and the exorcist said it had all started generations before. Every morning I would write down exactly what had happened during the night as if I were compiling a report for the FBI. No rapid heartbeat, no dry mouth, no descriptions of terror— just the facts. I was like an accident victim interviewing myself again and again.

I am a private detective. I deal in forensics, in facts. A rape, a murder, a stolen painting—I care deeply about the truth. I am at ease with a district attorney, not with a demonologist.

Years after leaving Coral Gables, I decided to write the story. My computer was wiped clean. Notes vanished, files were deleted. I suffered headaches so explosive I expected blood to pour out of my ears but I edited and rewrote and it became THE DEMONS OF CORAL GABLES.

If there are typos, I apologize. My good friend, Lisa, was one person enlisted to check for them. As she read about the incubus, her computer screen was suddenly flooded with pages she had never seen before. They whizzed past. Lights flashed. Finally the chaos stopped. In the center of the screen the cursor blinked on one word: LUCIFER.

My manuscript files had been deleted. Yet again. This was not an easy book to write.

I now live in an elegant hôtel particulier built four hundred years ago. Ghosts are probably here but haven't bothered me. Demons are my problem. Everyone loves a good ghost story but nobody wants to talk about the Devil.

There are thousands of books about ghosts and the supernatural. I have read none of them. This book is the story of what happened to me.

A portrait of Vasco da Gama hangs over my desk. He set sail in a small ship on a vast ocean that was filled with monsters of great size and ferocity. And if the monsters didn't get you then it was believed that you would keep sailing until you and your boat and all your crew plunged off the edge of the world. Da Gama courageously ventured into the unknown and returned to

Portugal a hero. Now we know that the earth is round but are you prepared to imagine that there might be another world, just beyond a veil that hangs invisibly within arm's reach?

I am only sure of a few things: that my birthday is in January and that there is geography. Time and space as we know them. Wristwatches, calendars, maps and plane tickets. But what if there are other kinds of time and space we know nothing about? I thought that death was the end.

But what if it isn't?

Chapter One

AUGUST, 2006
Crash! Crash! It sounded as if someone were pushing over furniture in my bedroom. Not just pushing it over but lifting it and throwing it against the wall. I was actually used to this but then the force was directed at the closed door. That frightened me. I stared at it down the hallway from my perch on the French daybed in the living room; with every crash I expected to see the white door splinter to pieces and for some unspeakably ghoulish creature to step through it. Then I saw one of the demons cross the hall and go into the kitchen. The clock said nearly 2 AM and all the lights were on but it didn't care. It was over seven feet tall, with a hunched back, the silhouette of a man with a tremendous head. An animal head like a lion's but I saw horns. It's that goat again, I thought. My eyes watered with fear as I punched in Cassandra's number. She'd be in the cemetery now with the exorcist.

JANUARY 2006
CORAL GABLES. Penthouse. Beautiful, spacious, one bedroom, one-and-a-half bath apartment with large private terraces in romantic, Spanish-style building constructed in 1998. Interior is 900 square feet. Central air, all new appliances including dishwasher, washing machine, dryer. Walk-in closet, terra cotta stone floors. Excellent location, a short walk to shops on Miracle Mile.

I was told that January was a good time to place the ad. Coral Gables had been my personal international headquarters since Halloween of 2003, but it was time to leave. I used to move when the refrigerator needed defrosting.

I was born and I grew up in Mississippi but couldn't wait to escape. As a journalist and a writer and just for fun, I lived in Toronto, Rome, London, Geneva, and Beverly Hills. There were stints in a fishing village off the coast of Tuscany, another fishing village in Portugal, and on the island of Cyprus. I traced the perimeter of Africa for a year, went round the world, have been to nearly every island in the Caribbean with lots of time in Haiti, have been pretty much all over Europe. Ventured past the Arctic Circle and as far south as Patagonia. As a private detective, I lived in New York City, spent a summer in Mississippi, and was now in Miami, but quite ready to move on.

I was reluctant to give 6% to a realtor and when I found an agency in Miami called Homes by Owner, I called them. "I work at home so I can show anyone through just about any time," I explained. The realtor, Raquel, said José would come over that week to take photographs for the website. I would owe them $2,000 for sending me possible buyers who had been pre-approved for mortgages. The fee also went for advertising; a great part of this was the internet listing.

José arrived and pronounced the apartment "great." He said he loved the Spanish architecture of the building right away— the fountain in front, the tremendous Spanish chandeliers in the halls, the archways, the big square Mexican floor tiles. "It was only built eight years ago so it's fairly new and my kitchen, the bathrooms are in good condition. No one will want to redo anything. There are twenty units but mine is the only one-bedroom in the building and the only one with a terrace. Plural. I felt so lucky to find it."

"Terraces in Coral Gables are rare," he said. He was very enthusiastic. "And you really have three of them! This is the ultimate penthouse!"

The living room was painted a rich lemon yellow; I'd taken a lemon to Sherwin Williams and matched it exactly. There was a Juliet balcony at the far end of the living room and a door on the left leading to a very large outdoor covered terrace. "Wow!" José began clicking away. This covered terrace was the largest open space in the apartment, about twenty feet by thirty-five. I thought of it as my outdoor living room. The same terra cotta floor tiles as everywhere but the walls were more like concrete. Maybe the best way to describe the space is to think of a large garage with one side open. This faced north and had a wrought-iron railing; it overlooked Coral Gables, palm trees and the Miami airport in the distance. At night one could sit and watch the planes take off and land.

I'd put the dining room table out there as it was under a roof but out of doors all the same. My old black, brass-trimmed trunk served as a coffee table. I'd had it since summer camp a thousand years ago. The rest of the room was lined with seven-foot-tall bookcases loaded with books. It was a triumph to have them all out of storage and with me at last. I had hung paintings on the walls and big round wicker chairs circled the coffee table trunk. It was dining room and library, open, airy. One wall was dominated by a large wardrobe that opened to reveal a tremendous television set. I loved sitting out there at night, my feet on the trunk, watching an old movie as if I were at a drive-in. José was clicking away.

We returned to the living room. To the right was a short hallway with a powder room on the left and a kitchen on the right. The kitchen window and one living room window looked out onto the communal terrace which no one ever used.

Straight ahead was my bedroom and my bathroom. French doors opened onto my private terrace separated from the 1600 square-foot communal terrace by a gate and a waist-high wall. I'd gotten enormous terra cotta pots from Home Depot up in the elevator, dragged them down outside and put palm trees in them. My space, twenty feet by twenty, looked like a terrace in Palermo.

Back in the living room, José took more photos. The room contained low, white bookshelves so that the walls above them were free for my paintings, my prints. One shelf held a small television and a CD player and there were more books, of course. Beneath the window that looked out at the communal terrace was my desk facing the room. Across from it on the left-hand wall was my French daybed, bought years before from my decorator boss in Canada. It was covered in fawn-colored velvet and banked with pillows to be used as a sofa. In front of it was the marble-topped coffee table that Mother had designed and had made using an old wrought-iron gate from the garden at our house. The original marble top had been my McNair grandmother's bureau top in Mississippi but that had been replaced with a newer, whiter piece by the movers who'd broken it on the way to Beverly Hills.

"What's that?" José was pointing at the hole in my ceiling. It was above my brass étagère.

I groaned. "That hole was here when I moved in and the condo keeps saying they will fix it and they never do. It will be fixed."

"Why is the condo responsible?"

"I know it's in my apartment but the leak came through the roof which is condo territory."

"Be sure and tell everyone exactly that. If they don't notice it then their inspection people certainly will."

We both stared up at it. The edges of the 5 by 7 inch hole were ragged with white plaster.

"It looks like that hole is the only thing anyone could be concerned about."

José wanted to walk through again. My bedroom was dominated by my mahogany Haitian sleigh bed, bought and shipped from Haiti twenty years before. The identical head and foot boards had been over a hundred and fifty years old when I'd bought it; a carpenter in Port au Prince had mended the side rails. It was a double bed for tiny Frenchmen. Over it arched a big, square, Italian market umbrella. I loved how white it was against the bright green walls and how it looked when I was falling asleep at night.

I felt safe and happy under it.

My eight, brightly-colored, Naïf paintings from Haiti dominated my bedroom. On the wall nearest the foot of the bed were my family photographs, all black and white, all in narrow black frames. There were photos going all the way back to the 1830s, lots of Mother and one of me at about age fourteen with our chihuahua, Tiny.

To the left of my bed, which was at an angle in the smallish room, was a window next to the French doors. On the wall behind the head of the bed was another smaller window. I hated air conditioning so these were always open. All my windows were always open unless I were going out in the car as thunderstorms could materialize in minutes. I'd go around closing windows with the car keys in my hand. There was also a walk-in closet which I knew would be a good selling point.

José was snapping photos behind me as I led the way and described each room. He thought it would sell very quickly. "I'll post the photos before tomorrow and send you a link. Meanwhile, call the office if you have any questions." He gave me his business card and I walked him to the front door.

I was really selling it, really leaving. I remembered the day I'd found the apartment.

OCTOBER, 2003

"It's beautiful! It's just what I imagined I wanted but haven't been able to find. The apartments I've seen have been pretty awful. But this!" I couldn't stop marveling at the terraces, the views.

The Demons of Coral Gables

Mr. Sanchez, the elderly Venezuelan landlord, was at my elbow, smiling and nodding. Actually he was only about as tall *as* my elbow. I spoke Italian and he spoke Spanish and, in some bilingual dance, we bargained. He wanted $1200 a month but I would not pay more than $1000. A thousand dollars a month it would be. We shook hands, both pleased.

It was October 31st, 2003. I had borrowed a straw beach mat and a towel and a sheet from a friend who had let me live in her apartment in North Miami Beach for a while. There was one last swim while the place was being vacuumed by her cleaning woman then I went back and changed; my two suitcases were downstairs in the Mini Cooper I'd leased the day before. I surveyed the immaculate white apartment with its 21st floor view of the intra-coastal waterway and the Atlantic and then I locked the door for the last time.

My wet bikini was draped over the front seat, the wind was blowing in through the windows and I was heading south on I-95. The radio blasted Norah Jones. End of North Miami Beach chapter and start of Coral Gables chapter. There had been a last minute snag when Mr. Sanchez's daughter had objected to the lowered rent. She was steely, a real estate agent, one of those wildly wealthy Venezuelans who purred around Coral Gables in a Jaguar. I got my way at one grand a month but it entailed standing my ground.

I steered the Mini Cooper I would dub the Chihuahua, shining, new, green with a white roof, off at the exit and on to Le Jeune Road. Many red lights later I made the left-hand turn at Adriano Avenue. There it was. A big, sandy-yellow, Spanish-looking building with a fountain in front. Four stories tall with a roof covered in red barrel tiles. The garage clicker worked and the iron gate slid open. I found my numbered space and maneuvered the Chihuahua in carefully

In fifteen minutes, I had unloaded the car and all was upstairs. Moving in was easy as I had so little. Furniture was in storage as I'd been on the move since my last apartment in New York. I stood in the empty living room and thought, I must paint but this place is going to be fabulous.

Halloween had always been a favorite holiday for me but this was a strange one because no one rang my doorbell and I'd seen no little kids in costumes outside. I went to bed lying on my straw beach mat on the tile floor; I had made a pillow of the rolled-up towel and felt reasonably comfortable. As I started to fall asleep I heard a gunshot. I sat up. Firecrackers? No. That was definitely a gunshot. I got up and walked through the living room door and stood on the covered terrace at the wrought-iron railing. I could see street lights and palm trees and little houses and the airport in the distance. I stood there for a few minutes gazing out at the sky. Again. Unmistakable gunfire. Two rounds. But it sounded as if the shots were behind me *in* the apartment. It made no sense. I was in a perfectly empty space except for my little island of a straw mat and an open suitcase. How could there be gunfire *in* the apartment? I was too tired to think about it and went back to my pallet and fell asleep.

The next afternoon I introduced myself to the Cuban couple down the hall and asked if they had heard anything. No. I met someone else whose apartment faced the back as mine did but on the second floor. No. It seemed I was the only person to hear what I still thought were three gunshots.

I was very ill that first morning after that first night. A terrible cold, a tight feeling in my chest, headaches, fever, aching arms and legs. My eyes hurt. It lasted four days and then I felt like myself again.

Chapter Two

I began my new life in Coral Gables. My things in Mississippi were sent for. Every New Year's Eve one of my resolutions was to get everything I owned out of storage. I'd paid storage for seven years to keep possessions in a warehouse outside Rome, always imagining I would go back there to live. I grew up in Mississippi so this shipment was mostly books, paintings, journals, and childhood treasures. It all arrived but weeks later than promised. I was delighted to see my French daybed and the Haitian sleigh bed again. I had actually forgotten I owned them. I painted, hung paintings, sorted books, and though I did miss all the New York stuff that was in storage in Connecticut, I decided to leave it there.

One morning, I sat at my desk and thought, Miami is full of crime so I will have lots of great cases. My first priority was to get a list of all the lawyers who did court-appointed work for defendants who couldn't afford legal representation. No one seemed to want me to have that list but I got it. Then I sat down with a Diet Coke and started to call, introducing myself, directing them to my website or faxing a printout of my website to them. I was charming to receptionists, pleasant to assistants, vivacious to everyone. I told them I had ten years of experience in criminal investigations, that I didn't mind working for less than my usual fee in order to work, to meet them, to become involved. One lawyer snarled, "Why do I need a private investigator? All my clients are guilty anyway." I kept punching in phone numbers and I kept telling myself that being professional and relentless would win out. One hundred and seventeen lawyers actually got on the phone with me, listened, two said they admired my guts and one hundred and seventeen did not hire me.

My first week in Coral Gables, I put on a Diane von Furstenberg wrap dress, high-heeled sandals and looked pretty much okay. I went to thirty-five law firms in two days and only one lawyer asked me to sit down. And he was the one who looked at me and said he paid his investigator $15 an hour so why should he hire anybody else? I had not mentioned fees at all. I looked at him and smiled. "Well, that's great if he does a good job." He then ushered me out. A lawyer who practiced aviation law actually sat down in the reception area and listened to me. He stands out in my mind because he had good manners. Usually they looked at me as if I'd arrived from Mars and took my card as if I'd offered to let them hold my pet snake. My whole idea was to let these lawyers see what I looked like and to not be simply a name. Those two days were a bit disheartening and I'd leave the dim, air-conditioned offices and step out into the blinding white sunlight and think, I'm showing initiative and energy and I'm willing to work and I have experience. Dammit! I'm good at what I do. Not one man hired me.

That previous summer in North Miami Beach I had been at an art gallery opening and a woman had admired my necklace. "I made it," I told her and was immediately enlisted to contribute three to be auctioned to raise money for a hospital. I did. I was asked again, for other causes. These invitations floated over into my Coral Gables life. I went to their lunches with TV personalities and women with perfect helmets of hair and pastel suits wielding microphones. My name would always be in the program. I went to afternoon fund raisers with women in flowered dresses, I was introduced again and again. Sometimes I would say I was a writer and sometimes I would say I was a private detective and sometimes women actually screamed—in surprise—at hearing this. But I netted no cases.

I joined the health club at the Biltmore which is a glamorous old hotel in Coral Gables and went every morning. I eased myself into that glorious pool and defied gravity every single day. For the first time in my life, I went to a Costco. I explored mammoth shopping centers and malls from the vantage point of a car. The Chihuahua was my first car. I joined Netflix. I kept going to the First Fridays which were art gallery openings on the first Friday of the month and giving out my business card with the green star logo. I went to Books & Books as often as three times a week to sit and listen to a writer discuss his new book. *The New York Times* and *The Miami Herald* were delivered every morning and I devoured them.

The greatest satisfaction of my time in Florida was my volunteer work with a marine biologist one day a week. I was meant to have a string of degrees and training but I talked my way into helping because they were short-handed and I kept assaulting the head man with letters saying how much I revered turtles, how strongly I felt about their being endangered. We both knew he was taking a chance on me but I wouldn't let up and he surrendered and gave me the job nobody wanted which was to oversee the North Miami Beach hatchery in the middle of the night several nights a week.

The deserted beach was considered quite dangerous and I was alone but I didn't care. I loved being under a starry tropical sky with the baby turtles, putting the newly-hatched ones, the size of Ritz crackers, into a bucket and taking them down to the ocean. My heart would ache when they would run into the water, be tossed back by a wave, throw themselves in again, be tossed back, upside down and struggling, and then right themselves and run across the wet sand towards the waves again. I wasn't supposed to help them, to interfere, but a few times I couldn't stop myself. When at last they passed the breaker line, I could only see a tiny head above the surface but I would always call "Goodbye! Good luck!" as these little beings disappeared into that vast black ocean. Fearless and excited, I thought. This was how we should all dive into life.

Living in Coral Gables, I was assigned to work at Key Biscayne. I'd arrive just after dawn and a marine biologist and I would patrol the beach in a dune buggy for the mother sea turtle tracks. It was locating the nest, protecting the eggs and taking careful notes of when and how many hatched over the coming months.

In early 2004, an old client somehow found me and began to call. Collect, of course, from the slammer. Sante Kimes had been extradited from New York to California to stand trial for a second murder. I'd been on her defense team when she'd been previously convicted in New York. Now, it seemed that her two Los Angeles lawyers found her confusing and difficult. "Honey, you are the only person to understand the case! These lawyers don't know what they're doing!" she would wail long distance. I was asked to be consultant to the defense team for her Los Angeles trial. I wisely did not get on a plane until my ticket had been paid for.

During the lunch break on the last day of trial, a writer for *Vanity Fair* I'd met in New York introduced me to a Los Angeles private detective. John and I saw each other for five minutes but would become close friends later.

The trial ended. Sante Kimes was convicted, given life without parole, and I flew back to Florida. John and I were on the phone a lot and worked a case in New Orleans together.

I had lunch with a Florida private investigator who said we were destined to work together; he was determined to make it happen. I always liked him, he was always a phone call away with advice but I never got a case from him. I met the chief investigator for the State of Florida, a former police detective. He checked my credentials to start my business. The first words he said to me when I sat down across him were "You're not like the other investigators who come in here." I asked what he meant. "Because you're smart." I smiled because I had seen my newly-licensed colleagues in the waiting room and thought most of them looked pretty low rent. None of them looked trustworthy. I'd discover that Miami is filled with licensed p.i.s who will sit in a parked car all night drinking beer. They'll charge you $15 an hour whether they are awake or not. Contacts in New York steered me to Miami colleagues. That seemed the only way for me to get work at first. Strong references. Pretty soon other Miami lawyers were hiring me. Things were going well.

It was March of 2004, when my landlord called—the daughter of the elderly Venezuelan, the woman who'd given me such a hard time about the rent. "Are you 'appy?" she cooed. "Very happy," I answered and waited to hear the real reason for her call. The condo was going up for sale that Monday. "Do you want to buy it?" she asked. It was three o'clock on a Saturday afternoon and I thought, I guess I'm losing the apartment I love and I'll never find another one this pretty with terraces for a thousand dollars a month. I was stung with disappointment but managed to say, "I have to talk to my...my banker and my lawyer. It's Saturday afternoon and I can't possibly reach anyone until Monday or Tuesday." I didn't have a banker *or* a lawyer but she did agree not to advertise it until Wednesday.

Every person in my life was adamant: buy the condo! Some of my friends used the word 'security' which is rather alien to me but I knew the price was right and I knew it was one of the most beautiful apartments I had seen in Coral Gables. Actually THE most beautiful. But to *buy* it? I had never bought anything more expensive than a laptop.

My neighbor across the hall was particularly vehement and directed me to his mortgage broker. I called Alan Bernstein and he asked a lot of questions and then he asked for the last year's income tax return. I said it was not anything I thought anyone should see. I told him my income and there was silence. "What about the year before?" he asked with a lilt of hope in his voice. "Worse," I said. There was no way I could buy an apartment. "Okay," he said. "Let me just play with the numbers and get back to you."

So that's the way it went with Alan Bernstein. He'd ask questions, I would give him simply devastating news and he would say, "Let me just play with the numbers and get back to you."

Week after week of this playing with the numbers and documents being submitted meant that, so far, the sale was proceeding. I waited to be told what to me was quite obvious: with very little income this year and for the previous three years, there was no chance of purchasing a penthouse in Coral Gables. However, in some mysterious way, the process continued moving forward.

One day Alan Bernstein called me and told me that all was in order and that the closing costs would be $ 4,000. I was horrified. "Alan, I don't *have* four thousand dollars!" Nothing deterred him. "Oh, I know that," he said, oblivious to my anguish. "We'll just ask the buyer to change the sale price on paper and you can borrow the closing costs, too." I was stupefied. I was *buying* a condo and not paying one dime for it. Then I told Alan, "I'm really afraid that I won't ever be able to pay back all that money!" How he laughed. "You won't ever pay it back! You'll wait two years and then sell it. You won't pay capital gains on your profit and you'll buy something else."

To my complete astonishment, the condo sale was on track. I would pay only interest on the mortgage and probably not live in Coral Gables for long which meant I wouldn't care when the balloon mortgage kicked in. That's when the monthly payments would balloon into lots more money to pay. I signed documents and became the owner of a penthouse on Adriano Avenue. I felt like a grown-up. But I also felt I'd cheated a little bit. It was too easy. Technically, I could not own it, should not own anything. In years to come, I would fear I was personally responsible for the entire American housing crisis.

Now was the time for my New York things to be brought from storage in Connecticut. An old friend suggested I use the Christian Movers in Mississippi but I could not imagine that the price would make sense. They would have to drive almost a thousand miles north to even pick up my possessions and then head south to Florida but the price was surprisingly reasonable. I hired them and Brother Wayne set off from Jackson, arrived in Greenwich, loaded everything and then began the trip to Miami during the aftermath of a hurricane when rain was lashing the entire eastern seaboard.

That summer of 2004, I experienced my first hurricane which was preceded by days of watching rather self-important weather people stand in front of maps. The dreaded cone was moving slowly, it was picking up speed, it was veering west, now east, this or that. I dragged the enormous terra cotta pots across my terrace so that they could be protected by the lee of the building. I gave my palm trees a pep talk and then told myself they'd be fine because hurricane zones were their natural habitat.

After that first one, I knew how to handle it and the experience of each hurricane took on the same qualities. I knew the drill. I would drive to the supermarket to stock up which is what all the announcements told me to do. There'd be a jam at the entrance as cars tried to pull out or get in. There would be at least one shouting match over a precious parking place. Inside, there'd be a fight over the last shopping cart, the last jug of water, the last carton of milk. A loud announcement in Spanish would inform us that the place was closing in ten minutes.

Heightened excitement overlaid with desperation. Plump Latino housewives jockeyed for position at the check-out pushing carts piled over-their-heads high, others mobbed the nearly-empty shelves. People in shorts and flip-flops ran up and down the aisles. I always seemed to have plenty of water, lots of tuna fish and Diet Coke so I stood calmly in line with batteries and Milano Pepperidge Farm cookies. I wasn't even sure what to do with the batteries but I obediently bought them.

Once I lost electricity for a week and went to bed early, lying under my big, white Italian market umbrella reading by flashlight. A change of batteries was never necessary but I was pleased that I had them.

The bad storms that season were Charley, Frances, Ivan and Jeanne. I'd watch the news every night and think about Brother Wayne. He arrived on the afternoon of September 9th at quarter past five— big and black and looking exhausted. He'd done the whole trip by himself, poor thing. I told him I'd been worried about him with all the bad weather. He grinned and said, "I prayed and there was sunshine all the way."

He brought every box, piece of furniture and painting from the truck to my apartment which took about four hours and he never sat down to rest. He had a drink of water but never stopped. I suggested that he spend the night at the Holiday Inn across the street and I offered to pay for his room but he shook his head. He wanted to get home to his family. It was dark when I went down in the elevator with him and told him to wait for me to get some cash from the ATM across the street. I stood on tiptoes and handed him the money as he reached out of the truck's cab. I said he'd done a great job and to drive safely. When I said goodbye, he said, "Oh, you're gonna see me again."

"What do you mean?"

"You ain't stayin' here. You'll be leavin'."

I thought of the hundred and something boxes to be unpacked, of all the paintings to be hung. "You're joking, aren't you?" But he wasn't. Suddenly I had a bad feeling.

He had started the engine. "No, ma'am. You won't be here long."

I watched the truck pull away into the night heading north towards Mississippi and then walked up the steps and past the gurgling fountain, thinking what an odd remark. A psychic mover? Was I going to fall in love with a South American sugar cane tycoon and move somewhere even more wonderful? I pushed the elevator button for 'four.'

Suddenly I felt marginally less optimistic about my beautiful new apartment. Brother Wayne had been so definite.

Two thousand four became two thousand five. We sweated on Christmas and we sweated on New Year's Day. I went to seven parties and talked and smiled and ate hors d'oeuvres.

I wanted the firms who had hired me to keep on hiring me and thought that New Year's presents would garner more attention than anything delivered in December. I went to Godiva and bought gold boxes of chocolates. Under each ribbon I tucked a very large magnifying glass with a note that said, "This is to look for the truth. Happy New Year, Cici McNair." Each gold box went into a glossy gold bag; they were addressed to the man I'd worked for and dropped off at the main reception desk of each firm.

A postscript: only one lawyer of the eleven firms acknowledged the present.

I wanted more work. One contact in New York sent me to a large international firm. It was a few very interesting cases; one led me to South Carolina and on several trips to Washington, D.C. This case went on and on and on for more than a year and it meant I had money. Another firm gave me work, then other firms called me.

One Miami firm hired me for a case that veered from police brutality into what I saw as cold-blooded, close-range, shot-in-the-back-of-the-head execution. I went back and forth to Ft. Lauderdale in the Chihuahua knowing that the Broward Sheriff's Office had already threatened the lawyer, my handler at the time. I was told to be very careful on I-95. I felt very little tension trying to get people to talk to me in the Haitian neighborhood even though I was the only white face. But I felt not good at all when I thought of the Broward Sheriff's Office knowing that I was gathering evidence against one of their trigger-happy deputies. People were very afraid of Sheriff Jenne and his gang and I heard stories that confirmed that they should be.

I worked on a money laundering case. Millions and millions had gone into the pocket of the president of a certain little Caribbean nation. Great fun. The case had big yachts, big condos, and a Miami mistress with a big bosom.

There was the case of the missing grandmother. Quite dead and buried. Never underestimate the hysteria of Cuban Catholics who have gone to visit a grave every Sunday for years and suddenly discovered that it was not there. The granddaughter and grandson were told they were mistaken but they knew they weren't and hired a Cuban woman lawyer who hired me. Seems the cemetery was moving the dead, stacking them several bodies deep and generally behaving badly. I got to the books, got the proof we needed and brought it like a big bone to the lawyer. This lawyer had been very helpful in drawing up a retainer agreement for me to present to my clients to prevent getting stiffed. Then *she* stiffed *me* and disappeared into the wilds of Latin America.

I was sent to Paris to find a missing person by a client in New York. A cold and tricky case as he'd vanished five months before, had money and spoke four languages. I found him. The few weeks away were heaven. I was tired of the sun, of the monotony of wearing the same clothes, and not knowing what month of the year it was.

I met the former publisher of *The Miami Herald* socially and he gave me a list of the top nine lawyers to contact and said to use his name. My website had been redesigned, looked impressive; I was prepared.

Every lawyer responded via email. I actually met four of them and all were enthusiastic, talked about hiring me. Only one actually gave me a case but he was considered, by many, to be the best criminal defense attorney in Miami. Waiting to see him one afternoon, I was introduced to his wife in the reception area who said she was so happy her husband had hired me, that the firm really needed someone like me and that she'd heard wonderful things about my work.

I thanked her, we talked. I happened to know the really shoddy detective the firm had previously used.

I was doing a sensitive case for her husband who *was* the firm, the top and founding partner, and for the other senior partner. I'd been praised for my interviews by the big cheese, given more and more assignments regarding the case, and today, after a few months, summoned for a meeting at the office with him and the other partner. I parked on Brickell and arrived on time. One lawyer was delayed in traffic and the other was busy with a client. Every forty minutes or so I would excuse myself to the receptionist and go down in the elevator and outside to put more quarters in the meter.

After more than two and a half hours in the waiting room, the main man (with the nice wife) opened the door to the reception area, looked at me and motioned with a curt hand gesture for me to come in. No 'hello' or anything, only a hand wave to follow him. I said, "Hi, how are you? I'm meeting with Len but he's been held up." I was remarkably nice given all that waiting time. The lawyer didn't answer. I thought, finally a trial date or maybe I'll be given more names for more interviews. I started to follow him down the hall to the conference room or to his office but he stopped and said, "We can talk in here." It was the firm's kitchen. I was practically pushed backwards through the doorway and stood holding my briefcase with my back to the coffee maker behind me on the counter. To my right was the refrigerator. He loomed in the door, in his expensive suit and tie, scowling, and angry. "If I'd known about this meeting I would have told you not to bother to come. We don't need an investigator anymore."

I was stunned. "So all the interviews are—"

"We don't need you so go home," he snapped.

"I don't understand."

Again, the command. "Get out of here! Go home!" He moved out of the doorway and I squeezed past him. Me in my favorite Diane von Furstenberg dress. The receptionist called "goodbye" to me and I tried to smile, waved my hand in her direction and then I left the office, left the building and drove home. Shocked.

I sat at my desk and reviewed the last emails from both men. I had done a dozen interviews, a few of them several hours long, all very sensitive, and been sent emails saying, 'Good' and 'Well done,' which I knew, considering the source, were high praise. It made no sense. A few days later, the other partner called and asked me why I hadn't been there for our meeting. No apology for making me wait for nearly three hours, no mention of his being late. I told him that I had been told to leave, that they no longer needed me. "He shouldn't have said that. We may need you." I told him to call me if he did require more interviews. That was that. Finished. I never heard from the firm again. I kept hearing the voice telling me to "get out of here!" It was the way you'd shoo a dog out of the house.

The head of the firm, this admired man in the legal community, the man who had hired me and complimented my work had treated me as if he had caught me stealing.

This experience shook me. I realized that my professional life had changed. Three other firms I had worked for had not called back. I talked to the administrative assistant of one lawyer and she confided that they were now using another private detective. She seemed in earnest when she said she had no idea why. My phone stopped ringing and there were no more emails for meetings, for new cases.

My biggest source of income and the biggest firm was headed by a man who would wave me into his office overlooking Biscayne Bay, close the door and tell me he hadn't had sex with his wife for five years. I would look down at my notebook and say, "That has nothing to do with me. What is happening with such and such company? Do you have any questions regarding my last report?" I started wearing trousers to his office so he couldn't pull his chair around to the front of his desk and ogle my legs. I changed appointments with him from noon to the morning to preclude his insistence that we talk over lunch or over a drink in the afternoon. But, the earliest he arrived at the office was ten and when I came at ten, he insisted we go out for coffee and it was the same language and questions I did not answer about my social life and my sexual preferences. I told him to stop it, but he did not. He insisted I come into the office and that he couldn't talk to me over the phone. I tape recorded him. I gazed out through the floor-to-ceiling glass at the wide blue sweep of Biscayne Bay as this pig asked me if I liked anal sex.

 I consulted a friend who was a lawyer. "You are not his full-time employee so nothing can be done about his behavior. You are an independent contractor and do not have to work with him." I said, "But I *do*. I have to deal with him to pay my rent." If I blew the whistle on him it would probably ruin chances of being hired by other firms, other private detectives. I might be perceived as over-sensitive and dangerous to have around.

 The despicable executive director stopped calling. No decision for me to make.

 Every morning, I would sit at my desk in a corner of the living room, answer emails from friends, and try to think of how to get detective work. I realized I had already done all I could. The groundwork had been laid and I had clients. They knew I was here, they knew my work was good but, for some reason, they weren't calling. I couldn't keep reaching out to lawyers or I'd risk seeming desperate which was the kiss of death for a private detective. One morning I slammed my notebook closed, turned off the computer and decided that my job was to sell the condo. Nothing else!

 As I sat at my desk, a window overlooking the big communal terrace, forty by forty feet, was behind me. It sprawled outside my desk window, my kitchen window, and my bathroom window in bare, sunny splendor. My bedroom terrace was open on three sides: north for the airport view, east towards Miracle Mile and south was the adjoining community terrace which had eastern, southern and western views. I had terraces stretching on three sides of my one-bedroom apartment—the crème de la crème of penthouses. Very private. Later I would think how *isolated*.

I went to the Miami Book Fair International, to dozens and dozens of gallery openings. I paid $75 to go to a dinner for international visitors to Miami.

There were other dinners and sometimes I sat between people who were so uneducated, outspoken and conservative that I was sure that, by dessert, they would insist the world was flat.

I had dinners with men who did not interest me. I had dinner with a divorced man from Palm Beach. Again and again. I had nothing better to do. He was well-read, had a passable sense of humor, was Ivy League educated, was Social Register and good-looking enough. But I couldn't shake a bad feeling about him and I did what I never do: detective research for personal reasons. He'd declared bankruptcy to avoid giving his ex-wife, the mother of his children, any money. A judge in Palm Beach had actually sent him to jail. My instincts had been correct. A first for me: I broke up via email. When he called me one morning after that, I pretended to be in South Beach with a waiter handing me a Bellini. "I can't really talk. I'm with people. Brunch," I said, praying that no one would go on the Costco public address system calling for a clean-up in aisle eleven.

Every few weeks, I'd hear from a private detective or a lawyer in New York and I'd be euphoric and handle the case and get paid and then it would be over.

An email arrived asking if I would be interested in joining a branch of PEN if there were one in Florida. I was enthusiastic and became one of the founders and then the co-vice-president of PEN Florida.

I kept trying to market myself and my newly-incorporated Green Star Investigations. Dinners for $50, Florida Bar lunches, Women's Bar Association meetings, panel discussions with judges, I went to all of them. If I saw a lawyer's name in the newspaper, I sent the clipping and a note expressing interest in his case and in working for him. I went to the Inn of the Court with the Ecuadorian money-laundering expert who was a great mentor I'd met doing a case. He introduced me with drama and flair as if I were the second coming of Sherlock Holmes. I met judges and a few hundred lawyers. I gave them my card and wrote personal notes to each of them the following day. Not a call. The money launderer could hardly believe it. A woman judge became a friend and took me to a few receptions. She, too, was amazed that I netted no cases and no clients.

It was September of 2005, when an old beau, who'd asked me to marry him ages ago, was now divorced again and calling me. Sometimes I sat out on the covered terrace with the phone to my ear and we watched *Law & Order* together, chatting during the ads, laughing. He called me during a stakeout as I stared through the car windshield waiting for someone to arrive. He called me as I sat in a parking lot, all dressed up and dreading the dinner for lawyers I was about to attend. The calls were more frequent; he wanted me to come to see him in Newport, Rhode Island, or he would come to New York. When was I coming?

His calls were long and ranged over a myriad of subjects. We talked about marriage. Marriage, in general. What we would want, how we had changed in our ideas after our divorces. I remembered every weekend that summer in Newport. The Friday drive from Manhattan. How his mother opened her closet to me that first weekend when I hadn't known to bring an evening dress, how Simon always wanted to leave the black-tie parties and dances early. We'd end up eating peanut butter and chutney sandwiches at midnight in his parents' kitchen. His proposal was decades ago. Had he changed *enough*? Had I? In November of 2005, I told Simon that I would fly to New York and we'd meet after my London trip. I was staying with my zany Welsh writer friend, Bronwen, and had appointments with a few contacts who might have work for me in the States.

He called to talk the night before my early morning flight. I thought he sounded rather sad on the phone. I hung up and wondered why.

I arrived in London, had a grand reunion with Bronwen and we talked all day. After dinner and wine, we talked nonstop until nearly midnight and then I went to bed on the living room couch. I dreamed I was in a vast white room filled with faceless people wearing white robes of some sort and they were all shouting and crying. A tremendous space like a white gymnasium with a high ceiling and people moaning and sobbing and screaming. Terrified, I was lost in this crowd and then Simon appeared, put his arms around me, and held me. I woke up and thought how real it had been. I had actually felt him pressing against me. Maybe I should give him another chance, went through my mind. Maybe we had each changed enough. Maybe we should start over.

Back in Miami, I received an email from a friend saying that Simon had died. Computing the day and the time, he had the heart attack when I was landing at Heathrow. He came to me the first time I slept. Maybe that was the first time he could have my attention. I cried for days which surprised me. All my comfort was long distance.

The climate, the way of life—Coral Gables wasn't right for me but maybe the catalyst to leave was the realization that I had no one to talk to in Florida about how upset I felt.

Chapter Three

I look back now and think I couldn't have dealt with Miami any differently. I introduced myself with a firm handshake and a smile thousands of times at hundreds of lunches, brunches, breakfasts, dinners, receptions, conferences and cocktail parties. I wrote all the follow-up letters possible, wrote thank-you notes, made phone calls right to the end of every list. I gave it all my energy and still cannot think of anything I didn't do that would have made a difference.

Now, after two years and two months, it was January of 2006, and my penthouse was going to be sold. I would kiss Coral Gables and Miami, "the capital of Latin America," goodbye.

The ad was posted with the really spectacular photos and three days later Patrizia, who worked with Raquel, called. "We have an offer!" It was outrageous— ten thousand dollars over the asking price! "This man is relocating to Miami from Arkansas for a job, saw your apartment, and wants it!"

The next day a Miami realtor arrived "to look it over for him." I led her through, she asked questions, left. Within a day the offer was withdrawn.

No explanation. Patrizia and I wondered if she thought she could sell him something else and get a higher commission. That was it, we decided. Never mind, they said. There was plenty of interest. My phone rang all day long. Homes by Owner had six or seven realtors calling me and asking if I could be home in two hours, at three o'clock, at seven that evening. People came.

The next week there were four different couples who said they were going to make an offer. The Argentines were euphoric. "A bidding war!" crowed Raquel. Two offers were made but within twenty-four hours were withdrawn. That Sunday afternoon, a Peruvian came and I showed him through and then told him I would be at my desk in the living room if he had questions. "Just take your time," I told him. I left him standing on my bedroom terrace gazing off at the view. Smiling.

Ten minutes later he came into the living room and said, "It's a terrific apartment and I'm going to submit an offer tomorrow morning. First thing Monday morning. I want it."

Patrizia called me at eleven o'clock on Monday and I accepted his offer. Hurrah! But the next day, he called and said he'd changed his mind.

Wednesday afternoon, a man named Bernardo came to see the apartment. It happened that I was making chocolate chip cookies. I laughed when I let him in as I'd read somewhere that the scent of baking was a way to seduce a buyer. "It's a coincidence, I assure you." And it was. I bake cookies when I'm restless. Bernardo was given the tour I knew so well and he said he was "crazy about this place." We sat in the living room and talked about the neighborhood which he knew well. And we ate cookies. "If I had seen this two months ago, I would have bought it immediately," he said.

"What happened two months ago?"

"I bought an old 1930s house in the Gables. It's always been my dream to find an old one to renovate. "

"That's quite an undertaking," I said. The condo had to get the roof fixed after every hurricane season and every roofing company who'd given us a five-year guarantee was suddenly out of business or simply unfindable. My guess was that they changed the firm's name to avoid lawsuits. Every year, the condo board started again with a new company and a guarantee that meant nothing and workers who rarely showed up or arrived without ladders and, in general, were irresponsible slackers. That was just a roof repair. A renovation? A 3-D nightmare in Technicolor.

Bernardo said there were problems. "But I have had this dream for so long and it will be magnificent when I finish."

So Bernardo left with two dozen cookies. Bad timing, that's all.

January was filled with prospective buyers. Patrizia would call and say, "There is a young lawyer driving down from Ft. Lauderdale who can be there at three o'clock. Is that okay?" I never said 'no' and was later told how much Patrizia and Raquel appreciated that.

We sold the condo three more times. This does not count the number of people who said, I'm making an offer tomorrow, then didn't. But within a day someone else was ringing the doorbell, walking through the living room, exclaiming at the view from the terrace and saying how beautiful it was. I had flown to Philadelphia to look at houses to buy. I would have the luxury of space and be less than a hundred miles from Manhattan. I was still deciding which neighborhood suited me but counting on the Coral Gables condo sale to provide a down payment of twenty percent.

January flowed into February then it was March. Another offer and this time there was a deposit of ten thousand dollars and another home inspection. The fourth one. The fourth inspector came through with a little bag of tools and proceeded to test every electric socket, turn every faucet on and off. Every light switch was checked. He ran the washing machine and then the dryer. These were in a closet with sliding louvred doors in the back of the kitchen. The oven and each burner were turned on. Door handles were twisted, locks were tested. Smoke detectors 'whooped' to life. The inspector dropped to his knees in my walk-in closet to check the tiles for cracks with a flashlight.

All fine. The bank had okayed the loan before the buyer had even seen my apartment. Patrizia and Raquel always made certain of that. Documents went back and forth, the closing date was set for six weeks away. I flew to Philadelphia for the weekend and looked at more houses. I realized I had just over a month to find what I wanted. Back in Coral Gables, the phone rang and it was Patrizia. Her voice told me everything. "The realtor called this morning. I am so sorry. I can't understand it but the buyer changed his mind." I nodded, not speaking, awash with disappointment. She was trying to be upbeat and told me she had a couple who wanted to come tomorrow at ten. Before she hung up, I asked "Why? Why did he change his mind?" Patrizia said she'd asked the realtor the same thing. "She said he got cold feet. He didn't really tell her anything either. Just a case of cold feet."

Four days later an offer was made and we were elated all over again. The inspection was completed the next day. Meanwhile I'd made an offer on a house in Philadelphia contingent upon the Coral Gables sale. I was happy and excited.

Then my buyer changed his mind. Patrizia and Raquel seemed as miserable as I was and I lost the house in Philadelphia.

Of course, there were people who liked my apartment and had legitimate reasons for not making an offer. This was typically "I want to sell my house first." But there had been a parade of admirers who professed to fall in love with it, had made offers, paid for inspections and then rescinded the offer.

I called Cassandra. "Something is wrong," I told her. "May I come and see you?"

Coconut Grove was always traffic-clogged and the sidewalks were usually crowded with tourists. Bermuda shorts, Hawaiian print shirts, shopping bags were all I saw as I slowed looking for a parking place. The sign for Donuts was next to Cassandra's doorway but I had to keep moving. Finally a parking lot and I was out of the Mini Cooper, had paid my $5, and in minutes was going through the glass door next to the doughnut place and rushing up the steep stairs.

In a long skirt and white T-shirt, she greeted me with an embrace. We sat at either end of the white sofa facing each other. Her skin was golden, her eyes an unusual greenish-brown flecked with gold; her hair which hung below her shoulders had been colored an unflattering shade in the blonde family. We were glad to see each other. "Tell me what's happening," she said.

I described all the potential sales falling through. I explained about Simon, the dream and how I realized I didn't want to be in Miami anymore. I didn't mention that all my clients had stopped calling as I was entirely focused on selling the apartment and my feelings about Simon as a catalyst to leave. "I put the apartment on the market in January and here we are two months later."

"I'm sure it's a beautiful apartment. I don't have to see it to know that." She handed my photographs back without a glance. "You said you moved in on Halloween three years ago?"

I nodded.

"You won't leave until after Halloween of this year."

I gasped. It was now March. I was shocked. "Oh, Cassandra! I'm running out of money. I have to sell it and get out of there!"

"You still have that aura around you. We must get rid of it."

I blinked. She'd said this the summer before and I'd done all that she'd told me to do. I'd obeyed the instructions scrupulously, looking at my watch, blowing out the candles after fifteen minutes. Why hadn't it worked? She saw my face. "You will sell the apartment. But it won't be until the week after Halloween."

"Oh, that's so far away! What can I do? Do you want to come to the apartment? Would it help to see it?"

She shook her head. "I don't need to see it. People love it but they are having bad dreams about it and then they change their mind."

My asking Cassandra for help was a turning point. In time she would come to my apartment and then she would realize that she was not strong enough to deal with it all by herself.

Chapter Four

"Cassandra the Psychic of Coconut Grove? Are you kidding me?" Melinda's voice was amused. We'd been close friends since college, through job hunts, love affairs, and then through our respective divorces. Now, no husbands, no children, we were closer than ever. I was on my way home in the Chihuahua when she called from Manhattan. I didn't want to lose the connection in the garage so I parked on Adriano Avenue near my building.

"Well, I didn't have any other ideas. Why should one person after another offer to buy it, already have the bank loans, deal with the mortgage craziness, the inspection and then back out? Actually they have mortgage approval before they come to see the apartment so that never screws up the deal. We get right to the closing and then it's over. Five times now. Maybe six." I sighed in exasperation. "And I'm not counting all the people who stood in my living room, gushing with appreciation, discussing where to put their furniture, who said they were making a bid the next day—"

"And they didn't?"

"No, they didn't. Or they did and then withdrew it within days. Patrizia and Raquel tell me that the realtor—every single realtor—always says 'they got cold feet.'"

"No such thing in Miami in summer."

"Ha. But they don't really give a reason. It's not like 'one hour after seeing your apartment, my husband was transferred to Guatemala.'" I sighed again. "And now I've lost two houses in Philadelphia because each one was contingent on closing here."

"What are you going to do?"

"I'm going to do whatever Cassandra tells me to do. Nobody else has any ideas."

"You really want to go down that road?"

"What other road is there?"

"Tell me how you got in her clutches in the first place." Melinda's voice dripped with cynicism but she was in New York, content in her own apartment so I didn't blame her.

"First of all, I'm not in her clutches. It was last summer when I had dinner in Coconut Grove with Victoria who was getting a divorce. She wailed the entire dinner over not getting enough money from her banker husband.

Highly irritating. We were at a little sidewalk place and I kept seeing this green neon sign that said 'Psychic' over her shoulder. Finally, dinner was over and I said, 'Let's do something fun and go over there. Come on! You can hear the details of your divorce settlement before it's even decided.'" I switched the phone from one ear to the other and turned to stretch my feet out over the front seat. "I just wanted a diversion from her litany of woes. We went across the street and through a glass door, up a flight of stairs in our high-heeled sandals to this phenomenal room with incense going and icons and paintings everywhere. Chimes rang to announce us. It was an L-shaped area with a sofa and all manner of bottles, herbs in jars, candles and little shrines. They ranged from a statue of Saint Sebastian full of arrows to the blue and gold funeral mask of Tutankhamen. Glass picture windows along one entire wall looked out over the crowded main street of the Grove." I smiled, remembering. "The Virgin Mary was all over the place. It was Catholic and voodoo and everything else."

"Did she look strange, ethereal, weird?"

"She's adorable! Maybe thirty or thirty-five years old, with this beautiful olive complexion and long blonde hair. In a T-shirt and a long skirt, barefooted. She looked like she could work at the Gap and would come over and ask you what size you're looking for." I took a swallow of Diet Coke. "The gist of this is that it would cost twenty-five dollars to read our palms and we just didn't want to pay that so we started to leave and she said she'd read us for ten dollars each. I went first. I left Victoria sitting on a sofa, looking confused, surrounded by all these statues and altars. The other part of the L-shaped room had a table and loveseat and chairs out of sight. So I went with Cassandra around the corner of the room and sat across from her. Before I had even put my hand out, she said, 'Your family has treated you very cruelly. This has gone on for years. The saddest part of this is that you have had no one to help you. You have had no ally.' I remember hoping my face was expressionless." I stopped. "I know what you're thinking and so was I: she could say that to 98 out of 100 people and it would be true." I frowned. "Then she said my biggest problem was—I waited for her to say 'money' since we had turned to leave and since this was always my problem. But she said, 'relationships.'"

Melinda didn't say anything so I went on. "Cassandra asked me to think about my last relationship. It was the Swiss money-laundering expert who was truly good-looking and brilliant intellectually but seemed very inexperienced about women, love, or anything emotional. He was romantic but childish. Cassandra acted as if I'd said my thoughts aloud and said it didn't work because he was so immature." I stopped. "That was actually interesting. She went on to say that the very difficult family situation had made me extremely strong and that I was very honest but that I had a negative aura around me and should get rid of it. That things were happening to me, that things were being taken away from me because of it." I hesitated. "She said she would have read me for free, she was not going to let me go down the stairs without talking to me. I disagreed with her, nearly argued with her. I said, 'But I'm such an optimist. I'm a positive person.' She said that had nothing to do with this. I felt chilled when she said, 'People are changing their minds about you.'" I hated thinking of this. "When we stood up, she said, 'Come back to me and we'll work on getting rid of this, getting it out of your life. I won't charge you. It might be as simple as burning a candle or standing in the ocean and saying a prayer.' I thought it was all a bit dramatic for an after-dinner bit of fun." I kicked off my sandals. "Victoria's turn. I sat by the stairs and five minutes later she walked towards me with a shocked look on her face. She was wearing a jersey top and I remember her nipples were standing up!" Melinda and I both started to laugh on the phone. "She couldn't speak but pointed at the hair on her bare arm and yes, it was standing up, too. We paid and I said goodbye because Victoria was simply stupefied. In the car, she would not tell me what Cassandra had said. Only that it was all true. She was shocked by the experience."

"I know you went back to her. And she had you light all those candles."

"I can't remember everything she asked me to do but candles were part of it. White candles, yellow candles. I have no doubt that she is psychic. I remember one afternoon I was to go to her at four o'clock to get more candles—"

"You had to buy these candles from her?" I knew what Melinda was thinking.

"No. She has never asked me for money and knows that my work has dried up, that I've got the balloon mortgage torturing me so she asked the church to give me the candles. She didn't want me to buy them."

"Really?"

"Really. She said she was doing something spiritual for me and it would be a sin to take money for it. She said, 'God gave me this gift to help people and I want to help you.'"

"So she was seeing me for free but charging other people and I was pushing my little cart around Publix feeling miserable for not being able to pay her. Suddenly I remembered when things were bad in New York and my computer was broken. I found these Bangladeshis with a repair shop overlooking Times Square and when I asked how much it would cost to repair the hard drive and they told me, I started to pack up my computer and the head man said, 'No, no, we will fix it for you. No charge.' I nearly wept with gratitude. When I went back to pick it up, I took several dozen sugar cookies I'd baked. The men, three of them, in this little closet of an office on the 25th floor, were thrilled. You'd think I'd brought them gold. I heard that all their families were back in Bangladesh and out came the photographs."

I stopped. "So I thought okay, I'll bake cookies and take them to Cassandra. Then I saw a stand of flowers near the cash register. I bought flowers and the ingredients for the cookies. When I went to see her, I hadn't made the cookies and I left the flowers in the car by mistake. I went up the stairs and the first thing she said was I know you are worried about paying me. I don't want you to give me any money. Bring me flowers because I haven't had flowers for St. Michael in a long time. Bake cookies for my kids."

"Bullseye," said Melinda. "I confess that I'm impressed."

"Melinda, she knew some things that I've never told anybody."

"Not even me?"

"Not even you."

I remembered how Cassandra had looked at me and said that my father had sexually abused me. I had not blinked.

"Now you are going to drive me crazy with that statement."

"Don't worry about it. I don't." I frowned. "Not anymore."

Silence on the phone. These were marathon calls.

"She told me something last summer that I didn't agree with."

"What?"

"Do you think I'm missing in relationships? Tell me the truth."

"You have a circle of friends like no one I know. It's become trite to say but you are someone who has made their friends their family. Nobody I know has such close friends."

I was silent. "She had me buy a yard of red ribbon and put a straight pin across the width of it for every male person in my life that I'd ever had any possible relationship with, with any man who has affected me."

"Did you?"

"Yes, I drove to some ratty little shopping center off South Dixie Highway during peak traffic time at five o'clock and went into a fabric shop and bought red ribbon and a box of 500 straight pins. And then I came back here and started thinking. The first pin was for Billy McCormick who kissed me in the middle of the Old Canton Road before the first grade."

Laughter. "You were slow. Nobody kissed you in nursery school or kindergarten?"

"I didn't go to either one. I would sneak home after the Graham crackers. Finally they stopped making me go."

"You walked home by yourself? At age four?"

"Yep. But we're off track here. I thought of all the boys and all the men I'd been engaged to, slept with, had crushes on, who'd had crushes on me and that red ribbon wasn't even red anymore. The pins were so close together it was like a silver snake."

"What did Cassandra say when you gave it to her?"

"I couldn't give it to her for three days. I had to sleep with it under my mattress and then I had to put it in a shoebox and carry it with me wherever I went. I asked her if I could leave it in the trunk of the car when I went to Key Biscayne on Friday and she said it was okay but otherwise to keep it on the front seat with me or on my lap all the time. I was so worried all Friday that someone would steal my shoebox while I was counting turtle eggs."

"So then I took it to her so that she could take it to the church. She was shocked at how many pins there were or men there were and told me God had given them to me so I would not be alone and I had pushed them all away. Each pin was a wound in my heart. I argued with her and said that they weren't ever right for me but she disagreed, said God kept sending me people. She said nothing had worked out for a reason." I frowned. "I told her that in the past ten years I have had no time for relationships, certainly no time to look for anyone, maybe not to even see anyone as viable."

I took a sip of Diet Coke. "I think you were in California when a lot of this was happening. We weren't in touch."

"I think it was 2002 and 2003 that I was incommunicado."

"That's about right. About four or five years ago, a few years before moving here, detective work fell to nothing, as if often does, and I left my apartment in John Barrymore's brownstone on 37th and Fifth; I simply couldn't pay the rent. But I was offered a terrific job: I was to write the script for a television house makeover show. Brand-new idea at the time and now, of course, it's really popular. It was perfect for me. I've got that degree from the New York School of Interior Design, used to be a decorator, I've renovated houses, know how to deal with contractors and the script would have been the greatest fun. So all my stuff was loaded into a moving van during a snowstorm in Manhattan and was unloaded in this magnificent house overlooking Long Island Sound. The house in Greenwich, Connecticut, was part of the deal. I was so happy that first—and only—night in the large bedroom overlooking the water. But in twenty-four hours it had all fallen through, the bank had pulled the plug, all my stuff went into storage and I started sleeping on friends' couches." I hated remembering. "Kevin let me sleep in the office on the floor for a while. I avoided security and took showers at six o'clock every morning down the street at a gym." I hesitated. "There were mornings I woke up and actually laughed. Lying there on the floor, using a flak jacket as a pillow, between the shredder and boxes of counterfeit T-shirts. None of my friends knew. I was on my cell phone, I was seeing people, I was offered things. But they would fall through. Without fail. I was trying to stay afloat. Kevin gave me a few hours sometimes but it was minimal. I had one idea after another. I was hanging by a thread but I kept working at creating projects, pitching magazine articles, book ideas, vying for jobs and, of course, hoping for cases. Not just hoping! I was always writing letters, meeting people, going to receptions, meetings, introducing myself and handing out my business card."

I paused. "Big chances and little chances. I pursued everything." I took a deep breath. "I was asked to submit a script for a TV talk show on ABC and I wrote it in two days and mailed it to the colleague of a man I'd met at an art gallery opening. I waited a month and then called him and he said he'd never received it. I printed it out again, sent it and waited a week. I called and he said he had been about to pick up the phone. He told me it was exactly what he wanted, the right tone, the right everything and I was hired as a writer for the new show. Then he went into a meeting and called me three hours later. He had been fired."

Melinda gasped, "My god."

"So that was big, the house makeover show was big but I had twenty-seven other things in the air. I went back to Johnson O'Connor, the human engineering firm. They looked at my old aptitude scores and said, you can do advertising, you can write copy. I found a California clothing company with a catalog in the style of J.Peterman. Remember Elaine on *Seinfeld* and the urban sombrero?"

"Who could forget the urban sombrero?" laughed Melinda.

"They tried me out, sent me five articles of clothing to describe. It was in the vein of 'perfect for morning coffee after dancing all night with the mysterious Texan.'"

"That is so *you*!"

"So I got the material on Saturday, wrote the copy on Sunday afternoon because it was easy and faxed it to the man on Monday. He couldn't believe how quickly I'd done it and he liked my work. I was hired. I was delighted. I was *saved*. I would be paid $100 a blurb. Within days I received a phone call telling me how sorry they were but two of their previous writers suddenly wanted to come back and 'we never really fire anyone. I am sure you understand.'"

Melinda was angry. "So you worked for free, gave them your good creative work and they liked it and you were hired and *unhired* within a week?"

"Not even a week. That's the way it went with one thing after another. But I never got that upset because I always had another possibility to play out. I never sat down and cried. Melinda, I do *not* feel sorry for myself but something should have come through. There were so many possibilities that would have changed everything and suddenly someone would change their mind. The jobs were there. The money was there. I was qualified. It would be a fabulous criminal case, the lawyer would say 'we all want you on the defense team' and then the lawyer would call and say they didn't need me after all. No exaggeration. More than a dozen times. Cassandra said this aura was causing things to be taken away from me. She said that the first time we met." I paused. "She was thinking of love and I was thinking of survival."

Melinda broke in. "I never knew you were that desperate. I never knew!" Her voice was anguished. "Why didn't you tell me?"

I stared out the windshield. "It...it is a horrible thing to just run out of money and to have every job, all chances disappear. Cassandra said that I refused to lie down and die and that I was very strong. All I know is I never give up. Remember when I was selling pashminas in that chic little shop?"

"Yes! But you made it sound hilarious and they paid you in cash and no one *ever* imagined you were desperate for money!"

"Well, I was and I couldn't tell anyone. I guess if Mother were alive I would have gone to live with her for a while but—" I paused. "So I came here, I borrowed money—for the first time in my life—from a very good friend and I rented the Coral Gables apartment and got lots of work and began to pay her back. Then I bought the condo in a deal too good to be true and here I am running out of money again because the work has dried up."

"It does seem that it's a pattern. Nobody works harder than you do and I know you are a good detective. And you're a really talented writer. Why hasn't that taken off?"

I laughed. "Writing! I love writing but I hate the world of publishing. The difference in being a good writer and selling books is something called marketing and it takes something called money." I rolled my eyes. "Publishers want to see your track record with previous book sales before they buy your manuscript. A lot of good writers have wonderful manuscripts but previous book sales don't impress the publishers enough." I suddenly remembered my big chance in the magazine world. "At one point, *Talk* magazine was flying me back and forth to L.A. to do a story on Sante Kimes, my murderous client and my favorite psychopath."

"Wow! That's national. That was big!"

"It was great. I'd never had luck with magazine writing before. Tina Brown and my editor, Phoebe Eaton, kept saying, keep writing. You're over the word limit but we love it. So it was a huge piece and it would have made a huge difference to me and led to other things."

"I read every issue of *Talk* but I didn't see that story."

"Nobody did. The magazine folded the month before my piece was to run." I heard Melinda exclaim and then I went on. "For me to think back on all the possibilities, the not having money and to say it aloud…" I stopped. "*It hurts me* because this is not how I run my life. I am confident, optimistic, always have ideas and this looking back and seeing this…it feels wrong. Even shameful. The opposite of *la bella figura*. Mother taught me it was bad manners to talk about money but this can't all be coincidence. I can't be blind to a pattern."

A gale-force sigh from the Upper East Side then a long silence. "Agreed. You live your life with such spirit. Really you do! No one would imagine that you struggle. But, it's money. You need it and you need to escape that gorgeous penthouse. First, sell it, take the money and run and then think about love and relationships."

"Remember when we were in college and the idea was that you would fall in love and get married to someone who would take care of you?"

The recently-divorced Melinda laughed. "How well I remember."

God, it was hot. I considered closing the windows and turning on the air conditioning. "Cassandra told me there was something I wanted to accomplish but I haven't done it yet. Then she asked what my profession was. I told her I was a private detective and she said it wasn't that. It was something else. But what rings in my ears is the idea that this negative aura is causing things to go wrong."

"Do you think so?"

"What do I know? She is *positive*. Very religious. Devoted to the church. Goes to a Catholic church in West Palm Beach. Every night."

"I can't believe she's Catholic. The church is completely against psychics."

"All I know is that my income has dried up, that lawyers who praised my work suddenly have zero cases for me. I thought I'd be in this apartment just two years and then sell it and boom! The balloon mortgage kicked in and now I owe $2,500 a month instead of $1,800 and it's all going on my Visa card."

"You have to sell it."

"We've come full circle. Now do you see why I've turned to Cassandra?"

"Because there's nobody else?" She hesitated. "But what about the negative aura? Did she get rid of it for you with the red ribbon and the candles last summer?"

"Evidently not," I wiped sweat off my upper lip. How could I hate air conditioning and imagine living in South Florida? "I went to her last week and she said I still had the aura which is the reason it's not selling."

"But you did everything!" said Melinda sighed. "More candles?"

"No, she says we are dealing with something much stronger than she thought and she wants to talk to someone at the church about me. She told me back in March that I will sell the apartment but—get this—it won't be until after Halloween!"

"What?"

"Melinda, there is so much I don't understand. By the way, she took my red ribbon and gave it to the church. She took all my candle stubs from last summer—I had to save them—and gave them to the church."

"This is so otherworldly. I have to hang up but call me. I want to know what she tells you to do. And do you really like those Argentine realtors? Can you pressure them to tell you more about why those buyers are changing their minds?"

"They just don't know any more. They're not keeping anything from me. As a matter of fact, last week when Raquel called me to tell me that the sale was off, she told me that Patrizia was crying at her desk. She could not make the call to me so Raquel had to do it."

"I feel like crying, too," said Melinda.

"No! To paraphrase Tom Hanks, 'There's no crying in real estate!'"

Laughing, we hung up our phones in unison. One thousand two hundred and eighty-four miles apart. She was on East Eighty-first Street and I was on Adriano Avenue.

Chapter Five

Dear Deirdre and Bronwen,

 First of all, here it is the 10th of July, and I cannot believe I am still here. I keep telling myself not to get hysterical. After all, I am taking a swim every day in the most beautiful pool in the world at the Biltmore Hotel and the Duke and Duchess of Windsor swam there and Esther Williams and Al Capone. Not at the same time. I am certainly warm enough and have enough food. Coral Gables is not North Korea so I should calm down.

 Cassandra thought all my problems might stem from the Haitian sleigh bed and that there was some evil spirit in it keeping everyone from buying my apartment. But now she isn't sure and I have never thought that. Though, in fairness, I must say the best times of my life have been when it was in storage and I was in Europe but maybe that was Europe. And both of you know there has been endless tension, if not quiet, subdued panic about money. Always.

 My Italian class at Miami-Dade is heaven. I love it, love la professoressa who is so chic she makes you want to fly to Rome and attempt the same chicness. I was meant to be taking French 2 but there weren't enough people so I said, do you have an Italian class? And the woman laughed and booked me.

 I think I covered my woes pretty thoroughly on the phone. Forgive me for being such a bore. No work equals no income. Every firm who used me has just stopped. No calls. And every firm I worked for—praised me. Really. I did good work, got the information they wanted. Many times what they didn't think I could get. They liked my reports. I don't understand it. My real focus now is to get this place SOLD and if it means getting the evil spirit exorcised first then I must do that.

 So I lost the house on Poplar but it's okay. I allow myself to be very, very, *very* depressed for ten minutes and then it's just not worth it. It seems like it's wasting a day of your life. I think all three of us are rather like that. Poplar was a disappointment, past tense, but there are other houses in Philadelphia. It was just bad timing. I'm not going to think about the house on Poplar again.

 Oh, how I miss you! Please write and tell me how you are! Wish I could open a bottle of wine and pour us all a glass and spend a lovely dinner talking talking talking! What is the midway point between Rome, London and Miami? I guess we'd be treading water...

                 Much love to you, Cici

It was that night, another muggy, summer night, that I lay under the big white, square Italian market umbrella in the dark. I had the heavy iron stand pushed against the Haitian sleigh bed side rail so that the umbrella was as centered over me as possible. My kind of canopy bed. Nothing fussy, Victorian or antebellum for me. Suddenly the white umbrella turned black. I watched it ink over from left to right. I blinked. Black. I rose on one elbow to see if lights were on in the distance outside, beyond my terrace. Yes, they were. But even after hurricanes when all the street lights were out, the umbrella had always remained white in the dark. Now it was black. I stared at it, thought how odd, and fell asleep. It was white in the morning.

That afternoon I met Tad, a cousin on my mother's side, and his adult daughter for a movie. He'd lived in Miami for decades; we often had drinks and dinner together and were having a good time getting to know each other as adults. As we stood in line for tickets, I told them about the umbrella. Tad seemed to physically stiffen then stated firmly, "We are Buddhists. We don't believe in that." Matter closed. I felt a prickle of annoyance. Don't believe in *what* exactly? Was he saying I was *lying*?

It was the next night that I awakened with a sharp pain across my face as if I'd been hit. I opened my eyes, it was dark and I was disoriented, not in bed but standing up in my nightgown. I touched my nose gently. It really hurt. I realized I was on the other side of my bedroom beside the open door to the hall. The next morning my nose was red and there was a mark on my forehead. I had never walked in my sleep before.

A few days later, another bright summer day and I sat at my desk in shorts, barefooted. The phone rang. "John! How are you?" I was happy to hear from him. I called him L.A. P.I. since I'd met him in the Los Angeles courtroom and had so many Johns in my life. We'd done two or three cases together on the phone.

"Are the movers coming tomorrow? Isn't the closing tomorrow? Wait, isn't it today?"

"The sale fell through."

"Again? How could that happen?"

"It keeps happening. This last sale and the sale before that and the sale before that. I don't even want to count them."

"But—"

"I know. It's a great apartment, everyone says so and they make an offer and they have the inspection and we set the date for closing and—they back out."

"Why?"

"You tell me."

I didn't know whether to tell him about Cassandra and the candles and the negative aura or not but I did and it all made perfect sense to him. He was unsurprised and all for Cassandra. John, of course, was a Californian and dealt in crystals and herbs in his everyday life.

"I told you about the sage awhile back. You have to heat it in the oven and then put some in each room. It will remove bad spirits."

"John, where on earth do I find sage?" I was smiling. John acted as if everyone had a bit of sage somewhere in the house the way you'd have salt and pepper.

"Probably in any grocery store. Actually maybe not in Miami. Go to Whole Foods. Any health food store will have it."

We talked about our last client. "Do you think he'll go ahead with the lawsuit or drop it?"

John nearly laughed. "I advised him to drop it and get out of Dodge."

I nodded. "Case closed."

As we hung up, he said, "Sage should do the trick for the apartment. Don't worry."

A few hours later, I found a Whole Foods on the internet and decided there was no sense in putting it off. I hadn't heard from Cassandra in a few days. Maybe sage would change everything.

I decided to start the washing machine before I left and patted my white shorts pockets for change, yanked the tank top over my head and stripped naked in the kitchen. I grabbed detergent and tossed everything, plus underwear and a few white T-shirts, into the machine. It roared to life, I pulled on white Levis, a shirt, scuffed my feet into sandals and was out the door.

South Dixie Highway I hated. It was a close second in sheer awfulness to I-95. Creeping along between traffic lights, the south Florida sun shimmered in waves on the roofs of the cars in front of me like heat from a stove. I thought of growing up in Mississippi, of being a little girl when no one went outside between noon and four in the afternoon.

I spotted the shopping center, made the turn and drove within a hundred feet of the Whole Foods to park. I noticed about forty people on the sidewalk in the distance. A magician or a mime? In New York, it might be someone selling gold chains or counterfeit handbags.

I put on lipstick in the rear view mirror from force of habit and got out of the Chihuahua. Clickety-thunk, doors locked. The crowd was there when I went into the store but it was at least seventy feet away and I still couldn't see what they were looking at.

Amazingly, Whole Foods was empty. I was directed to the sage, found it and was paying within two or three minutes. Then I was out the door and into the blazing heat again. I looked to the left for the crowd and saw no one at all. I'd counted the rows so as not to lose the car and headed right for it. Between me and the car were a couple of people, standing beside something. A pony? A big dog? All of those people gone so quickly? In three minutes?

It was a goat, with black and white markings, decorated as if for a parade. Colorful scrunchies that one uses for ponytails were around his legs, red ribbons tied in bows decorated his horns; he wore a necklace of ribbons and bells and he sported a crown of white flowers on his head. "He looks like a goat from a story book!" I said.

My first attention was directed towards this adorable animal about waist tall, with flowing colorful ribbons. Then I noticed the man and woman beside him, obviously the owners. They were tan but I didn't think they were from Florida. They both wore shorts and cotton shirts but something about their clothes was not Florida. It was as if their clothes were made by hand. Something was not quite right. He was quite tall, over six feet four and lean with a sun-beaten face and very white teeth and bright eyes. She was not as tall as he was but taller than my six feet in my espadrilles which was unusual. Very tan, she had that same healthy outdoor look, no make-up. They were both attractive, perhaps in their sixties and of course, we spoke English but I remembered thinking the man had no accent. No accent at all. He made no mistakes, the English was perfect but it was flat somehow. The woman may have had a Dutch accent. They told me that they had a pot-bellied pig and many animals and lived outside Miami on several acres of land. I told them about the pigs that my mother and father had seen in the Delta before the dinner party. How intelligent they were and how the man had put them through their paces even asking them to bow their heads and pray before going to the feeding trough. We all agreed that humans underestimated animals.

One or two people stopped and spoke to the man as I talked to the woman but they left quickly. I was alone with them for maybe eight minutes. The conversation took a strange turn. The woman told me that it was the last week of—maybe she said 'fixing it' but I was unsure. I didn't understand. She said, "All you do is put a rubber band around it and it dries up and falls off." I felt disturbed and must have conveyed this because she said, "It's nothing but if you don't do it, they go from place to place and put an odor on everything." I didn't say anything as I didn't want to know anything more.

The man turned to us and said, "This is the last week of having the rubber band on him. This—" I said, "Yes, I know." The woman said, "I told her."

The woman kept talking about this and I felt uneasy. I wondered if the animal were in pain. It didn't appear to be. I patted the goat, looking right into those big eyes, noticing the face, the snow white fur, the pattern of black fur, thinking it was a lovely animal. Again, I noticed the twisted rubber band. I said goodbye.

The Mini Cooper was right there, one car away. I slid into the driver's seat and put the key in the ignition. Then I twisted around to look back and they were gone.

Gone in twelve seconds? I scanned the parking lot. They were tall and should have been visible above the cars' rooftops. They had vanished. Then I wondered why that couple had been there at all. Between parked cars in the summer heat, with a goat decorated like that. They never said why there were there. That tan. Was it fake? After three years in Miami, I knew a sunbathing tan from a sailing tan and a sunbed tan from a spray-on. Their color was certainly glowing and rich and deep but somehow off. Why didn't the woman have a handbag? A tote bag or a basket? Where were they from? They were definitely not from Florida, not even American. Not Canadian. Swiss? No. I would know that.

Imagine going to buy sage and ending up petting a goat in a Miami parking lot! Life was fun and events were unexpected and ridiculous! I didn't think I'd ever petted a goat before. I'd seen them in Ethiopia, in Egypt, in Ireland, in lots of places but never stared into one's face. I started the car and drove home.

The washing machine cycle was over and I reached in to pull out the clothes. Sometimes there'd be a dime or a penny lying in the bottom so I wasn't surprised when I saw a flash of metal. I grabbed the silver coin and was amazed that it wasn't a dime but it was big like a Kennedy half dollar, like a Susan B. Anthony dollar. It was a Haitian 50 gourd coin and the date was 1908. Where had it come from? The pocket of my shorts? No, I'd checked and they'd been empty. There was nothing else with a pocket in the wash. Besides I'd have seen it if I'd put it in my pocket. It was heavy. I tossed everything into the dryer and put the big coin on my desk.

The sage was green, like grass. It had to be dry or I couldn't light it so I turned on the oven to 350F and emptied the little bag onto a baking sheet. Should sage be baked or broiled when it's for banishing a bad spirit? I went for bake and in half an hour I thought it was dry and ready. John had told me to light it and then, with the smoke, draw a protective clockwise circle around myself. I started with my green bedroom. Face the east and with the smoke draw the star of David in front of me chanting "Earth, Air, Fire, Water, in the name of all that is Good and Right, I command you to leave." Then I did the same chant facing south and then again facing west and then north. Then I went to different sections of the room and repeated it all and then did the same thing in each room. I did it more times than he told me to. John told me to do it in doorways and windows, too, and I did. I was chanting like a maniac and my arm was tired so I switched from right to left. John told me that I would notice an immediate change in the energy.

I didn't have any red brick dust to pour on the windowsills and in the doorways; John had said that it was an old voodoo trick that he really liked. I thought the sage would be enough and anyway, where does one find red brick dust?

I finished, my arms ached and I thought, okay, I have done all I can. I did not notice any change in the energy.

Cassandra called and said that she and Father Gabriel were working on my apartment. I told her about the coin and she said she didn't know what it meant, maybe nothing. I liked that about her. I was mystified enough for both of us and she could have told me anything and I would have been receptive.

Then I told her about the sage and I thought she'd be happy but she seemed upset. "You never should have done that!" Her voice was sharp. "That was the worst thing to do. We are dealing with something much too strong for that. The sage will anger it. You are confronting the spirit and it's going to attack you if it feels threatened. The spirit needs a ground, a resting place. The bed is your resting place, your safe haven when sleeping. Now it's throughout the whole house and it's why things go wrong."

"But I thought we got rid of the negative energy with all the candles last summer?"

"I thought so, too."

"I have the parsley out. Since last week. Should I leave it out?"

"It won't help at this point but leave it out anyway."

As Cassandra had directed, I had little saucers piled with green sprigs in every room. My bedroom had three dishes of it and the living room had four. We hung up. I could still smell the burning sage. Maybe John was right. After all the phone calls and candles and the red ribbon…maybe the sage would change everything.

Chapter Six

JULY 14, 2006

I was getting ready for bed when I suddenly felt a pinch in my lower back. I couldn't remember lifting anything but I decided to put my pink and white striped sleeping bag down on the floor beside my bed. I love sleeping on the floor and did it for years in my tiny Manhattan apartment filled with books. The Mexican tiles were cold under me at first and I turned back and forth to get comfortable. I was lying between the bed and the walk-in closet staring up at the underside of the bed. Something bothered me. I didn't like lying nearly under the bed and I didn't like turning my back on it either. I got up and took the sleeping bag into the living room. I laid it near the outdoor living room door, fluffed up the pillow and prepared to turn out the light. For some reason, I went down the hall and closed the bedroom door. I never did that and I wondered why I was doing it even as I pulled it closed.

Back to my pallet and I lay down thinking that this was exactly where I'd slept the first night. It would be three years come Halloween. Today was Bastille Day, I thought, as I fell asleep.

CRASH! I was awake and sitting up and ready to run. CRASH! It was something huge on the other side of the bedroom door, charging into it, trying to break it down. It sounded like an animal with horns, with a great head, with massive shoulders. CRASH! A bison? A tremendous bull? Then I thought of a rhinoceros.

I stood up, shaking, turned on a lamp, and grabbed my cell. Without thinking, I called Cassandra and panting with fear told her something terrible was in my bedroom.

"We know all about it. Don't be afraid. Do you have a Bible? Get it. I'll stay on the phone with you."

I was terrified. I wondered what it was, what could be so tremendous, and would that door splinter to pieces at the next blow? I went to the outdoor living room. I'd seen the Bible that very morning. It was on top of a box that had been packed, but not yet taped closed. My little white leather Bible from the First Presbyterian Church. I'd gotten it at age twelve in spite of refusing to memorize the silly catechism. I grabbed it.

"Now, Cici, listen to me." Her voice was authoritative. "Turn on every light in your apartment. I'm staying on the line. Do it."

"But I can't go in the bedroom!" I flipped on the kitchen light, the laundry room closet light, the powder room light and then backed down the hallway staring at my bedroom door.

"No. Don't go in the bedroom. Don't open the door. We know it's there. We are taking care of it."

"But what is it?" My voice cracked.

"You are going to be alright. There are angels all around you. They won't let anything bad happen to you. Sit down and open the Bible and hold onto it, keep all the lights on and call me in an hour. I'm in the cemetery with Father Gabriel and —"

"What are you doing in a cemetery? In the middle of the night?" I gasped into the phone.

"I told you we are working on this. I have to stay until six tomorrow morning. We know what it is. We are binding it. It did this to prove to you that it existed, to make you believe in it because you never really believed in it before."

I was trembling with fear. My hand clutched the phone in an iron grip but shook anyway.

"Now, call me in an hour. I won't pick up but just leave a message that you're okay. I am sending angels to watch over you. You're safe. I will come and see you tomorrow."

"You will?" I'd asked her to come and she had seemed to think it wasn't necessary. Things had changed.

I hated having her hang up. I sat in one of the Chinese Chippendale chairs with the Bible in my lap and stared around my bright yellow living room. The bookshelves were empty, the packing boxes pushed at one end of the room but I'd left the pictures on the walls. My hands were ice cold, gripping the white leather-bound book. The crashing had stopped but there was something moving around in the bedroom. Not footsteps but a shuffling noise as if it were so big it was brushing against the walls. I went into the kitchen and suddenly it seemed like a good idea to grab a can of tuna fish. Solid white albacore with water. It was more familiar to me than any Bible. I went back to my chair and sat, clutching the can with the Bible in my lap. I listened to the sounds of movement on the other side of the closed door. An hour passed very slowly but finally it was one-fifteen. I called Cassandra's cell and left a message saying I was okay and I would be glad to see her tomorrow. Even hearing her recorded voice helped me.

   I looked at the sleeping bag but could not get down on the floor again. The apartment was bright but the loud rustling noise in the bedroom continued. I found myself staring at the Aubrey Beardsley poster on the wall. It was black and white, of course, and more than three feet tall and maybe two and a half feet wide, framed, with glass. As I watched, a face materialized. It was an old man with long hair and a beard. It looked like Leonardo da Vinci. I was fascinated. I watched the face change. Now it looked like Kris Kristofferson. I blinked, wishing the lines of the Beardsley poster would return. I watched the face blur and then become a very angry, dangerous-looking man with fiery eyes. I tried to stop staring but it was mesmerizing. I resolved to turn my head away, and, with difficulty, I did. I clutched the can of tuna and the Bible and waited for sunrise.

Chapter Seven

JULY 15, 2006

It was the next morning. Saturday. I stood outside the bedroom and listened. Be sensible, I told myself, then I held my breath, turned the doorknob and pushed the door open. I really thought I'd see marks on the walls and broken furniture but all was normal. The air was very still but otherwise the room was just as it had been last night before I closed the door. The white umbrella, the Haitian sleigh bed, my framed family photographs on the emerald green wall were all in place, where they were supposed to be.

Cassandra had not called but John was on the phone. I stood on the covered terrace at the wrought-iron railing watching a plane land in the distance. Another plane was taking off. "Whatever happened last night changed me. I do believe there is some spirit around me. I felt rather good after burning the sage and I do think the coin means something but what? I had no odd feelings going to bed the night before last or last night."

"You're tough," said John.

"I don't know how tough I am but in the bright light of day I can talk myself out of anything the least bit dark. But I *did* see the black umbrella and the coin is there on my desk and the noises levitated me right off the floor! So, if burning sage forced a confrontation— great!" I stopped. "Even if I did have about nine heart attacks." I was sounding a great deal more brave than I felt; I felt weak when I thought of the noise on the other side of my bedroom door. It would sound in my ears for the rest of my life.

John laughed. "So are you going to sleep in your bedroom tonight?"

"I will never sleep in that room again," I stated. "It's definitely time to move."

John said he'd never known the sage not to work. He told me about his book collection, talked about spirits.

"But, John, why would a spirit want to follow me?"

"It's like a vampire. You have a lot of energy and it wants to be with that energy." He agreed with Cassandra saying, "Yes, you can get rid of it. You can get rid of it forever."

I thought of all the candles, yellow, white and lavender that I burned last year. The red ribbon with all the pins. The white handkerchief under the mattress. I thought of sleepwalking and slamming my nose into the door frame.

"I think you should trust Cassandra but meanwhile I will try to get in touch with a witch I know out here in Santa Monica."

"Oh, John!" I cried in exasperation. "Do you really think we need to get a witch involved?"

"What do you think Cassandra is?" he demanded. "The tooth fairy?"

"Well, she calls herself a psychic and I've heard her say she's a spiritualist—"

"She's a witch," John stated definitively. "She is probably a white witch but she's a witch all the same."

"Oh," I said hollowly. A witch in Coconut Grove, a priest, something huge and dangerous in my bedroom and a detective in L.A. offering to contact a witch in California. Life was interesting.

"I went into the bedroom this morning and I couldn't believe that nothing was disturbed. I felt shocked that all was in place. I stood there, amazed."

"Then what did you do?"

"I got into a bikini, brushed my teeth, washed my face and drove to the Biltmore to go swimming. Just like I do every morning."

"Good for you." He paused. "Ask Cassandra about the sea salt around your door since you couldn't find the red brick dust."

I rolled my eyes. Are there stores that sell things like *red brick dust*? Maybe in California but not in normal places. He went on about the influence of Christianity and gave me websites to look at but I told him I didn't want to go any further. "But knowledge is power," he said. How many times have I said that to myself as a detective?

The call waiting beep sounded. "I heard that," he said. "Maybe it's Cassandra. I'll let you go."

It was. "Do you want me to pick you up? I can come right now."

"No, I can't come to you today," she said. I could barely understand her. She seemed to be having trouble enunciating. "I was attacked last night."

"What happened? Are you alright?"

"When you called me I was in the cemetery with Father Gabriel but I was some distance away from him when something grabbed me and tried to suffocate me."

"Something? What was it?"

"It was huge but I couldn't see anything. It was on top of me. I only felt it. We struggled. I was screaming."

"Were you hurt?" My palm with splayed fingers was over my chest. I wanted to shout 'Is this true? Why are you telling me this? How could this happen?' Instead, I heard myself say, "But, Cassandra, I don't understand how something you can't see could do this!"

"You know something was trying to break that door down, don't you? That is what came after me. I've never had this happen to me before but I have seen women thrown across the room in a church." I was silent. "Whatever was in your bedroom last night attacked me in the cemetery."

I felt cold. I watched another plane take off in the distance heading east over the Atlantic. She went on. "It's a male entity. It's huge and it's very angry. I told you before that the spirits in your apartment were much stronger than we first thought."

"Last night—" I stammered. "It's amazing that I would have a pain in my back and—"

"God wanted you to be safe."

I didn't say a word. Personally, I didn't think God had much to do with what happens to any of us and these people who have lost twenty-seven relatives in a hurricane and then thank God on the six o'clock news that their dog is safe are just fools. "I'm closing that door tonight and I'm not going in there until tomorrow morning."

"Get everything you need, close that door and don't go in there after dark."

"But what about the windows?" I asked. I wondered if this *thing* was like a cat burglar.

"It can't get out the bedroom window or get on the living room balcony. We've isolated it in that one room. At least for a while." I wasn't sure if I felt better or not. "Have a glass of wine and try to relax. I will come tomorrow. I will call you. I'm going to church now. I have to go as two of the women who were working on this have refused to go any further." I felt frightened at this news. "Now that it's gotten physical they are afraid." She hesitated and then said, "Call me if you hear or see anything."

We hung up. I was very glad she was coming to the apartment. I was sure that she could deal with it and my apartment would be fine and someone would buy it if only Cassandra would come.

I poured a glass of sauvignon blanc, put it on the marble coffee table and stared at it. Oscar Wilde always called white wine yellow wine and it was. I didn't want to drink it. I vowed to not have anything to drink unless I were out with a friend and it would have been cause for comment not to. I wanted to be alert and lucid for whatever might happen.

It was getting dark. I went into my bedroom and grabbed a bikini, my hairbrush, tooth brush, face cream, everything I needed to prepare for bed and my morning swim and moved it all into the hall powder room. Then I closed the bedroom door. Firmly. I pushed against it and made sure it could not swing open.

I went through the living room and then out onto the balcony of the outdoor living room. Below me was Coral Gables, a quiet, wealthy, upper class suburb of Miami. Enough miles inland from the ocean so that there was no forced evacuation during hurricane season. That's why I'd picked it. That and Books & Books. Roof tops of pastel houses peeked through palm trees, little streets with Spanish names criss-crossed the landscape. Another plane took off in the distance leaving a white vapor trail in the deep blue sky. Darkness came suddenly here. I went back inside to the living room and turned on all the lights.

Chapter Eight

Lying on a chaise in my wet bikini, I felt as if the sun were healing me. My muscles faintly ached from doing more laps than usual and maybe from not enough sleep. I reached down for the Arts section of Sunday's *New York Times* as someone laughed on the other side of the swimming pool. The largest one in the continental United States, it was surrounded by jungle greenery and flowers of yellow, orange, and pink. I swam in it every morning, and counted it as one of the best things in my life.

At a little after eleven, when I was home, Cassandra called. She said she was feeling much better and we arranged for me to pick her up later. She asked how I was. "Nothing happened last night. Except that thing with the picture changing into a man's face."

"Don't look at it!" said Cassandra sharply. She didn't deny that it happens, I thought. She isn't questioning my sanity.

"I tried not to look." I wanted to be upbeat, to disguise my fear. "I didn't sleep but who cares." I had sat in a chair all night long, in my clothes, my feet up on the coffee table. I'd watched television until about one in the morning and then turned it off, thinking I would close my eyes and rest them. I dreamed of an animal with its head in my lap. I petted it as if it were a dog but suddenly I saw that it was a goat. I jerked awake. The room was silent but I felt that someone else was there. "Cassandra, I didn't see or actually hear anything but I felt that I wasn't alone."

"You aren't alone," she said. "Even now. I don't want you to talk on this phone anymore. Use your cell and leave the building, go outside."

"I'm out on the terrace. Isn't that good enough?"

"No, you must leave the apartment and the building. They can hear you." She hung up.

Who are *they*? I wondered.

I was in front of her office at three; she got into the Chihuahua adjusting an ankle-length, blue skirt. I'd never seen her wearing sunglasses before; they were the big Jackie-O kind and she looked very different.

"How are you?" I said as we stopped at the first traffic light. She lifted the glasses and I saw the two black eyes. One was swollen almost closed. Then I noticed that her top lip was puffy and split. I was aghast. There were black bruises on her neck as if someone had rubbed charcoal on her golden skin. A

Band-aid on her arm partially covered a cut and I saw more bruises. "Oh, Cassandra, all this happened to you in the cemetery?"

"Well, my husband doesn't beat me." I stared at her as she started to laugh and then said, "No! I can't laugh! I really hurts."

I was profoundly shocked. I apologized and then thought, am I to blame? What does this have to do with me?

I paid attention to the Sunday traffic but kept asking her what it was, to explain it to me. All I kept hearing was that it was more powerful than they thought. "We isolated it last night. We tied it down. It can't come back to your apartment."

"But you couldn't see it? You could feel it and it could obviously hurt you. Cassandra, I think of spirits and I think of air. Not something that could leave bruises on you."

"Spirits are not just air. It's male, it's huge and it's angry. The entity was trying to break the door down and when you called me and I put a circle of protection around you then it knew we were linked. I was confronting it and it came after me. It showed itself to you. You've never really believed in it before and it's been with your for a long time. You are very lucky nothing happened to you when you saw the black umbrella." She tentatively touched a bruise on her neck. "You have been ignoring things because you have not been able to grasp the idea of the spirit. It is now crossing over. It can hurt you the way it hurt me. When you saw the umbrella turn black, it was there."

I felt as if she were talking about something that had nothing to do with me. This was not real. This was the plot of a movie she once saw. She kept talking. She had seven people with her last night watching her. "I will give you a phone number to call immediately if I tell you to. You are looking at me now but if I change in any way because I'm going to confront it then you have to run out of the house and call the phone number and the nuns will come and get me. But you have to get out of the house."

Her phone rang and she answered. "Yes, we're on the way." She turned to me. "Where are we exactly?"

"We are nearly on Virginia and then we'll be on Bird Avenue."

Cassandra repeated it. "What kind of car is this?"

"It's a green Mini Cooper with a white top," I said and she repeated it. Then I added, "It's called the Chihuahua." Cassandra laughed and repeated that into her cell.

She snapped the phone closed. "They are praying for us. I wouldn't go near your house without their knowing we are there. They will be with us. They are praying for us right now."

We turned on Douglas as she told me that I must do as she says. I will enter the apartment first and then invite her over the threshold. But I must leave her there if I am commanded to. I didn't say anything. For once, I had no questions. Cassandra was in charge. She had been doing this sort of thing for years; she was a pro. "Aren't you afraid?" I said, looking at the marks on her neck.

"No. I've done this so many times."

I clicked the garage door open with the remote and we glided into the underground garage. I felt like going into my spiel of "this is the mailroom" and "we are going to re-do the elevator," as we stepped in. What if she didn't find anything at all? I had seen or heard nothing out of the ordinary on this sun-filled Sunday afternoon. The fourth floor was quiet. I unlocked my front door and went in. Then I motioned her to come in and went behind her to stand on the threshold as she had directed. Cassandra handed me her cell phone "because it will disturb it." She stood for a moment in the middle of the living room as if listening. Then she walked to the left to the outdoor living room. No one ever did that.

Somehow it was more natural to veer to the right in the living room towards the hall, the kitchen, the powder room and my bedroom. She came back and sat in one of the Chinese Chippendale chairs and stared into space. I thought she was listening but the apartment was silent. Then she got up and went to the hall and the kitchen and the bathroom and then she motioned for me to come with her and went toward the bedroom. She opened the bedroom door and then she shouted, "Go to the door! Quickly! Stand with one foot outside and one inside!" I hurried back through the apartment to the threshold.

"Can you hear me?"

"Yes, but you didn't give me any phone number." I felt very calm. I was even casual. This all seemed a bit theatrical.

"Just a minute," she called. Cassandra came out and sat on the chair again. "There are four spirits here."

Later she would say that it was like two kids who run to you and can't wait to say, you'll never guess what *he* did! That's exactly what two of the spirits did. One was talking but it didn't really speak clearly. The other one was easily understood. She said one was from my childhood, had been with me for so long, knew me so well. The other was a black boy now a man and later she said she thought he was Haitian and maybe the painter of a painting. "He left the coin for you. Neither of them want to harm you but there are two others who are hidden in the apartment and won't show themselves."

One attacked her the other night. She explained that it was trying to break the door down because they had tied it, captured it and it was struggling. She stood up again and said, "Come with me," and we went into the bedroom and I explained about the windows always being open. "But I still feel there is something odd about the air in here."

Cassandra opened the terrace door and we went outside. She didn't want a chair but wanted to stand. "In case he shows himself."

"But what will you see?" I asked.

"I don't know. Maybe a man, maybe a dog. I don't know."

We stood on the terrace and looked back at my apartment. Leaving the doors open we could see through the bedroom, down the short, straight hallway and into the living room. Above the French daybed was a large gold-framed mirror from Rome. It was thirty feet away but in our direct line of vision. Cassandra was facing the apartment, standing beside me. "I'm here because I believe in you and because I want them to know that you are not alone."

"Why are we out here?" I asked.

"Because the apartment frightens me," she said. "I don't want to be in it."

Cassandra was frightened? The umbrella had not frightened me and sleepwalking was simply out of the ordinary. The coin was strange but I had not been frightened until I'd heard the noise.

"I want to know what happened here. What happened to the building or to the land it's on. When was it built?"

"This building is only eight years old. I am the second person to own the apartment. The first owner rented it to me and to other people the whole time.

I don't think she ever lived in it." Silvia, the Venezuelan in the Jaguar. Coral Gables was thick with both. It had been her father who'd shown me through and it had been her father who had lowered the rent from $1200 a month to the $1,000 that was my maximum.

Suddenly Cassandra said, "Oh, oh, come on! Let's get out of here! I saw it!" She was upset. "Come on! Close the door because you aren't coming back here!" So I locked the French doors behind us and we rushed into the living room closing the bedroom door behind us.

"Holy Father, protect us! Holy Father, in the name of all that is good!" Cassandra was talking really fast, seemed panicked as she rushed around my living room putting out little blue stones on my packing boxes and on chairs and under the cushion on a chair and under the mattress of the French daybed.

In the middle of all this chaos, Cassandra turned to me and lifted a large gold cross on a chain over my head. "Never take it off!"

"What about swimming?"

"Swimming, in the shower—never take it off!"

So that was settled and then she started racing around again saying, "We have to get out of here! Get your stuff!" and I was thinking what stuff? "You left your Bible," I said and she grabbed it off the chair and then demanded, "Where's yours?" and I pointed to it on top of one of the brown boxes and she opened it and put it back. I grabbed my basket purse and we ran out.

In the hall, at last, I locked the door. "What was it? Did you see something?"

She punched the elevator button, the doors slid open and we stepped in quickly. "Let's get away from here," she said pushing the button for the garage.

We went downstairs, got in the Chihuahua and slammed the doors. Two women sitting in an underground garage in a Mini Cooper with the bright Florida day outside. Another spectacular Sunday afternoon.

"It was an incubus. I saw it in the mirror. It was walking past the mirror."

"What is an incubus?" I demanded.

"It's...uh...it was over seven feet tall."

"That makes me feel ill."

"Your apartment made me feel ill when I walked in. Very sick at my stomach." I looked at her face and she did not look at all well. Under the bruises, her face was pasty. "Let's get out of here and get some fresh air," I said and then I remembered and opened my pocketbook. "Let me give you this. Here's the mortgage broker's card, some photographs of my bedroom and do you want the coin?"

"Yes." I handed everything to her and she put it all in her lap.

"I've had it on my desk all week and I play with it while I'm on the phone and keep wondering where it came from." I took the Haitian coin from my shorts pocket and gave it to her. She had her hand out. I didn't see it fall but somehow it did. "Oh, sorry," I said. I looked in my lap and then raised up awkwardly and felt under myself on the seat. "Maybe it fell here," I said looking at the gear shift between us. I fumbled around and came up with a dime. We opened both doors and got out of the car. I took the flashlight out of the glove compartment and we shook out both black rubber floor mats and came up with two hair clips.

"You are never going to find it. Now I know it's connected to all this. If I had not believed you before this then I would believe you now."

I was out of the car with my door open, bending down and staring under the seat.

"It has to be here," I said. "It was in my hand. You saw it."

"Stop! You aren't going to find it because it was not meant to come to me. It was for you."

I got back in the car and slammed the door, feeling frustrated, confused. Things do not disappear into thin air in a confined space. Cassandra said, "It's gone. Look at me." She took both my hands in hers. "I'm making a promise to you that I will not desert you, I will help you. You are the only case for me now and you come before anything else. Before my family, before anything." I nodded, not knowing what to say.

"Hold the cross," she directed. "In the name of the Father and the Son..." she prayed with her hands around mine and mine clutching the big gold cross around my neck. "Amen."

I faced forward.

"Bathemus is there. The heaviness in the air...it does not want to let you go. When I walked in there were all those voices but the one I felt was most important was of a little Haitian boy. He has been with you for a long time."

I turned in my seat to stare at her. "Little boy?"

"He's older now but he came to you as a little boy. He is good. He won't hurt you. But he is not strong enough to fight the others."

I understood nothing. "Others?" She didn't answer. "So let me get this straight," I said, clicking on my seat belt. "There is the Haitian little boy and one other who can come with me, be with me…" Cassandra interrupted. "Yes, they are okay. They won't hurt you. And now we know about this goat but the fourth one is a mystery."

We exited the garage, turning left at the Holiday Inn on the corner of Le Jeune Road. Again, I asked what she had seen. "There are very strong powers there. I saw Bathemus."

"What is *that*?"

"It is part man, part goat. It's used in Satanic worship. The head is a goat and it has horns. It crossed in front of the mirror and I saw the reflection. It was huge."

"How huge?" I demanded.

"Like a linebacker."

"Six feet tall?" I demanded again.

Her voice was serious. "Taller. More than seven but it was hunched over. It is the Devil. We need documentation of this entity to know what to do."

My mind was racing. The Devil? Walking around in my living room?

"I told you that two women who were working on this case didn't want to after Friday night but I've talked them into continuing. I have others who have been called to work on it but they don't know any details yet." She sighed. "I'll have to explain it to them." We were both silent. "Father Gabriel doesn't want to come to your apartment and when a priest is afraid then…"

"How many people are working on this?"

"Seven not counting me."

I said, "Okay. You are the best so you count as three of the others."

She started to smile but didn't because she really couldn't with the deep cut on her lip. "Something may have happened on the land where this building was built and the spirit there—whatever spirit there was—had the power to call other spirits. When you moved in it was fine but now that you want to go they don't want to let you go. The house has a lot of demonic entities."

"Cassandra, this past week I've had vivid dreams—before Friday, before that thing tried to break the door down. I dreamed that I was bitten on my hip and it was like a pony nipping me. Not like a horse, much smaller. But definitely a bite."

"It wasn't a dream," she said. "A goat's mouth is not unlike a pony's."

I changed lanes, forcing myself to concentrate. The place still hurt. "But this thing you saw..." I said. I wanted specifics.

"I saw it cross in front of the mirror, only the reflection. It's an incubus. It's not human exactly but it won't hurt you because it wants you. There is something called possession, you know..."

I knew of no such thing but her voice told me it was fairly horrific. I had no idea what questions to ask. I felt confused. She saw an incubus but she also saw something called Bathemus and that was the Devil? All I really knew was that it was not good, it was in the apartment, and once it was gone, I could sell the condo and leave.

The traffic on Sunday afternoon was slow and thick. I had to pay attention as Miami drivers are notorious. The saying is that everyone obeys the laws—the laws of their own country. The thought flashed through my mind that I was sitting next to a witch who'd been attacked by a demon who lived in my penthouse and we were in my Mini Cooper on the way to Coconut Grove. The year was 2006. Didn't demons live in gloomy English castles filled with cobwebs, bats, and winding staircases, two hundred years ago? And witches, most assuredly, did not live in Coconut Grove. They didn't have offices next to doughnut shops.

Cassandra touched the bandage on her arm. "I'm going to ask Father Gabriel to come to your apartment. I can't do this alone. I need help."

Sounding tired because I was tired, I asked, "And when all this stuff is gone from my apartment then someone will buy it?"

I remember exactly where we were when she answered. We were just making the turn onto Douglas Road. "It's not the apartment. It's you."

I felt a wave of fear. The sun was bright, it was afternoon but I felt lost in darkness. I heard her voice as if she were far away. "You *have* to sell that apartment but if this will move with you to wherever you go it will ruin your business, your life, whatever you try..."

We were crossing Highway 1. "Then why don't I just kill myself?"

Cassandra became very upset. "God does not forgive suicide. You didn't mean it. I know you didn't mean it."

"I guess I've had other times to do it if I were going to. Things have been worse in my life." I put on my blinker and changed lanes. "But if there is no hope?"

She said, "I'm glad you said this in front of me because it tells me more about you. Do you think I would spend all this time on you if I didn't think you were valuable, you were worth it? Maybe you are going to write something about what is happening to you now, you are going to do something very important when this is over. But you must be patient."

I didn't want to be patient. I wanted to leave Coral Gables forever. I wanted to sleep. I tried to sound reasonable, to make sense of it. The goat at Whole Foods and the strange couple suddenly flashed into my mind but I felt too tired to tell her about it. My God. A goat. The animal I'd been petting in my lap in the dream. Another goat.

I said, "This probably isn't important in light of everything else but I have someone coming from New York to see the apartment on Tuesday at 11 o'clock. What am I going to do with all that parsley?" Not to mention all those blue stones and the four spirits.

"Tuck it out of sight. When you go back now I want you to walk in with no expression on your face. I know it's hard but don't think about me or about any of this."

I looked at her as if she were delirious.

"Pretend you're on a case," she said.

"Okay. Undercover in my own apartment."

Cassandra kissed me on the cheek before getting out of the car in front of her office. "I love you," she said solemnly. Suddenly I felt emotional. Maybe it was some sort of love for her or it was the realization that she was the only person helping me and I was in serious trouble that I didn't understand. "I love you, too," I said.

She closed the door and leaned with one bruised tan forearm on the window frame. "I'll be in church tonight. Once we get rid of it we will be rid of it forever."

Sounding tired because I was tired, I asked, "And when all this stuff is gone from my apartment then someone will buy it?" I remember watching her lips move as she said it again. Definitely. Clearly. "Cici, it's *not* the apartment. It's you."

I drove home trying to focus on traffic lights, stop signs, turn signals and the speedometer. Basic, predictable activities to notice when driving a car. Driving a car with a tank full of gas, with a bathing suit on the back seat, with a spare tire in the trunk. I am a reasonable person leading a normal life, I told myself. I proceeded over a familiar landscape back to Coral Gables.

I entered the apartment trying not to think of running away from it. I went into the bedroom and made sure the French doors were locked. In twelve seconds I'd grabbed a bikini, a fresh towel and was out of the room. I closed the door behind me and went into the living room. I knew I was not alone. I was being watched, someone or something was standing by my desk. The room was silent but it was there. A siren sounded outside, probably over on Ponce de Leon, and I heard laughter and voices on the sidewalk below.

Okay, I thought, you stay here. But I'm not staying here. I went out to the covered terrace and read the rest of *The New York Times* in one of the wicker chairs. I always saved the Sunday magazine and the Travel section for last. Several times I looked up at the sky and noticed that the light had changed. Soon it would be dark.

Chapter Nine

Half past eleven. Before all this started, at this hour, I would have been asleep in my Haitian sleigh bed under the Italian market umbrella. Now I was in the living room, with all the lights on, sitting on the French daybed with my legs stretched out straight admiring my pedicure. I wore a white T-shirt and white shorts, my hair was in a ponytail. I'd washed my face, brushed my teeth and was ready for sleep in case I decided it was okay to risk it. I started to read the fat, new biography of Benjamin Franklin for, after all, I'd be living in his city soon. I heard a little pfffffft noise a few feet away. It was like air escaping from a bicycle pump.

I stared at nothing as if expecting to see some shape materialize but I saw nothing and then I started to read again.

A moment later, I heard it. I looked at my watch; it happened again in fifty seconds. I stared at the second hand and, after three minutes, I put my arm down. *Pfffffft*. Yes, something was standing right there about two feet to my left. Then there was a different noise. It sounded as if someone was holding a piece of typing paper and giving it a little shake. I could see nothing except my brightly-lit living room.

I went back to Ben Franklin but I couldn't concentrate. My T-shirt scratched against my chest and I winced. Cassandra had put the cross on me on Sunday afternoon and oozing, open, red blisters had formed within hours. Wet, angry, bleeding sores in the shape of the cross. I put the chain and the cross outside my clothes so it couldn't touch me and the next day went to see her.

"Take it off," she said. "They don't want you to wear it." Most of the 18K gold cross had turned black. Cassandra lifted it over my head. "This has never happened before."

My poor chest was healing but the new skin was still sensitive.

I started to think that this isn't nearly as awful as Rome was. Maybe I've had some experiences that don't happen to the average person. I went to a palm reader once who said, "You are so psychic that you could put us all out of business if you ever wanted to." I'd shrugged cynically. Maybe she said that to everyone.

I have sometimes imagined some communication flying from another person to me. I cannot explain why I awakened in Rome from a very sad dream, turned on the light and looked at the clock. It was 4:20 in the morning. I lay back in the dark and thought of Cousin Clare in the dream calling out my name and saying "Goodbye! Goodbye!" and I knew, absolutely, that she had died. The next afternoon when the phone rang, I knew it was my cousin about to tell me that she had died at 10:20 in the evening Eastern Standard Time precisely when I was dreaming of her in Italy.

Mother came to me on the day she died and rode shotgun with me from New York City to a location in New Jersey. Just as she had the summer of 1994, when I was a detective in Turtle Creek. I did my work with the cops and she and I drove back together in my rented Avis car. I could not see her but I could feel her presence. My T-shirt damp with tears, I talked the whole way and a few hours later, in my apartment, she came to me and embraced me. It was the sweetest sensation I have ever experienced. My body felt enveloped in silk, in wings, in silent music. I knew it was Mother. I would be told, the next day, that she had died in Mississippi but I knew it already.

Mother came to me after that, several times. I saw her face over my shoulder, smiling, in the mirror of an apartment building lobby. She appeared at night in my New York apartment. I haven't seen her for a long time but maybe it is because she is within me always, her voice, her laugh, what she taught me, her ideas about doing 'the right thing.' So I don't need to see her. I know she is with me.

My brother Stirling came to me after he died. It was in Rome and he was sitting in the living room as I prepared dinner in the kitchen. The living room was dark and I did not go to look but I knew he was there.

When I was married and lived in Ottawa, I was on the second floor when I saw a woman with dark hair wearing a white dress or nightgown. I watched her descend the stairs and vanish. My husband said I spent too much time alone. One day two seventh-grade girls rang the doorbell and asked if they could see the house since it was on the Canadian Register of Historic Places and was their school project. They told me about the young woman who had died there and I told them what I'd seen on the stairs. They were thrilled.

At one point, in between apartments in Rome, it was arranged that I would stay at a friend's apartment on the Lungotevere. The rent was reasonable, the location was central and the place was enormous. Plenty of space for me to set up an office and write. I'd met Eve, who was Czech, at lunch a few times with a mutual friend. She had decided, at about age forty, to go to Vienna and study to become an opera singer. Her apartment would be empty; her husband and three sons lived in Germany. I'd been living in London, arrived at Fiumicino, and took a taxi to the Trastevere address. Elated as I unlocked the big front door, I entered the long wide hallway that was the spine of the apartment. Rooms with closed doors lined the hallway. Behind me, with closed door, was the kitchen, another door was the bathroom, the door in front of me was the living room, the next was the library, the next was Eve's and her husband's bedroom. On the opposite side of the hall were her sons's bedrooms. Every door closed.

I was euphoric to be back in Rome. The apartment was freezing so I opened my suitcase in the hall to dig out a sweater and then called my friend Judy for dinner plans.

The January afternoon was fast fading into evening. I peeked into every room and closed each ten-foot-tall door again.

Dinner with Judy and her husband Giovanni was at their apartment a short walk away. A celebration of my return. I came back to the apartment feeling very happy but when I opened the front door I noticed again how strangely cold it was. I unpacked a few things in the bathroom, put on my nightgown and wondered where I should sleep. Eve had said to sleep in her double bed but I decided not to and her boys's rooms were covered in sports posters and felt very personal, too. I saw a daybed in the library, found clean sheets and a pillow. There was a grand piano in the large room, bookshelves extended from floor to the high ceiling; a large chandelier presided over it all. The outside air was warmer than the strangely chilly room and I tried, with no success, to open a window. It should have opened inward and I pulled with all my strength but it wouldn't move. I hate not having fresh air in a room where I'm sleeping but I'd already made the bed and thought I'd have to forget about it for tonight.

I lay down and realized I had to sit up and turn, leaning on one elbow, to reach the lamp. I felt exhausted, clicked it off and pulled the covers up. It was quite cold but I felt my whole body relax as I realized all that I'd done since leaving London that morning. I was delighted to be back in Rome, the apartment would be great for me once I set up my computer and tomorrow Jay, my fiancé, would arrive. As I drifted off to sleep, I felt joyful.

Something touched my face. I slapped it away, sat up and reached for the lamp. I threw the covers off me, thinking it had been a spider. There was nothing. I turned off the light, lay back in the dark but again, something touched my face. It felt more substantial this time and I sat up and reached for the lamp. Blinking, staring around the room, examining the blanket, shaking it, I could see nothing. Again, I turned off the light, settled myself and closed my eyes. This time the touch was definitely a hand on my face. I was so frightened I felt paralyzed. I wanted to leap up and race from the room but I was too afraid to sit up because I thought I would actually bump into the owner of that hand in front of me in the dark.

At last, heart pounding, I sat up, turned on the light and pulled the blanket and sheets off the bed, grabbed the pillow and went down the hall to one of the son's rooms. I left the hall light on, fixed the bed, got in then got up and tried to lock the door. No lock. I put a chair in front of it. I felt ridiculous.

I didn't sleep well. I stared at the door far too long. A disembodied, invisible hand? I stared up at the soccer poster and thought, I'm in Eve's apartment in Rome. I love this city and Eve is a friend. I'm okay. I fell asleep at some point and woke in bright daylight.

Stumbling into the hall I saw my open suitcase where I'd left it and thought I'd wash my hair, get ready for Jay. I was about to step into the shower when I realized my shampoo was still packed. Out in the hall, the library door was open so I closed it. As I turned away, I saw the lever handle move downward and the door open again. Slowly I reached for it, closed it and again, the handle moved and the door opened. Then I watched the living room door open, then the bedroom door where I'd spent the night. All the handles were moving down and all the doors were opening. I was so frightened that tears were pouring out of my eyes and my teeth were chattering. I pulled the towel around me and wanted to run screaming out the front door, down all the stairs and into the Roman traffic. Instead, I ran into the bathroom and slammed the door behind me. I turned the lock and stared into the mirror, whimpering. My hair was standing on end, my scalp prickling with an ice-cold sensation. Teeth chattering, heart going like a trip hammer, eyes wide with tears that seemed to be splashing out of them and my hair on end. I was like a dog with all the fur standing up.

I showered, washed and dried my hair, got dressed in the bathroom and when I came out it was time for Jay to arrive. I decided to tell him the minimum and maybe nothing else would happen with him on the scene.

The doorbell rang, he came up the stairs smiling, talking about being back in Rome, what was the apartment like, had he ever met Eve, etcetera. After we embraced, I told him that it was best that we kept the doors closed and maybe just used the living room and the kitchen and bathroom until we decided where to sleep that night.

We popped open a bottle of Pinot de Pinot, settled ourselves in the large living room, talking. As always, we spent a lovely day together, invited friends for a lunch the next day, went food shopping, went out to dinner. That evening, we walked down the marble hallway opening doors, peering into each room. He agreed that the library was impressive. I told him what had happened there and he went in and looked around and tried to open the window as I had done. Even exerting all his strength it was impossibly stuck.

We decided to sleep in Eve's double bed. Before we turned out the light, I asked if all the doors were closed and he said he had tried every handle twice.

Later, I woke up and saw that the hall light was on outside our door. I woke Jay and then we heard the piano. It wasn't a song exactly but someone was playing the piano. "Maybe Eve or her husband…? Could they have come back?" he asked. The clock with luminous dial said that it was just past midnight. "Yes. Maybe they did," I agreed. We were lying there, absolutely still, staring at the light under the bedroom door. "I'm going to see who's in the library," he said. I didn't want him to go but I was dying of curiosity. He turned on a light and then, only wearing boxer shorts, opened the bedroom door. I watched him turn left and disappear. When he came back all the hair on his chest was standing out straight. I thought it was hilarious and rocked with laughter but Jay was alarmed. "There's no one in the library but the lights are on in every room, every door is open, and the window in the library—the stuck one—is open and all these papers are blowing around."

I got out of bed and walked down the hall behind him. The library was a mess with sheet music everywhere, the chandelier was ablaze but the piano was silent. The window was wide open. We went from room to room turning off lights, closing doors, and then tried to sleep the rest of the night.

The next morning we made sure all the doors were closed except for the living room and the kitchen as we prepared lunch. Chantal, Judy and Giovanni arrived with wine, with great good humor. I was back in Rome and all was right with the world. It was a winter afternoon and the room was dim. We lit candles. Suddenly they began to flicker. Chantal said, "The kitchen window must be open." I got up from the table and saw that no windows were open. The flames blew back and forth wildly, the temperature in the room dropped radically. The door slammed. We were all a bit perturbed as there were no outside windows or doors open. The wind was originating inside the room. Jay and I told them about our eventful night of very little sleep and we all made very bad jokes but laughing about it helped. Wine helped.

That evening after everyone left, Jay and I went out to dinner. When we came home all the lights were on, all the doors were open and the apartment was very, very cold. We barricaded ourselves in Eve's room. The next morning I told him that I couldn't stay there on my own writing a novel. I had to find another place to live.

I moved to Porto Ercole immediately, taking over a villa that was usually a summer rental for what was left of January, for February, March and April. It was a good place for me and where I wrote *Dancing With Thieves* from start to finish.

So now this craziness was happening in Coral Gables. The clock said half past one. I closed my eyes but opened them when I felt movement near me. Nothing so obvious as a footfall or breathing. Just the sense that something had moved closer. I could reach out and touch it. Or it could touch me. I thought of Cassandra's fear when she saw whatever she saw. Please, please, please, don't touch me. Please don't let me see you, kept running through my mind.

I thought of Eve's apartment again. That spring when I was living in Porto Ercole, I often came into Rome to have lunch with Judy. When Eve was in town from Vienna she joined us. I told her about the apartment and she told me that she thought it was her mother who had come to look for her. "We were very close. During the War, when I was a little girl, she and I went all over Europe, getting off and on trains, avoiding the Germans. She died a few months ago and my brothers did not tell me until after the funeral. I think she came back here, the last place we were together, to see me. The hand on your face was like a mother's stroking a child's forehead. She thought you were me," said Eve.

    The Florida night air was cool. I realized I couldn't go into my bedroom for a sweater. Yes, something was definitely standing beside me. It was rather like being in line at the post office and knowing, without turning around, that there is someone behind you, maybe standing a bit too close. You don't hear anything, nothing touches you, you don't smell them, but you know. I didn't close my eyes again but readjusted the cushion and moved a few inches closer to the wall. I pulled my knees up, balanced the book on them and began to read. I told myself that the spirit of Benjamin Franklin would keep me safe.

Chapter Ten

L.A. P.I. and I emailed back and forth. I called him that because there seemed to be about thirty-seven Johns in my life. I wrote him:

"I still feel shocked about what happened on Friday night. Cassandra told me to pray and that she was praying, the nuns were praying. I haven't prayed in a long time but I do believe in God. If one is not in awe of the ocean and the sky then there is no hope.

I think I might have to risk sleep. Wondering if Cassandra is in the cemetery tonight. This is something she grew up with (and so did her husband because his mother is a psychic, too) so it's not as strange to her as it is to me. I must look on this as another adventure!

Thanks for listening to me and for understanding this. C"

L.A. P.I. wrote: "While I don't know details, I do intuitively know your journey has been anything but mainstream. The world needs us renegades. What you are experiencing now is difficult. But the Universe never gives you more than you can handle. You'll come out on the other side of this with strength you have, up to now, only been able to imagine.

Strength, wisdom and courage to you!

Hugs,

J"

I disagreed with John's 'the Universe never gives you more than you can handle.' Why did my brother kill himself? Why does anyone?

L.A. P.I's next email arrived with Cassandra's full name, Social Security number, her husband's name and his Social Security number, their home address and the criminal background checks which had come up clean. I had resisted doing it but had known I had to. It was due diligence, and now I must trust in her and move forward. What choice did I have?

Chapter Eleven

I kept showing my immaculate apartment, kept being enthusiastic with Patrizia and Raquel on the phone about the next potential buyer. I knew they were sworn to tell all they knew about a property so I couldn't say a thing about my problems. The last thing I did before answering the door was to tuck the saucers of parsley under the bed or into a bureau drawer. Once an electrician from the condo came unexpectedly to check something and stared at one little dish. He probably thought I had some sort of vegetarian pet.

Cassandra didn't want to meet in her office so it was Starbucks in Coconut Grove. I sat at a little metal table outdoors thinking that it was as hot as Africa. However, I'd experienced far worse that very morning.

Cassandra asked me how I was. "I'm great if you count sitting up all night in my clothes, knowing that I'm being watched by invisible *things* walking around the apartment."

"Anything unusual?"

I rolled my eyes. "This morning I went swimming and came back around eight o'clock. I opened the bedroom door and wham! The heat was overwhelming! It was like a fire. I couldn't breathe, I thought my eyelashes had been burned off."

"What did you do?"

"I rushed to the windows and opened them all the way. Cassandra, my skin was burning! But the air outside was cold in comparison. The air in the bathroom next to the bedroom was normal but this…" I shook my head. "And there was the really strong smell of sulphur."

"Stay out of the bedroom. Are you still closing the door every night when it gets dark?"

I nodded. "But what about all that heat?"

"Your bedroom has a portal to Hell."

"My bedroom has a porthole to Hell?" I repeated. I wasn't sure I believed in Hell. Hell with a capital h? I believed in hell on earth but not the hell of Hieronymus Bosch or the Bible. Hellfire and brimstone and pitchforks—definitely not. A porthole to Hell?

Cassandra's cell phone rang and she answered it instead of me. "Yes, I'm coming tonight."

Then she started to speak in a language I'd never heard before. Romanian? Portuguese? No. Her English was nearly perfect. I noticed a few errors in grammar but then I noticed that in nearly everyone around me. I'd heard her speak Spanish but this was guttural. She clicked the phone closed. "I know you are tired. I shouldn't be telling you this but Father Gabriel is coming. Soon."

"Finally!"

"His plane arrives tomorrow afternoon. He has more power than I do to get the others involved."

"Others?"

"People who help us. The nuns." She knew I wanted to know more. "He will explain a lot that I can't explain. Just know that you are not in danger. Do you think I would let you stay there if you were in danger? No. I would have you come to my house."

"Are you coming back to my apartment?"

"Not alone. The two spirits know that we are shining a light on them and they will be quiet. Father Gabriel will come and any time three or more are gathered together in the name of the Lord then He is there. He will be with us."

I stared at her. "How do you know Father Gabriel? Is he from Miami?"

"We've worked together before. He travels all the time."

"Where is he from?"

"From Puerto Rico but he is affiliated with a church in Montreal. He understands Haitian and Brazilian rituals."

I noticed that she didn't use the words voodoo or santeria.

"He performs exorcisms."

My God. An *exorcist*. "You know, Cassandra, I'm not a Catholic but I worked at Vatican Radio for two years."

She was surprised. "We've asked the Vatican about this situation. Do you know people there?"

"It was twenty years ago. Father Borgomeo hired me. My mentor has died." I added, "I adored him. Admired him. I have great respect for the Jesuits."

"I'll tell Father Gabriel about Vatican Radio." She paused. "He can do things I can't do. I'm unclean because I have borne children."

Like what? What can he do? I wanted to scream. "Do you think he can help me?"

"Yes. He can. What is happening to you is unusual but it's not unknown. It can be taken care of and then it will be gone forever." She paused. "It is the cause of people changing their minds about you. It is the cause of things going wrong. This spirit can cause problems for you, could keep things from happening, just when something is within your grasp it will be pushed away."

"I've written a book and there are people in Los Angeles who want to make it into a TV series."

She shook her head. "I don't think this will happen," she said.

Yesterday, I'd gone through my notebooks from New York and the more recent Florida one. Names, email addresses, phone numbers. Client after client explaining they had decided not to move ahead. Assignments quietly cancelled, behind my back.

I thought of all the lawyers who had praised my work. And then? Changed their minds about me?

I sat up all night thinking this would be the last night like this. Help was on the way. Where was he coming from? Was he getting on a plane right now or was he closing a suitcase in some faraway time zone? Father Gabriel had been spoken of with awe. He was a priest with power, he was an authority and he would know what to do. Cassandra had once called him a demonologist. I wondered why, if he'd been in the cemetery with Cassandra on Bastille Day, he hadn't come before this.

Pfffffft.

Okay, I know you're there. When I looked up, expecting to see nothing as usual, I saw a huge dark figure in the shape of a man with a giant animal head cross the hall from the powder room into the kitchen. I stifled a scream; the shock of it seemed to permeate my entire body. My very skin seemed to shrink with fear. I felt so small, so weak. It was taller than the door frame, it was over seven feet tall and hunched over. I blinked and thought, no, no, no. Please don't be that big. Please don't let me see you. Whatever it was it was now in the kitchen. It didn't care that all the lights were on.

I tried to decide if I should keep staring at the spot where I'd seen it in case it came out again and came towards me or if I should never look at that bit of air again.

I stared all night long, rarely blinking, not moving from the French daybed as if it were my life raft adrift on an ocean of terror. And this ocean of terror was my brightly-lit, yellow living room in Coral Gables. I heard the pfffffft noise every few minutes and knew that something stood beside me. I saw the Beardsley poster change into the face of a fiercely angry old man and I tore my gaze away and stared at the hallway. Please don't let me see you, was my mantra.

At dawn I grabbed my bag with my bikini and hair brush and wallet. Clutching the car keys I left the apartment and drove through the quiet streets. "This is okay," I said aloud, before turning on the radio. Anastasia Avenue had never looked so beautiful. The sky was lightening with every beat of my heart. A new day was being born. I could hear birds when I stopped at a STOP sign, could see flowers. No more darkness, I thought. Everything was going to be okay. The exorcist was coming tonight.

Chapter Twelve

"He had to change his plans," said Cassandra. I was sitting in the Chihuahua parked on Minorca. Out of the apartment, off the land, as instructed. I clutched my cell and thought, okay, don't whine. Don't complain. Cassandra is doing this for me.

"When can he come? Tomorrow?"

"It's going to be at least a week. He's in a place where I can't talk to him so I have to wait for him to contact me."

"Cassandra, I saw something. Last night. I don't know if it's what you saw but it was seven feet tall, at least that, and it was the outline of a person, of a man. A huge man. But the head—I don't know what it was but it wasn't a human head. Maybe it was a lion head."

"He's getting stronger if he showed himself to you. This is not good," she said slowly.

I knew it was not good. "Is it dead? Are these things in my apartment dead? The one that stands next to me and shakes the piece of paper? The pfffffft character? That giant shadow? The face in the picture?" I was insistent. "Are they dead?"

"Yes, they are."

"Glad to have that settled," I said sarcastically.

"Cici, I'm sorry about tonight but Father Gabriel *is* coming to see you. Be patient." I didn't answer. Another night like last night. I could take it. Sure. I hadn't died of fear yet. Cassandra said, "You are not in danger. Believe me."

"I do believe you."

"I love you."

Suddenly I felt my throat thicken with tears. "I love you, too," I sighed into the phone.

I sat there for a long time after we hung up. The occasional car went by. A woman crossed the street holding hands with a child of about five. They both wore flip-flops and shorts and purple T-shirts and were chattering in Spanish. The sun was out. As usual. I was thoroughly sick of the sun, rejoiced in the rare cloudy day or thunderstorm.

I called L.A. P.I. who answered on the second ring. He got up early to go surfing sometimes. "John, it's so normal here," I said.

He caught on immediately. "I know."

Another day of bright, blinding sunshine.

Barbara, one of the realtors, called about Big Dog client. We called him that because he *has* a big dog and keeps mentioning it. You'd think the dog was buying the condo. He wants to bring his girlfriend between 2:30 and 3 which is fine. Then Melinda called from New York and said there was an article in the Metro section of *The New York Times* about a very wealthy, educated man who got scammed by a fake art dealer. A*nyone* can get scammed. She asked me to call her after the exorcist left. "He isn't coming." My voice was leaden with disappointment. "I don't know when he's coming." Suddenly I felt childlike. Pathetically dependent.

The night was uneventful unless you count sitting in a chair in my clothes all night in a state of high, ready-to-shriek alert. Both phones a few inches away, consumed by the idea of that huge, hunched creature, and thinking, oh, please, don't let it be standing in this room just staring at me. I now wonder if it watches me in the shower. Have these ghouls seen me make love, eat a peach over the sink? Could it be possible that I have not been alone for most of my life?

Pornochef called from Long Island to see how I was. Another John in my life. He's a world-class chef who is also a writer and, long before I met him, once wrote pornography. We had long talks when I was so despondent about Simon. I told him that the condo was still on the market and he said it is not selling because of Saturn. Evidently it's in retrograde. He said it wasn't necessarily a bad thing. It was slow-moving but forced one to look inward. If you are in traffic, for instance, and cannot change that, then you are forced to take stock, be introspective. I told him I was consulting a psychic and then he said something that surprised me. "It might have something to do with your friend who died."

I stood on the balcony daring to talk to Melinda. "My reasoning is this: if you and I are talking with twelve hundred miles between us and I don't understand *how* then I should believe in things I can't see and can't explain."

Melinda said, "I do believe in things I can't see."

"I believe in a god of nature. The tiny baby turtles, the vastness of a galaxy, but I don't know if I believe in angels," I said and then changed my mind. "But what about the mountain climber who is suddenly pulled to safety by invisible arms? So if I do believe in angels then why is it impossible to grasp what is happening now? The thing I've seen isn't human. What more do I need to believe? I saw the black umbrella, the coin and I heard the horrible noise. I didn't imagine it. I saw Cassandra's bruises and her cut and swollen lip."

Melinda and I went back and forth. "I keep thinking that the huge crashing at my bedroom door, a turning point for me, was *after* I told her I was having problems with the sale. But she had never been to my apartment. She came two days afterwards. There is no way I can imagine that the noise was fake."

Melinda agreed. "Plus you have had all those inspections. If there were wires or microphones anywhere—" I chimed in, "They would have been discovered." After agreeing that we understood nothing of what was happening, the two of us hung up.

Bronwen called from Italy and I sat in the car and filled her in. She exclaimed, "Ohmygod, you are so brave! I couldn't stay there!" I started to tell her about the coin and she interrupted, "And then it disappeared." Bronwen caught on instantly.

The next day I called Cassandra at two o'clock and left a message and then I called again just before four. "I have to leave the house," she said, "because I don't want to talk about this in front of the children." I, of course, didn't want to talk about it in front of the roommates so I was sitting in the Chihuahua parked on Alcazar. I heard her walking on a tile floor and then a door slammed. "In the next hour they are going to be doing some heavy meditation," she said.

They? I guess she meant nuns. "I'm going out for awhile anyway." "Good. Father Gabriel said it was not a good idea for me to go back there so maybe you could come to the Grove late tonight."

"Oh, sure. Anytime," I said. Who sleeps?

"I'll call you at eight. Be sure and answer the phone. Father Gabriel will tell us what must be done."

I hung up and drove home. I thought I'd take a cold shower before dark. Humidity in Florida was one thing but the heaviness in my apartment was different. Cassandra said it was from the spirits.

It was ten of eight and the sun was setting. I stared at my cell phone on the front seat of the Chihuahua and then flipped it open to make sure it was on. I was parked on Madeira again with the windows open watching pedestrians pass the car, walking dogs, chatting. These were people who weren't afraid of the dark. I waited until nine but Cassandra did not call.

Every single night after Bastille Day felt as if it lasted a week but the days were passing. All I could think about was the exorcist. One night, feeling very restless, I called Cassandra at a bit after ten o'clock. I told her I had seen the gruesome figure with the head again. "I have to tell you," she said. "The bite. It was trying to do something sexual to you."

Of course. Love bites from a dead half-human, half-goat. No matter what she said, it made me feel better just talking to her. She was being picked up to drive to church in West Palm Beach in thirty-five minutes. I love it. A woman who will spend all night in a cemetery ready to face the Devil is carpooling with three psychics because she is afraid to drive after dark. And is Coconut Grove simply rife with psychics?

I watched the news and then Jay Leno. In between the waves of audience laughter, I heard the pfffffft noise a few feet away. I thought of Cassandra. She said that this demonic spirit was very jealous, wanted me for himself and would make sure that nothing went right with anyone. "If you had married it would have fallen apart, it would not have worked." I didn't agree with her. Demons wouldn't be to blame. It would have been me. I like my freedom more than most people and marriage always felt like having a leash around my neck. Even the finest silk cord studded with emeralds would still be a leash.

Even when I disagreed with Cassandra, I was grateful to talk to her. I understood my dependency on her, the sense of intimacy. Perhaps my arrested clients had those same feelings towards me. I'd hear their stories and hope they were telling the truth, holding nothing back. They trusted me and often regarded me as capable of saving the day, even saving them. Fear and helplessness in the face of the legal system. And me? Now? I was Alice who'd fallen down the rabbit hole and had no friends except a psychic and an exorcist who had yet to appear. Would they rescue me or not?

Chapter Thirteen

JULY 20, 2006

I parked in front of my mailbox place on Ponce de Leon and called Cassandra. It was voicemail nine times out of ten so I was surprised when she answered. "All is happening tonight. I'm waiting to be picked up because we are going out to prepare. Go home and I will call you later and you will come out of the house. We are coming after nine o'clock."

I understood that she would call, say 'hello,' and I would leave the building. They would come and we three would go in together.

I went to the Biltmore in the late afternoon for a second swim of the day. In the shallow end of the pool I talked with a very blonde, darkly-tanned man from Sweden named Thor. We chatted about Miami, about Florida, and he told me he was on vacation, staying at the hotel, of course. Thor was meeting someone in Miami Beach at 6:30 and I offered to drive him. It was getting dark but my bedroom door was closed and I had time. I dropped him off and on the way home my cell rang and it was Cassandra. They were early, waiting in front of the building.

I parked the car in the underground space and then walked through the iron gate to the driveway so that I could approach them without going inside. There was no one there. The fountain was splashing, the lights were on in the flower beds and highlighting the palms but no one was sitting on the steps or in sight.

I turned and saw Cassandra and a slender man in black walking towards me up the steps from the sidewalk. I told myself that I could tell if this was really a priest or someone on his break from Radio Shack wearing a dog collar. After all, two years at Vatican Radio meant I had been surrounded by priests. I knew the way they walk, I knew a genuine priest. Dark hair, dark eyes, glasses, early forties, slender in a black shirt, black trousers, with a white collar. Cassandra, in a long skirt and a T-shirt, introduced us but we didn't shake hands. Her eyes looked terrible, surrounded by yellow, gray and lots of purple.

"Finally I meet you," I said to him. "It seems as if so much time has gone by."

He didn't smile, did not answer, was staring at me as we three got into the elevator. He seemed to be assessing me, making up his mind. I sensed he was the real thing. Cassandra explained, "It's the same as before. You must cross the threshold first and then invite us in. Then you and I will stand in the doorway. Don't turn the lights on."

The fourth floor was empty, as usual, and I was relieved. I knew it wouldn't be helpful for my neighbors to know that I needed an exorcist to sell my apartment. Property values would plummet, I supposed. Or maybe I'd start a fad like feng shui and everyone in South Florida would be trying to get exorcists to come. I turned the key in the lock and went in. The lights from the street outside the French doors reflected on the glass of the pictures, in the mirror from Rome over the daybed, on the marble-topped coffee table, on the Mexican tile floors. I stepped aside, motioned them to enter and then went behind Father Gabriel to stand in the doorway. He did exactly as Cassandra had done and turned to the left to go to the covered terrace off the living room. Then he returned to the living room and stood in the middle and looked around as if getting his balance. Cassandra was holding my hand. She whispered, "I always feel sick in your apartment." We watched the priest disappear down the dark hallway towards my bedroom and then we heard him open the bedroom door. Cassandra was clutching my hand tightly. We both strained to hear. Nothing. A car door slammed on the street below. We waited. "Father Gabriel?" called Cassandra with fear in her voice. "Are you okay?"

He sounded panicked as he ran towards us in the dark. "We have to get out now!" The three of us, like a cartoon, all tried to wedge ourselves out the front door at the same time. In the hall light he looked upset. His eyes were bright and he seemed to be out of breath. "We have to get off the land!"

Cassandra was pushing the elevator button and staring at him. He was pacing under the big chandelier, back and forth in front of the floor-to-ceiling glass window that overlooked the fountain outside. The elevator came, we hurriedly got in and ascended. "We have to get off the land," he kept saying.

"There's a Holiday Inn on the corner," I said. We got out of the elevator and rushed through the lobby and outside. The exorcist and the psychic were nearly running towards the street. "I have to go back and lock the door," I said. It sounded stupid at the time but everyone always talked about crime in South Florida so I was being responsible. "Go into the bar and I'll be there in a minute," I called. They were already crossing Adriano Avenue.

I went up to the fourth floor, put my ear to my front door and listened. Silence. I locked the door and stepped into the waiting elevator. Walking towards the motel, I thought, this is insane. A psychic comes to my apartment and runs out, an exorcist comes and runs out and I have to go back and spend the night there.

The Holiday Inn. Americana at its most pedestrian. I walked past the reception desk and into the bar. Empty. Father Gabriel and Cassandra were sitting at a table way in the back of the deserted restaurant; I sat down across from them. The priest's face was absolutely white but he was pouring with perspiration. Cassandra handed him a white damask napkin and he mopped his forehead with it but droplets still ran down his face. Great, I thought. The exorcist had finally come and he was now having a heart attack. He was going to die before he could help me.

"Here," said Cassandra putting a glass of ice water in front of him. His hands were shaking when he reached for it.

I watched him, waiting for him to speak.

"It's your father," he said, after one swallow. "He's very angry. He's shouting."

I was cavalier. "Oh, he's always angry. Always shouting." Then I leaned back in the chair. "But he's been dead for about forty years."

"It's your father with Bathemus and there are other spirits they have drawn to them. They are in the apartment."

I didn't know what to say. He was obviously sincere, white as the tablecloth, trembling with the import of whatever he had experienced. I had never seen a man so frightened.

He opened a small book on the table between us. The cover was faded a pale red, the pages were tissue-paper thin, yellowed with age. "This is what is in your apartment. This is what your father has invited in." He turned the pages pointing at pen-and-ink illustrations of creatures half-human, half-animal. There was one with horns. I kept hearing "this" and "this." I turned away in revulsion and said, "I don't want to see any more."

"This is the strongest evil entity I have ever encountered," said Father Gabriel wiping his face again.

Cassandra reached over and closed the book. "I know Cici and I know that you can't tell her all of this because she has to go back."

He nodded. The three of us were silent for a moment and then he said, "I agree with Cassandra that we must get you out of there because otherwise you will spend the rest of your life there."

"But why? Why is any spirit interested in me? My father is dead! Why is this happening?"

Cassandra and I waited for him to speak. "Everything in your life has led you here. To Coral Gables, to that apartment. Everything, all your life. This was meant to happen."

I felt chilled. I would later regret not asking more questions but I couldn't think of anything but selling the condo and leaving forever. "What happens next?"

"We will work on releasing you from these entities, separating you from them."

"How?" I asked. This was an exorcist. I imagined pea soup shooting out of my mouth.

"By prayer."

Cassandra chimed in. "You have no idea how many people are praying for you every day. And every night."

"Should I be burning candles?"

"No. We are going to take care of all that."

"What did you mean when you said that everything in my life has led me here?"

"It was all planned a long time ago. Your family has been involved for generations in this. You were meant to come to Florida, to Coral Gables, to that specific apartment to live."

"Florida was the last place I'd ever thought of coming until a few years ago and suddenly I had problems with my apartment in New York, problems with where to live, then I was given an apartment in North Miami Beach and..."

Cassandra said, "You told me how the rent on Adriano was lowered for you. You also told me about buying the apartment with no money. It was all so easy."

Father Gabriel said, "It was too easy. It was all ordained. You were meant to be in that specific apartment."

Coral Gables? I thought. But I'm such a New York, such a Rome kind of person. I'm an anywhere-but-Florida kind of person. It was far more likely that

I would live in a Swiss chalet or a Portuguese fishing village than here. Actually, *I have lived in those places*. Cassandra and Father Gabriel were talking softly and I heard Cassandra say, "Don't tell her any more."

"When you moved in it was fine. The problems started when you wanted to leave. They don't want you to go. We must research what to do with this entity. The house has a great number of demonic entities. The strongest one is your father."

"Cici had a dream a few nights ago," said Cassandra. "She was outside an apartment—"

"Not this one but another one," I interrupted.

Cassandra went on. "And she knew that bad spirits were inside. She put her key in the lock to lock them inside so she could leave without them but no matter how many times she locked the door, it would come open. The lock would not lock."

"They will go with you. We know that a ritual on the property is not enough." Father Gabriel was beginning to look reasonable again; the color had returned to his face. "It's just like your dream."

"When will this be over?" I asked.

"When it's over you can sell the condo." This was not an answer.

"I told Cici it would be after Halloween of this year. The week after," said Cassandra.

"We have work to do," he said solemnly.

No waiter or waitress had approached us, there was no bill to pay, so we got up and walked out into the hot July night. I looked at the quiet street and the low houses and thought, where am I? I felt disoriented by what I'd been told; the benign landscape seemed foreign.

"When you go in," directed Cassandra, "try to relax. Don't think of us or of anything negative."

I nodded. The building loomed against the navy-blue night sky. The water in the fountain splashed softly, there was the scent of honeysuckle coming from somewhere. Father Gabriel's collar looked very white. His complexion was tan again. "But what should I do? What can I do?" I asked.

"Cassandra and I will be working on this. She will call you."

That seemed to be the last word. And right there in front of the Holiday Inn at the corner of La Jeune Road and Adriano Avenue, we three bowed our heads as the exorcist said a prayer. It was to protect me and I felt better. I really did. Cassandra threw her arms around me and said she loved me and I did the same. I think I did love her. Father Gabriel made the sign of the cross in front of me and I said, "Thank you. Thank you for coming," like some absurd hostess after a successful dinner party. I turned and left them, walked across the street and up the steps, past the fountain, to the front door and then I went into the elevator where I would ascend to the fourth floor. I would stand outside with my key in my hand, take a deep breath and then enter my apartment full of demons.

Chapter Fourteen

July 23rd, 2006

Dear Cassandra and Father Gabriel,

The chronology of events might be helpful.
I am approaching this as I would a criminal case. What happened, where and when, and creating a time line. I want to document all I can and to be as precise as possible.
The other evening I did not want to hear about Bathemus.
WHAT or WHO seemed secondary.
All I want is to feel safe again. I just want it out of my life.
It was impossible for me to absorb anything intellectual—I felt raw from worry and fear and I wanted comfort from you and you did give me a measure of that. I also wanted to be sure that whatever happened to me or happens in the future was or is REALLY happening and that I remain unsusceptible to any pictures I've seen or descriptions I've read or heard.
I must write about this. After all, I'm a detective and a former journalist and this is my approach to anything new.
Someday I would like to know more. Not now. Questions are swirling around me all the time. Not a day goes by that I don't think of that terrifying noise.
Cassandra, I know you said suicide was what God could never forgive but the brother emotionally closest to me killed himself. He was very attractive and bright and kind and no one could tell a story the way he could. A gently hilarious sense of humor. Enormously popular...so many friends who loved him. Daddy cut me and Stirling out of his will. Stirling was his oldest son and namesake and I am the oldest daughter named after my mother. I didn't care. I was twenty and in college. My brother was 33, thirteen years older than me. Daddy was actually clever and gave us each one thousand dollars so that we could not contest the will since he had mentioned us. By the way, calling him Daddy is not affectionate; we called him that because Mother called her father that.
It was a despicable act. For everyone in Jackson to know that the illustrious eye surgeon (whom everybody thought was a hero) had done this inferred something was wrong with my brother. Daddy did his last terrible thing with that will. My two other brothers were jealous of Stirling and when they inherited the money they

suddenly saw it as power and refused to divide it with him. Each of them came to me several times and said, 'I've always loved you so I'm going to give you this check.' That repulsed me. I asked if they were giving Stirling the same amount and they said, no, or they hadn't decided yet or 'Dad said Stirling couldn't handle money and he didn't want him to have it so I don't think I am giving him anything. Dad didn't want him to have any of his money.'

They were intoxicated by this situation. Once Curtis handed me a check and I tore it in half and handed it back to him. I told them both I would not take anything unless they gave the same to Stirling. All I could think of was how much pain they were causing him. Daddy hurt him by doing this and then— to have his own younger brothers become so arrogant! A few years later I was told that they were giving money to Stirling and I did take a few of the checks when I was sure we were being given the same.

My sister did give the same to me and Stirling at the onset but none of the three gave me or Stirling what would have been our share. Not at all! They had the power to dole it out or not and how they relished that!

After the reading of the will, Stirling left Jackson and never came back. He lived in Houston, liked to sail and joined the yacht club, had a beautiful apartment, a respected job. He always had very wealthy women asking him to concerts and dinners. So many times, he told me and Mother that he thought this woman or that one was in love with him and he would like to be married and have children but he worried that he didn't have as much money as her family did. Though he was making quite a reasonable living, he suffered and felt insecure because he felt it wasn't enough.

Mother and I talked about it. Stirling found it abhorrent that anyone would ever imagine that he married for money. Other men would have thought it perfect: I love her and she loves me and her father and I get along and he's offered me a position in his firm. The fathers of these girls were always crazy about Stirling. Often he was treated like the son they never had.

Stirling felt a deep need to keep up appearances. He always had a new car and he dressed very well. He was the escort for this young woman or that one to the most glamorous balls, to barbecues on huge ranches, to charity benefits. Queen Beatrix of the Netherlands came to Houston and Stirling was one of a dozen people invited to meet her and have dinner.

Anyway, not having A LOT of money troubled him and I think it kept him from being content.

When he was in his mid-40s, something happened to his job—Houston suffered a full-scale recession because oil prices dropped—and he went from one job interview to another. Mother said that he was often one of five candidates being considered. Then they would call him back and say he was one of two men being considered for the position. He would wait for the phone call and be told that the other person had been hired. The next thing, the next thing, and he would be passed over. He was trying so desperately and nothing would come through for him. This went on for several years. It was time after time that he would be told that he was the favored candidate and then—someone else would be chosen. He borrowed money from Mother (she had inherited some money when her father died) and I think that when he couldn't get a job, and so much time was going by, that he suddenly realized he couldn't pay Mother back and he was so ashamed and despondent that he saw it as the end.

I was in Rome and I dreamed that he killed himself and I wrote him a long letter telling him how much I loved him and that I knew what he was thinking and that he could not, please don't. The letter arrived a day after he died.

A few months ago, here in Florida, I received a check from my brother Rob. It was odd. Something in a short note said he had enough money and he had congestive heart failure so he was sending me a check. My initial reaction was disgust. Keep your money, stay away from me. But my close friends, Bronwen and Deirdre, pleaded with me to take it. I did not want anything from him, anything to do with him. Deirdre was especially insistent. I needed the money badly so I cashed the check and wrote a 'thank you' note on a postcard. Though he sent another check I soon realized he wanted nothing to do with me either. When I called him in Texas and tried to thank him on the phone, he hung up in my face. So the checks were sent to make himself feel better, to assuage his guilt. There was no benevolence in the gesture. The money had nothing to do with me.

I am not a wonderful person—my refusal to take the checks when offered after Daddy died was not a big decision at all. The money was really not important to me. I graduated from college, had several jobs in NYC and was living in a large, old, high-ceilinged apartment with either heat or hot water (but never both at the same time) and it was four flights up which was quite a lot of exercise but I had a hundred friends and a very large, eccentric rabbit named Daphne. I flourished on nearly no money and I never saw the will as a money situation. I saw it as an act of cruelty to an oldest son who was a very good person. It was not ever the money. My rent was $134.88 a month and I never went to the grocery store because I was always going out to dinner and I had marriage proposals all the time and was having such FUN. On the first of the month, I'd find my German landlord in the gloom of the corner bar and I'd put the cash in the breast pocket of his filthy plaid flannel shirt. He was never too drunk to not find the humor in my dropping the last three pennies in.

I think that having Daddy as a father and being in that family made me want only one thing: to ESCAPE. To take care of myself and to not have anyone control me or make me unhappy. Only recently have I understood how much I need to be economically okay. I have tried to take care of myself financially and it's been tough going.

Mother was from such a wealthy family (I think Daddy married her for her money) that my grandfather never worked. The background was Quaker and money was never talked about. Mother had a positive outlook, a radiant spirit, and was gracious with everyone no matter who they were. She was the same with the governor's wife or the clerk at the Brandon post office. She talked to everybody and never thought of how wealthy anyone was and would never judge anyone by their clothes or their house.

Of course, I am ambivalent about money.

Daddy worshipped it and Mother said (when we'd come home from the grocery store) "Wash your hands! You've been handling money!"

Daddy used to change his will on his prescription pads. Often. He'd tell one son that he was leaving all his money to his two brothers and he would call his lawyer and have the silly will rewritten. Only one specific reason comes to mind. Three times over the years, with all three of them, the unforgiveable transgression was daring to say that they did not want to go to medical school, did not want to be a doctor. Daddy bellowed and changed his will. This was a mighty act, he was showing force, his authority. Knowing him, he probably delighted in the idea of inciting jealousy between the three boys.

All five of us survived Daddy but with our own scars. I don't know if the money from the will changed them or if the three of them were at a turning point in their lives and merely became who they were destined to be. I am not in contact with my two brothers or my sister. After some very bad experiences it's safer for me to stay away. I wish them only good things but I don't trust them. They are not my friends.

When Mother was in her 80s, she was silently enduring excruciating pain and should have been given a hip replacement but Curtis snarled, "It idn't worth it" so she did not have the operation. He lived near her in Mississippi and made that decision. My active Mother who swam every day well into her 80s would spend her last years in a wheelchair.

When she was 86, I thought it was so nice of Rob to invite her to be with him and his wife for Thanksgiving and to stay for Christmas at their house in Texas. Mother was very excited and we talked on the phone about the clothes she would take, what to pack. Rob is an educated person. Both my brothers have master's degrees. Rob and his wife would leave the house at 8 a.m. for work and come home at about 6 p.m. I called Mother every day she was there to chat and see how she was. I don't think her time with them was very enjoyable.

Back home in Mississippi, she received an invoice for the food she had eaten. I think it was $14 per week. My brother had computed the electric bill for the time, Monday to Friday, that she had been alone in the house. She was charged one dollar and some cents for a box of Kleenex.

My other brother is every bit as parsimonious, but more duplicitous, more dangerous. Curtis is known in Jackson as a successful multi-millionaire businessman and a man of great charity. He is the only person I know who actually manages to brag about how humble he is. Like Rob, he describes himself as "a good Christian." He is a very important man at his Baptist church and even donated a million dollars to start a missionary fund in his own name. But this is the same man who, when it was still expensive, would sneak into his mother's house when she was out, and make all his long-distance calls. The same man who met his mother at a restaurant on her 84th birthday for the Early Bird Special and then asked for two checks. "But," Mother told me blithely, "afterwards, he had me follow him in my car to the filling station. He got a full tank of gas and gave me the coupon for the free car wash." I sent her a present and called (which is how I know all this) but neither my sister nor my other brother even picked up the phone. I guess, in comparison, Curtis should be commended for giving her the car wash coupon.

Both of her sons wrote anonymous letters to the Mississippi Highway Patrol in an attempt to have her driver's license revoked. She lived in the country and all her activities, yacht club, choir practice, Caledonian Club, meeting someone for breakfast at the Beagle Bagel and simply going to the grocery store, depended on her driving. Those brothers of mine knew this. I had a Mississippi detective friend arrange for a driver's test which she passed with flying colors.

A few years later, Curtis would even take away Mother's small joy of her mail by having delivery rerouted to HIS house. The scene was described to me: Mother in her wheelchair frantically trying to catch up to him in the driveway, crying and shouting, "I want my mail!" as he ignored her and got into his brand-new truck and drove away. I intervened and Mother's mail was delivered to her house again.

It was many degrees of unkindness—from evil intent to small disappointments—inflicted on her by her children. Mother was thrilled that my sister, the corporate lawyer, was arriving in Jackson for business and couldn't wait to see her, to have her stay overnight. However, she opted to stay at Curtis's much larger house and breezed in and out of Mother's in Turtle Creek in a big, important hurry. I lived with Mother for three months in the summer of 1994. My sister did not write or telephone one time. Mother always said how busy she was and that she understood.

This is the daughter who borrowed and never repaid many, many thousands of dollars from her mother, depleting her financially, all the while pulling down a hefty income as a lawyer. I cannot bear to write what the money purchased.

Maybe the most cruel thing one could do to anyone, Curtis did to Mother. He claimed that no one should believe a word she said. "She has Alzheimer's." When I was in New York we talked long-distance nearly every day and she was entirely lucid. Once she happened to mention that she would see me in Destin. Florida? I asked. She then gave me the dates of what she claimed was to be a family reunion. I told her I had no plans to go to Florida and felt panicked that maybe Curtis was right. I knew from Mother that he would not buy her a cup of coffee or even speak to her if he saw her having breakfast alone at one of the local places but he did live nearby and did see her so I called him. Curtis said she didn't know what she was talking about, and that I had to come to terms with the fact that her mind was going. I spoke to her all the time and she was insistent about this family reunion, that we were to be all together in condos right on the beach. It had been arranged months before. Whenever she mentioned it on the phone, I felt a wave of sadness.

Later I would learn that my two brothers, my sister, their spouses, and their children from Texas, Oklahoma, Florida, and Mississippi, had all gathered with

Mother, in Destin, on the dates she had specified. They'd kept it a secret from me. I was stunned. It was like a one-liner from a stand-up comedian: my family had a reunion and didn't invite me.

Curtis nagged Mother for months trying to get her power of attorney. He'd even asked me to try to persuade her but there was no need for her to give it to him and she was adamant that he not have it. But he wanted it and, with his connections, actually had her admitted to a psychiatric ward in order to get it.

So, if Daddy has friends who are demons, it is perfect. He, himself, was pretty demonic.

I look at my brothers and my sister and think *he has left his mark.*

You two are my rescuers. Let me know what happens next.

I send you all my gratitude. love, C

(I reread the letter and put it away.)

The next morning the sun was out, I went swimming, and Patrizia called with people to see my apartment. Yesterday had been a normal day except for the professional confirmation that I had roommates from Hell. I called Cassandra and asked her what I should do about the pretty blue stones. "You can leave them out, I think." But should I put a few in the bedroom? "No! Don't put any in the bedroom. We don't want to antagonize him." Oh, okay, I thought.

My dependency on Cassandra appalled me. The phone calls went back and forth. Usually I got her voicemail and often it was full and I was unable to leave a message. Every day I longed for news and at night I wondered if she were in the cemetery. She was driven all the way to West Palm Beach to church every single evening. A certain church, a certain group of women. Nuns? I thought of her praying and reminded myself that praying worked. All those years ago, wasn't the Tiny Tears doll I'd prayed for under the Christmas tree? Then I wondered where Father Gabriel was. Then I'd look at my watch and see that it was eight o'clock, my bedroom door was closed and *she* must be getting into the car with the other psychics of Coconut Grove. I'd pace the apartment and end up staring out at the planes taking off at the Miami airport and wish I were on one. Then I'd torture myself imagining an accident on I-95. What would I do if Cassandra died?

I left the Biltmore, drove to Publix and parked the car, thinking this was another normal day in a normal place. People in shorts were walking to and from their minivans, pushing carts, carrying babies and shopping bags. I'd had my swim and was wearing white shorts over my wet bikini. I would buy groceries, go home, put the food away and then open the bedroom door and put on a clean pair of white shorts. I had three identical pairs.

I was a master of compartmentalization. It kept me in my bad marriage longer than I should have stayed and it kept me hopeful when otherwise I might have been depressed to the point of paralysis. Now I compartmentalized again.

Though Father Gabriel and Cassandra claimed it was the strongest entity they'd ever encountered, they vowed they would get rid of it. I believed them and I believed in them. I also believed that Raquel and Patrizia would send me someone to buy my apartment. Really buy it this time. I told myself that I was lucky to be surrounded by people who were all working on my behalf. It was going to be fine because they were, each in their own way, capable professionals.

My cell phone rang in the frozen food section. "Patrizia! Hi! No, I'm not home now but I can be." I listened. "Sure, it's immaculate. Give me twenty minutes." I listened again. "Perfect. Thanks so much."

I paid at the checkout and got into the Chihuahua. Cassandra had told me to go into the apartment not thinking about her or Father Gabriel or anything that had happened. Only happy thoughts. "We don't want it to know we are getting rid of it," she said. I had looked at her and wanted to laugh. "Don't be tense or it will hang on even harder. Just relax." Of course, relax when something over seven feet tall is walking around, when your Beardsley print becomes vicious faces at night, when you are so frightened that sleep has become a luxury.

I remembered a case in New York. I'd been contacted by someone I nicknamed Laser Woman in my mind. Poor thing. I'm changing nearly all details though she was never my client. I was invited to the Junior League clubhouse on the Upper East Side for a drink where she introduced herself and said she wanted to hire me to find the source of the lasers assaulting her vagina.

She swore the torture was being orchestrated by a handsome and brilliant dermatologist in Kansas City whom she had rejected romantically. Now he was punishing her with lasers beamed down via satellites, all night and all day. Doctor after doctor could find no physiological sign of injury, no source of the pain she swore she was suffering. I listened to her for twenty minutes, all the while trying to decide how to say I could not help her, how to suggest she see a psychiatrist.

She was sure she wanted a private detective, someone she claimed "could think out of the box." This woman was anguished, in deep trouble, and I felt sorry for her so I didn't allow myself the suggestion of a smile. I never took money from her and kept telling her I had no idea how to help her. We met several times but I would not let her hire me, would not take the retainer check she extended across the table again and again. Maybe listening helped. But at some point, so drawn in was I, I remember looking up and saying, "Do you think we should move away from the windows?"

Now I wondered if this were the same sort of situation. I was being pulled deeper and deeper into something I did not understand and though intellectually I was rejecting all this talk of spirits, I was closing the bedroom door.

But, no. This wasn't the same. Something existed. I had heard it. The crashes that sounded like ten sledgehammers at once cracking into the wood. I knew sledgehammers. I'd seen the men use them in New York during counterfeit raids, saw them every single day hanging on the wall beside my desk like a row of crochet mallets. I'd used a sledgehammer last Friday to slam posts into the sand to secure a clutch of turtle eggs. But the noise at my bedroom door had not been ten sledgehammers. It hadn't been a rhinoceros and it hadn't been a human.

I stood outside my apartment door, fumbled with my bag of groceries and key in hand, took a deep breath. I closed my eyes for a second and tried to summon a happy thought.

Chapter Fifteen

Jim Rhoades called from Chicago. He had been a special agent of the F.B.I. specializing in stolen art recovery and was now retired. We had done two stolen art cases together when I was in New York, had a long-time friend in common, and we trusted each other.

He wanted to me to join him in starting a small firm dealing with museum security. I listened to him and, of course, was delighted to be a part of it. I told him I was not going to be in Miami for much longer, that the condo would be sold any minute. That was fine. Where was I going? Back to New York? I told him I was pretty sure it would be Philadelphia. That was convenient because he was often in and out of D.C. and Philadelphia was a short ride on Amtrak. Emails would follow with his ideas but as soon as we chose a name I was to get it incorporated as a limited liability corporation in Florida. I was all for the new company, wanted this to fly. Finally! A project!

The phone rang two minutes after we'd hung up. I was taking notes about the call when Cassandra was suddenly on the line telling me that my father was evil. Out of the blue, she had decided this. I closed my notebook and listened. "Very evil and he was very, very materialistic."

Not ever enough money, I thought. I confirmed what she'd said. "He was an eye surgeon and he was very wealthy by Mississippi standards. Mississippi is the poorest state there is so he wasn't Rockefeller-rich but he was well-off. But more than that, he had us five children when three was typical and we were all attractive enough and healthy and he had a wife who was loyal and loved him. At least in the beginning."

"Your father knew you were special and he was jealous of you. You were different and you were strong."

Maybe not. I couldn't understand the jealousy at all and second, I did not feel strong these days. She said, "I love you," and hung up.

It was getting dark. Cassandra, on her way to West Palm Beach, now heading north on I-95 to pray with the nuns, was my only hope. A woman spirited to mass every night by the witches of Coconut Grove in a white Toyota.

That night I had the dream again. I was petting the dog, with its head in my lap, and suddenly I realized it was a goat and jerked awake. No more sleeping. I would stay awake and pray: don't let me see you.

L.A. P.I. called the next day as I walked in from the Biltmore; it was one of his days to get up early for surfing. Cassandra had decided it was okay to talk outside on the covered terrace so I dropped my bag and walked out and closed the door. I was thankful to be able to confide in him. I had one or two women friends in the building but, of course, could not tell them anything about this. As I sat in my shorts, bare feet up on the railing, I heard John's voice and thought that this was another world. We were walking around in sunlight, buying groceries and watching the news on TV. What do we know of spirits? Nothing. But John insisted they are always here.

John went on about a witch named Raven he was trying to reach, his crystal collection, the influence of Christianity on all of this. He wanted me to write down websites to look at but I didn't want to. "I don't think I want to go much farther with this."

In true detective form, he said, "I'd like to put up cameras in your bedroom for twenty-four hours and really investigate."

"Be my guest," I said, thinking too bad he was in California. "Odd little things are happening. This morning I saw that my wooden ring, I bought it in Paris years ago, was on the bottom shelf of the empty bookcase in the living room. Not in the jewelry box. I also saw a rhinestone earring that I rarely wear on the windowsill in the bathroom. Taken out of my jewelry box which is closed and in the bedroom."

"Poltergeist activity," he said.

As if I didn't have enough going on.

"John, this fear. It's something new for me. Something we never experience. Nowadays we worry about a mammogram, there is tension about money but this fear that is visceral right down to the blood in my veins is new." I paused. "Or very, very old."

"When you told me about the Haitian coin my spine went cold."

"It is a different experience to feel such primitive fear. Maybe it's what a cave man felt when he saw his first sabretooth tiger." More than a million years ago, flashed through my mind. The year is 2006 and I am terribly afraid. John and I kept talking. As we were hanging up, he said, "Be brave. You will survive this."

Bronwen called from Italy then Deirdre called from Oxford. It was so freeing to laugh, to feel far away from Coral Gables. Bronwen knew but I decided to confide in Deirdre. Told her the whole thing since she had told me, ages ago, about her experience in the thousand-year-old castle. It seemed that the men were going off to join the Crusades and had one last dinner in that castle. Then Deirdre arrived hundreds of years later and was nearly overcome by the scent of incense and candles. No other guest smelled anything!

But curiously, she seemed disbelieving of what was happening to me now. I told myself that I must resist the urge to talk about this. Even with someone I had known for twenty years.

Cassandra called on Sunday afternoon and we spent a long time on the phone. I was out on the covered terrace. The psychic said that God had plans for me, that I had been chosen for something very big and "you have not lived your life. Not the life you were meant to live. You have lived a false life for all these years but after this you will have peace and love and happiness. Maybe you are going to write something about the existence of the Devil. You are going to do something very important when this is over. But you must be patient." She'd said this several times. I thought it was strange, never responded, and never took her seriously. God? A plan? No.

Then she said that she had something to tell me about Rome and I said, "But what I have to tell you happened in Rome." She said, "I wanted to talk to you about what happened in the apartment." There was no need to tell her for she appeared to already know. Then I told her about Eve and her mother on all the trains going across Europe. Cassandra said, "No. Eve's mother did not think you were her daughter. The spirits know. Some part of that spirit may have stayed with you." I felt the sun on my arms, looked out over the railing at the placid sherbet-colored houses of Coral Gables and shivered.

Cassandra repeated that I was destined to do something great. "All of this is making you who you are. All of this, even from childhood, has made you stronger. You are a very strong woman."

Just keep telling me that, I thought. We hung up. It flashed through my mind: if I don't really believe all this in the light of day then why do I keep walking out on the terrace to talk about it on the phone?

No phone in the apartment proper but I was allowed to send email. Okay. And when are *they* going to start using the internet? One morning I'll have a hoofprint on my desk. It would seem logical that the demons would *already* be online. *Long* before anybody else.

I found it was a relief to go out in the car and sing with the radio. Loud singing. Just me and the Chihuahua cruising up and down Ponce de Leon and then onto little side streets. Worth the price of gas. It was not that I forgot; it was more like something pleasant washing over a grim sort of darkness that I now carried with me. Fresh lipstick on chapped lips. A chic hat over a bad haircut. For a few songs I could subdue the awful idea that there were spirits, maybe the Devil himself living with me. Oh, yeah, and don't forget Daddy. I hated living with him when he was alive.

It was hot. I thought of turning on the air conditioning and I thought of Daddy. His presence. The very air seemed to change when he came home. Speaking of air, Daddy was one of the first people to have central air conditioning installed. Because of his asthma attacks which he would screamingly blame on me and Mother. A window open half an inch would inspire an hours-long rant along the lines of "Whaddya think? Ya think Ah'm made a money? Is that what ya'll think? Ya think Ah'm gonna pay good money to air condition the entire goddam state a Mississippi?"

No. Not the whole state. As a teenager, I fantasized about pushing the thermostat down to fifty-five, opening every window as wide as it would go and having Daddy pay to air condition Hinds County.

Chapter Sixteen

I grabbed a pareo, a bikini and made sure each window was open just two inches and then I closed the bedroom door. Preparing for tomorrow's swim by preparing for darkness now. I decided to drive to the grocery store and splurge on smoked salmon. I parked at Publix thinking I'd misjudged the darkness as it was still very light so I called Melinda. We talked for nearly an hour. Should I lower the price of the condo? Should I add a perk the way other people in Florida were doing? Other sellers were throwing in club memberships, even cars. Maybe I could offer a coupon valid for finding a missing family member. We discussed the practical and not the metaphysical.

I bought cream cheese, salmon, capers and onions and went home. Kept checking the clock, looking forward to *Hustle* at ten. In the kitchen I wondered if anyone were watching me move around. The salmon was marvelous, *Hustle* was well-done. I started to feel a little lighter, a little bit like humming. I tried but I was too self-conscious. I can't hum unless I'm alone.

Music cheered me in the car but I didn't like listening to it in the apartment. My Scarlatti harpsichord music or Johnny Cash, whatever it was, it didn't matter. I felt that *they were listening, too.* The notes hung in the air differently. With any music, any song, I experienced a sharper awareness of not being alone.

My phone was charging so I didn't hear it ring; the message from Cassandra said to call her. It was past eleven but I did. She asked how I was and I said I felt okay. She told me that the women had told her nothing was happening in my apartment.

Then I said I wanted to explain something. "The other day when I was telling you about introducing myself to all those lawyers and wanting to work for them and no one ever hiring me, I was very calm and very polite. I realized when I was telling you the story that I'm not beaten down by this or angry but I actually felt it was their loss. I'm capable and they were losing out."

"I understand," she said. "I interpreted this not as anger but as the reaction of a woman who is trying so hard and hitting a wall." Cassandra paused. "I understand you very well. Maybe better than you understand yourself."

I wasn't sure of that so I did not say anything.

We both said "I love you" and it seemed very natural. We never even said that in our family until after Stirling killed himself and even then only on the phone and it was so hokey I wanted to make a face. But with Cassandra, I did feel some kind of love.

I got on top of the sleeping bag on the daybed with the little green flashlight. Up again to get the tuna. Bible. Cell phone. Emergency survival equipment. All in order. My ritual. Kitchen light on. One more night, I kept thinking. Unless this is a scam and I'm to be tortured like this until the fright is ratcheted up to the screaming point and the phone rings after dark and I drop dead of a heart attack clutching a can of white albacore.

The pfffffft noise. About two feet to my left, I estimated. Someone, something standing beside that end of the marble coffee table. Pfffffft. I tried to keep my eyes closed for a count of five pfffffts which was about seven minutes according to my watch. I couldn't do it. It was not only the noise; it was the certainty that something was standing there, could reach out, could touch me. I turned on the television, turned it off, reached for Ben Franklin and tried to concentrate. I suddenly felt very tense, more tense at midnight and I saw the man's face on the glass of the Beardsley. It didn't seem to be the same man as a few nights before but it was also old, with a high forehead and long hair. Just staring.

Slept a while and opened my eyes, still there. I blinked and he didn't go away. I saw the reflection of the ceiling fixture in the hall, could see the black and white lines of the Beardsley but that face was right there. Clearer than before. More detail. More wrinkles. Staring. As I watched it became twisted and full of rage. I put my hand over my eyes and only then could I turn away. At last, I slept.

Patrizia and Raquel kept calling, kept sending people to see the apartment. Sometimes I'd think how much fun it would be to be entirely honest. I'd greet them enthusiastically and begin my spiel. "This is my bedroom. It can get a little hot in here but don't worry it's just a portal to hell and once in a while a seven-and-a-half-foot tall half man-half goat walks around but other than a little bite at night he won't bother you. He might try to have sex with you but just push him away. There's also a little black boy who wanders through and something so big and so terrible nobody can figure out who he is but look at the view! Three terraces! Plus you're only four blocks from Miracle Mile which is fabulous. It's a beautiful penthouse but you'll never sleep again..."

Every morning I left the apartment, drove to the Biltmore, swam then lay on a chaise and slept. In an hour or two I would go home and begin my day. Usually on the internet checking real estate in Philadelphia. I had long lists with addresses, prices, square footage and there was a way to compute mortgage payments. I was organized. I also kept a detailed record of what had happened in the previous twenty-four hours.

Another night, waiting for Cassandra's call. It was past eight and *Law & Order* would keep me occupied for an hour. I finally called her on my cell phone at half-past eleven out on the balcony and her voicemail was full but she called me back right away. I grabbed the phone and practically flew over the railing I was so nervous.

"I only have two women with me but I have two more nuns coming from Tampa who will arrive around midnight. I can't come to you because I wouldn't get there till two or three in the morning and I can't go in the house then." She stopped. "How are you?"

"Okay, I guess. I'm afraid of the darkness but even in the daytime I have the feeling that I'm not alone."

"You're not ever alone but I want you to know that at midnight I will be with you. I have to wait for the nuns to come to watch me but I am placing angels in every corner of the house and a circle of protection around you. Try to get some sleep."

Maybe, I think. "I have a woman coming tomorrow at eleven to see it for the first time and someone else coming at twelve for the first time."

Cassandra said, "I wasn't going to say this but it'll make you feel better. I've been working with people in Canada and they are trying to find a client who has enough strength to withstand the spirit." I didn't respond. "I love you," she said and I echoed that and added, "Be careful."

I closed the phone and went inside. The kitchen light was on. I lay down on the French daybed watching David Letterman thinking, oh, he could *not* show himself during *David Letterman*. She said she'd be with me at midnight and the clock said 11:48.

I turned off the TV and arranged the Bible. I kept it open and rested my sledgehammer elbow on it. It still hurt from pounding in a post last Friday. I had the little green flashlight and I had the cell phone, the tuna, and the landline. My shoes were in place for the speedy exit that I never seemed to make.

I didn't feel particularly calm even if it was after midnight. Actually, I felt so wired that my skin ached. I was waiting for Cassandra's prayers to kick in the way you wait for the internet connection. She wasn't with me; I didn't feel good. I kept looking at the clock.

Then I looked at the Beardsley print and saw a different face. It had the same long hair and a beard and it was staring at me. I kept blinking and it was still there. I stared and it stared back but this face looked kind, gentle,benevolent. I must have fallen asleep because the next time I saw the clock it was five. The face was gone.

At just before seven, I got up and pulled on a bikini, brushed my teeth and drove to the Biltmore. I did the breaststroke in that glorious water and wondered how the Devil could possibly end up in a one-bedroom penthouse in an upscale suburb of Miami. I swam and read *The New York Times* just like anyone who lives with demons.

I lay in the sun and wondered if Cassandra would want me to become a nun, to join the order with all those women in West Palm Beach? She did not answer direct questions but she'd divulged that she was Syrian, with a mother and a grandmother who were both spiritualists. A word that seemed to be more acceptable to the Catholics. Her sister, too. "People would come and ask her things when she was ten years old."

I went home. The doorbell rang at eleven and in walked the newest possible buyer. Lexie was trim, athletic, tomboyish, and stunned by the outside space. At noon, she was still there when Barbara arrived. "Can I come back later as my client is still in a meeting and just can't get away?" Absolutely, I said, thinking this is working out very well. Lexie left and then the doorbell rang and it was the realtor named Audrey with the fiancé of the sweet girl I met the other day. As they paraded through, I polished my mental spiel: Washer, dryer, dishwasher, all new. The bedroom has a walk-in closet, a portal to Hell and ensuite bath. The French doors open onto a private terrace...

Then they left and I called Raquel about the confusion and not being told about the noon appointment. I told her it turned out just fine. Lexie called. "I'm having lunch with a friend and he is dying to see it. Could we come?" Her friend was an associate dean at FIU and he loved it; they both particularly admired the outdoor room off the living room. All this talk about what it was meant for, what could be done with it, could the covered terrace be air-conditioned, what about doorways, extending the living rom to include the outdoor covered terrace.

Then Barbara arrived with her client who was enthusiastic and wanted to come back with his girlfriend. "She has all the power," he smiled. I heard Barbara saying on the terrace, "You just don't have this in Coral Gables."

Everyone left and I called Cassandra and she said, "I couldn't get into your apartment last night. I told you I'd be there at midnight but I kept trying and it wouldn't let me in. I tried to push so hard I got a nosebleed. I woke up and there was blood all over my shirt." Woke up? Does she go into a trance? I pictured her physically pushing against a wall of what? Of air? "I was afraid that the women would be afraid. I was only with two of them last night. But I couldn't get in." She sighed. "Do you know how when you...no, you wouldn't know...when you go into meditation and the air is muggy? That's how it was." I listened. "It did not want me to come in. Since I've confronted it, it's harder for me, they know me. We are going to have to call on spirits from the cemetery."

This was all so foreign to me that I didn't even know what to ask. I told her about the face. "Maybe it was an angel looking out for you. I said I would send them." Yes, she had promised that on the phone. "I can't go into your house again unprepared. I am gathering information about this. I was unprepared, not in uniform. I have to take something of the church with me. When I was attacked I was alone and had gotten too far away from Father Gabriel."

The cemetery? Uniform? I had a dozen questions but Cassandra was forever elusive so I only asked the most urgent one. "Why am I keeping the bedroom door closed when you saw it in the living room? Can it get out of the bedroom?"

"Yes, it can go anywhere." She paused. "What I saw in your apartment I've only seen in books. God wanted me to see it. Do you remember when I came to your house and walked right in to the other living room?"

"Yes. People never do that." Father Gabriel and Cassandra were the only ones to ever do it.

"It was there. Later, when I saw the reflection in the mirror it had come out of that room and rounded the corner as if it were coming to see what we were doing. I only saw the reflection in the mirror. I could not see the real thing or I would have been hurt. It would be like looking at the face of God. You can't."

The face of God? Had I seen an angel in the Beardsley poster? I told her it had been a terrific day with a woman coming back for her third time and bringing a friend who loved it, the fiancé of someone else also liked it. Another man wanted to come back with his girlfriend. Calls from brokers, everyone so positive. "But," I said, "this always happens."

"No," she said, "this is different. I have the entire staff in Quebec working on this. God is working on this. That's the difference."

She said she would call me around nine o'clock to make sure I was alright. "If that place where you were bitten still hurts then I want to put holy water on it." It did. "I love you," she said before hanging up. I said it back and closed the phone.

Cassandra didn't call but it was okay because she was busy and she was doing this for me. That night I took off one peridot earring from Rome because it bothered me. I put it beside the flashlight and in the morning it was gone. I checked everywhere. That same day the cable was out. Black and white snow and a very loud hissing noise.

The next morning I saw the earring under the TV table. Later, I saw my turquoise ring on the bottom shelf of a bookcase.

The Comcast man arrived. It was simple: the big dial was on eight and not three. When he flipped it back, using force, I had color TV again. He asked, "Did you turn the dial? It's very hard to move it." I shook my head. He was insistent, "Well, somebody did."

The next morning I walked in from swimming and heard loud voices behind my closed bedroom door. I walked down the hall and listened. The voices were flat, odd, not human, and it was not any language I had ever heard. It seemed that at least twenty people were in my bedroom having a meeting of some sort.

It was eight o'clock in the morning, and I refused to be afraid. I grabbed the doorknob, turned it and pushed the door open as fast as I could. Standing on the threshold I stared into the bright, sunlit room. No voices. My sleigh bed, the paintings, the umbrella, all were in place. There was a very loud, hissing noise which I realized was coming from the television. It was on, the volume knob was turned as high as possible, and the screen was all gray snow. Maybe the dial had been flipped away from the cable. I punched it off, decided to deal with it later. Silence. The eery voices, the garbled language made me think of Martians. I stood there another moment sensing the air was different. The sunlight streamed in and my bedroom looked the same but something had disturbed the very air.

Chapter Seventeen

The day. He's coming he's coming he's coming, danced through my mind. Someone called at 7:20 and hung up. It was probably Adam, my lawyer friend in New York, calling to say 'good morning.' No swim. Pouring rain. All morning I thought of the exorcist. Is he getting on a plane? If I believe in angels do I believe in devils? I looked at the Beardsley. No face. Then I looked over my head and could see black mold on the ceiling on one side of the hole that I wanted so desperately to have fixed. A few minutes later there was more of it. It was actually marching across the white ceiling! I stood on a chair with a steak knife and began scraping. It was not coming off. Then I got down, got up again with paintbrush, hair dryer. Of all days for Lexie to decide to come with her air conditioning man and, of course, he would probably be looking at the ceiling to discover where the present ducts were. Damn. Painting the edge of the ceiling white I then went over the line onto the yellow wall so then I dried it and went and got yellow from the can in the kitchen closet and then went over the line into the white. Had the hair dryer roaring on 'high' and I was on a chair waving it back and forth over my head. Emergency. Doorbell. I jumped off the chair, stuffed the hair dryer under a cushion, took a deep breath and opened the front door with a smile.

Lexie came and went. She and her a.c. man were out on the covered terrace the whole time. Patrizia called and said Ann, the realtor from South Miami, said her clients were seeing other things over the weekend but mine was their favorite so far. If there was nothing they liked better, then they would make an offer on Monday. Same thing with Barbara and her young married couple. Lexie wanted to know if anyone else had made a bid and described herself as "definitely serious." She had come three times.

The day seemed to last twice as long as it should have. This was going to be over, I told myself. I looked at the clock every twenty minutes. *He is coming he is coming he is coming.* The sky changed color, and I walked down the hall to the bedroom. I found a bikini and a pareo and got out. This would be the last night like this. The exorcist will fix everything.

The entire concept of spirits and dead people frightened and repulsed me. I didn't want to die and be with bad characters for all eternity in a condo in Coral Gables. How hideous. I didn't even have a man I wanted to have dinner with but now a goat wanted to have sex with me? I did not always feel that particular presence but I was definitely not alone. At least once a day, when I returned from errands, from Publix, from the library, I turned the key in the front door and wondered if the spirits were all lined up waiting for me. Or were they in various rooms doing their own private things until I returned? What *did* they *do*?

At eight o'clock, Cassandra called and said, "I'm sorry. He couldn't come. That's all I can say. Don't worry, he wants to come. We can't talk about this anymore right now."

I hung up and told myself to not be devastated. He wants to come. He and Cassandra are doing all this for me. Don't lose faith. I reheard her voice: He wants to come.

I went into the kitchen and decided to cook the pork and even though the sell by date was two days away and it was in the fridge—it was rotten. That happened with the hamburger on Sunday. I bought it and three hours later took it out of the refrigerator and it smelled rank and actually had a greenish sheen to it. I'm not buying any more meat.

Jim and I conferred on the phone but mostly we traded very detailed emails. He was meticulous, very detail-oriented, and, like many FBI men, had a law degree. We were hammering out what needed to be on the website, shooting emails back and forth.

No matter how often Cassandra and I talked it was never enough for me. I had so many questions but often she didn't answer or she told me something she'd said before. Twice she told me that the noise I'd heard in the bedroom was the goat man ramming his horns in frustration at the door. Sometimes she encouraged me. I heard the word 'strong' again and again. "Your childhood, your family have been difficult but you have never given up. All of it has made you a very strong woman."

I never felt strong after dark. When I professed to feel confused about all that was happening, she would say, "This is unusual but it's not unknown. That's why I called Father Gabriel. It can be taken care of. It will be gone forever. It is the cause of things going wrong, of things being taken away from you." I could not hear "it will be gone forever" often enough.

Many times she ended a conversation with, "I'll call you tonight and make sure you're okay. This might be a difficult night because they don't want us to come." A psychic reading the minds of spirits? Do the spirits plan things? It's Wednesday so let's terrify that woman in the penthouse on Adriano Avenue. No, we are going there tomorrow night. Let's go to that house in Vero Beach and drive that couple crazy.

Sometimes it was arranging a phone call around Cassandra's time at the church. In the car, no one liked her to talk on the phone so she would say, "I'm in the car and I can't talk" or it was "I was on a break but have to go in now." She might tell me to be sure and answer the phone at ten o'clock. "I'm going to hear from Father Gabriel about what to do next and I'll call you after that." Then she might *not* call and the next day I'd hear that *he* had not called.

The days passed in a constant exchange of admonishments to be patient, to not talk on the phone in the apartment and waiting for word from Father Gabriel. The nights passed slowly, one at a time, usually in fifteen-minute increments with my prayers usually voiced as "please, please, don't let me see anything" or "please, don't let anything touch me." I'd gotten used to the routine of grabbing all I needed before dark from the bedroom, closing the door and pulling the knob, pushing the knob to make sure it could not possibly swing open. The long nights were spent with old movies, *Law & Order*, and three men: David Letterman, Jay Leno, and Benjamin Franklin. Long, long nights.

One morning I woke up with this disgusting smell in the crotch of my white shorts. I jumped up, gagging, and tore them off. At first I thought it was urine but it wasn't. It was on the outside of my shorts, colorless. It reminded me of those two male cats I'd been housesitting in New York. They'd sprayed something in my open suitcase when they were upset I was going away. Holding the shorts at arm's length I tossed them into the washing machine on 'hot' and then washed my hands for a long, soapy time.

"Tomorrow," I told Cassandra, "two or maybe three different people are coming to see the apartment."

"Good." She didn't say it but her prediction of the sale always hung in the air for me: the week after Halloween. So these people were probably not the ones. "The Haitian coin was all about money and all your money is in the apartment. You have to sell it. It's a fair price."

"Exactly," I answered. "I want to pay back the bank, have money to get my stuff up to Philadelphia and enough for a down payment on a place for me and my office. That's it."

"If you were a greedy person I wouldn't be on the phone with you."

I felt a twinge of worry once in awhile. She did take money for her work. She did read palms, she did have clients and yet she was doing all this for me as a gift. What if we got to the end of this and I sold the condo and she said, 'Father Gabriel, the nuns and I have done so much for you so now we want you to contribute the money from the sale to the Catholic Church.' Would I be demon-free and broke? Or would I thank her profusely, get on a plane with all the money, and hope I could get a decent night's sleep once a year?

Chapter Eighteen

A realtor named Lourdes was supposed to come with someone named Daniel and his fiancée but now it is not until tomorrow. I prayed the ceiling would stay white and that it wouldn't rain and that the mold would stay away. Mold is a four-letter word in Miami. Then Barbara the realtor called as I sat with Thor at the pool and said, "I know it's short notice. First of all, Stephen got cold feet but I have another couple who really want to see it. How is five o'clock?"

I dashed home, and saw that the apartment was in perfect order. They came, they raved about it and they left.

The next afternoon Thor was here for a drink, we were talking and I offered to drive him to South Beach. We were in the Chihuahua, he was charming, the radio was on. Cassandra called and told me to call her when I was back. I did. "I'm pulling up to the building." She said not to go in. "Park the car where you usually do and then go and wait by the fountain." I did as I was told and time passed and I called her and she said she would call me back. I waited, taking deep breaths of the fresh, flower-scented air. Yes, something was definitely wrong with the air in my apartment. Out of the darkness came two figures; I embraced Father Gabriel and then Cassandra. He said, "She told you I was coming before and then unforeseen things happened and we didn't want to disappoint you again." Cassandra said, "I wanted to tell you but I couldn't. Should we go in?"

As we went up in the elevator I explained about having a friend over. It was the only time I had not closed the bedroom door before dark. I clutched my key then heard a pfffffft noise on the other side of the door. Cassandra said, "You heard that. So did I." I was very used to it. I would later be told it was Daddy.

So we went in and they told me that Father Gabriel was going to Paris, to look in the archives about Bathemus.

"How long will you be gone?" I asked. "As long as it takes," was the answer.

I offered them wine, fruit juice, water. Father Gabriel said he did not drink alcohol so I gave him white cranberry juice. Cassandra lit two white candles as I moved Thor's and my wine glasses off the coffee table. I sat down again as they prayed. Light came in from the French doors of the living room balcony but otherwise we sat in darkness.

While we were sitting there on the French daybed, beside the marble coffee table, the mold started again. Of course, I didn't hear it or smell it but somehow I *felt* it. I looked up and said, "It will be over six or seven inches long in less than an hour." They stared with upturned faces. We could actually see it moving.

Then I looked at Father Gabriel and asked, "May I come with you to Paris?" and he laughed and said, "We won't get anything done." It wasn't flirtatious, it was just 'no.' Father Gabriel had a quiet intensity. His frame was slight and he was no taller than me but he looked hard and lean like a runner. Behind the glasses, his eyes seemed black. He was solemn and yet, he could really laugh.

As I understood it, Bathemus was bound and in a new location. They couldn't bind my father before but he was bound tonight and angry and screaming at Father Gabriel for separating him from Bathemus. He was furious but behind a wall. If I hear anything, any noises, I am not to be afraid. I can even shout to shut up, to leave me alone, to let me sleep! Well, yes, I was told I could do that but could I really do it?

"My flesh, my skin feels different," I said. "I don't know what it is. Not aching with tiredness but with a new feeling. It's entirely different from what I've ever felt before."

"You are not used to being alone," said Father Gabriel.

"And I am not used to feeling afraid," I said. "I have actually been called fearless when I go undercover. I am wearing a wire, spinning a story and I know I'm on enemy territory but I am not afraid. I am very focused on what must be done. I walk into those situations and take chances but this…"

Cassandra said, "It is amazing that someone of your calibre could have this happen to you." I didn't know what she meant and before I could ask, she had stood up and walked over and lifted the Beardsley off the wall. "I can look into mirrors and summon spirits and you can, too. They can't come through but they are there showing themselves to you."

I was not to be afraid, they both told me. There was nothing more here. Daddy was bound.

Father Gabriel told me not to feel weak. "You are very, very strong or you would have given in, been taken over a long time ago. They are angry and trying all they can to get you but they can't. You don't know how strong you are. They haven't gotten you yet and this has gone on for years."

I tried to absorb that idea. I thought of Stirling. I thought of Mother. How I wished I could talk to them about this. I thought of Big Momma, Daddy's mother. How frightened I was of her as a little girl. They told me that there was something in Daddy that made him do these things.

I told them about the pearls. "My sister and I were told by Mother that Daddy said that any child who went to his house to wish him 'Merry Christmas' would be given fifty dollars. I laughed. My parents were divorced and I was glad that I never had to see him again. I was nearly twenty-one and my sister must have been eighteen. We were home from college for the holidays."

"My sister went. She came back and I joked with her. 'Did you get your fifty dollars?' She was upset and my sister was never upset. I was the one who burst into tears, who slammed doors, and she was the one who never cried. She held out a long, narrow, leather jewelry box and said, 'Take it! I don't want it!' She opened it and inside was a string of pearls. She pushed the box at me. 'Take them! I don't want them!' I said I didn't want them either. She was crying which was very unusual. I threw my arms around her. She said, 'He gave me the pearls so that you would want them and hate me for having them!' I kept insisting that we had fooled him and that I could never hate her, that I loved her! She kept saying she didn't want the pearls. I told her to put them away. 'Someday you will wear them and forget where they came from. Keep them. Put them away.' She was very upset, she didn't want them and I didn't want them. I pulled them from the box and went into the bathroom and held them over the toilet. 'Then let's get rid of them!' Her hand shot out and rescued the pearl necklace from disappearing forever."

Cassandra said, "This isn't normal. To want his daughters to hate each other. This is in his blood. Your brother was weak and your father got to him but he couldn't get to you. He has not gotten to you."

I wondered what she meant by saying my brother was weak. Did she know about Stirling's suicide? How could she?

I told them about the pearls but I didn't tell them that about ten days later, he would be dead. Quite possibly murdered by his second wife. That

Christmas Eve of the pearls would be my last chance to see him and I didn't and I didn't care.

"A lot of things we know but when you tell us a story like the pearls, it all fits." Cassandra turned to Father Gabriel who said, "We are coming to the end of this but some things have to be done. Cassandra is unclean, has had children, so there are things I must do."

Cassandra said that there are people praying for me. "These women sew their own clothes, don't know who the president of the U.S. is, but they are praying for you. I wear a uniform when I go to church and I rarely speak because they wouldn't understand or approve of my slang. You would not recognize me when I'm in my uniform."

"This is part of the Catholic Church?" I asked and she nodded. I didn't know what to say, what to ask.

"Every morning," I told them, "I think I've come through another night. If I know it will end, I can deal with anything."

Father Gabriel said, "Every beginning is the end of another beginning." This did not comfort me. Didn't Churchill say it better? He embraced me twice and we prayed and he kissed my hand. "We are in complete agreement that you write about this but you must not use my name or the name of my church or Cassandra's name." I said it would be a long time away and Cassandra said, "This isn't about a book, let's take care of this first."

They stood and we walked to the elevator. "We will see this through," said Father Gabriel. Then he smiled slyly and asked, "What did you call her?" I looked at Cassandra, each eye still ringed with bruises. "The purple raccoon," I answered. He reacted to that with a loud bark of a laugh.

I went down with them and we sat on the bench in front of the building next door and talked quietly in the darkness. I didn't want them to leave and I didn't want to go upstairs again.

The apartment felt empty when I went back. Maybe this was the final act. I turned on the laundry room light and got my little green flashlight, the Bible, my tuna, my cell phone and suited up in white cotton shorts and a white tank top. I fell asleep watching television and when I woke up my left hand was in a cramp, all fingers curved like a claw. I could not move it. I massaged it then I banged it against the wall. My cell phone said 1:22 AM so I'd been asleep for an hour. I woke up again exactly an hour later with the same hand in the same cramp. A claw. It happened a third time, 3:22 AM. I massaged the feeling into it again and my fingers started to move. Then I went into the kitchen for a drink of water. A door slammed in my bedroom. Since the closet had louvred doors, it had to be the bathroom door. Then it happened again, loud, hard! There was a heavy thump against the bedroom door as if someone had used their shoulder on it, the way cops do in the movies. Then the bathroom door slammed. Again and again. I sat cross-legged on the French daybed staring down the hallway at my bedroom door as the bathroom door kept slamming. Someone was in a rage! Was it Daddy? I realized that my heart was not pounding at all. I put my hand on my chest. No heartbeat. Could my heart have simply stopped in fear?

At dawn, I grabbed my bikini and bolted out of my apartment.

Later I talked to Cassandra and hated it when she said, "We could see him moving around the apartment but we never saw your hand in a claw like that."

I interrupted. "He? Daddy? But I thought he was behind a wall!"

"No, he got out. He moves all around the apartment." I grimaced. "He is angry like a kid kicking a door. We knew there would be some activity. We had to do a lot to prepare Father Gabriel for his trip." She went on. "There are so many things we cannot tell you yet. There are revelations. Things will become clear to you. Not now but—" Her call waiting sounded. "I have to take this." We hung up.

I stood on the terrace outside my bedroom and stared out at the bright blue afternoon sky. I thought back about the last few weeks. The umbrella turned black. I slammed my face into the wall in the middle of the night or someone hit me. I went to buy sage on a Friday afternoon. I saw these odd people with a goat in the parking lot of Whole Foods. The goat was decorated with ribbons and flowers. I went home and found this big Haitian coin in the washing machine. I burned the sage and that night the door was nearly broken down by a goat ramming his horns against it. Cassandra was attacked in the cemetery at the same time. She was too hurt to come the next day but on Sunday she came and saw a seven-foot tall figure with a goat head in my apartment. A goat. I felt the sun burning my bare skin. A goat. I turned to go indoors. Detectives don't believe in coincidences.

Chapter Nineteen

I wrote this letter the day after their second visit. And I did give it to Cassandra.

Dear Cassandra and Father Gabriel,

It is astounding how different I felt after your visit last night. Physically different.

After Daddy died, I really tried to think of one good moment with him—and I could not.

Dinner, every single night, was something to endure. The dining room walls were covered with lovely ice-blue wallpaper. Pale, oyster-white Chinese figures in kimonos floated over bridges, among delicate flowers. The chandelier sparkled above the long polished table set with Mother's silver. Any topic of conversation could evoke Daddy's rage which was directed at Mother or at me, not ever my younger, blonde sister. I ate carefully but was criticized for taking a drink of water. "Don't wash your food down!" I was criticized for not chewing enough times, for not taking a second helping when Mary the maid circled the table with a serving dish. I was called "scrawny." Often, apropos of nothing, I was shouted at for not being competitive. "You have no sense of competition!" I never understood it. But he was right. I am only in competition with myself. I want to do my best. That's all. I didn't care about winning a contest unless it was sailing, a Saturday race in a Blue Jay. Daddy used better as a verb. It was the first time I'd heard that. "You'll never better yourself!" But maybe worst of all and most often, shouted at me nearly every day, was the pronouncement that I was stupid.

When I was in third grade I remember telling a friend that I never added salt to my food because my tears dripped onto my plate. At age fifteen, one evening I left the dinner table. This was after the required, "Mother, may I please be excused?" and Mother saying, "Don't you care for dessert?" and my saying, "No thank you. May I please be excused?" In tears, as usual, I went up to my room and stared out the window. Suddenly I thought, "There is nothing wrong with me. It's DADDY. Even though the world thinks he is charming and wonderful. I'm not stupid, I'm not an awful person. Something is wrong with Daddy."

At that moment, I decided I would never speak to him again unless I had to. I would say, 'good morning' and answer any questions but nothing else. I would never volunteer anything again. Those were the rules and they were MY rules. MY secret. MY plan. And that's what I did with my father and at last I felt that I had some power over what happened to me. But the household being what it was——chaos—with Daddy screaming and Mother trying to hold her own without further antagonizing him and the barrage of temper tantrums and criticism, NO ONE EVER NOTICED that I never spoke to him again.

My sister is very bright...she knew the pearls weren't a Christmas present to her but were a weapon. "He wants us to hate each other." Thank you, Cassandra, for saying it isn't normal.

I didn't tell you that he died a week later around the new year. Maybe the 2nd or 3rd of January. Mother and Stirling and I talked and we all thought he had been murdered by his 2nd wife. The others said "we don't want publicity so keep quiet." Mother was divorced from him, of course, and Stirling and I didn't care.

I couldn't believe that he was really dead. I kept waiting to be told that it was a mistake. I used to pray, when I was little, that he would be struck by lightning on the golf course or that someone would shoot him in a hunting accident.

Now I look back and think how annoyed Mother was and how upset Aunt Frances was about the 2nd wife not writing thank-you notes for the flowers. Bad manners—in my family that's worse than murder. The second wife was last seen driving west towards Louisiana in Daddy's black Mercedes.

That Mercedes. Shipped all the way from Stuttgart so that Daddy could preen at stop lights and tell curious and very impressed onlookers what it was. The first Mercedes in the state of Mississippi.

I think the will changed my two brothers and my sister. They weren't the same or maybe who they really were became more clearly defined.

Mother's last years were heartbreakingly sad. I'd begged her to move to Vero Beach to be near her sisters and away from Curtis but she wouldn't. She could never have imagined her children behaving as they did. Mother created a busy and independent life for herself after her divorce yet those three treated her as if she were a nuisance. They wanted to control her, they wanted her to be dependent upon them so they ripped away everything that made her who she was. They did a great job on her. This person who was naturally joyful was destroyed. That last summer she no longer wanted to live.

I felt that IF I had had money or a husband—IF Stirling had been alive—none of it would have been allowed to happen.

When I was a little girl I rescued her from Daddy several nights a week. He would be shouting at her and I would go downstairs into the kitchen and start banging pots and pans to give her an excuse to say, "Cici is making popcorn and I want to make sure she's okay with the stove." But I couldn't rescue her at the end—from her own children this time—- and I ache with regret that I was not able to help her.

It is now Friday morning and I slept better last night than I have since all this began. At one point, it started to rain so I got up and closed the balcony door, very firmly as I do all doors, and a few minutes later I heard it open. Maybe the wind. I told myself it was.

I am thinking of you, Father Gabriel—so far away—and hoping that the research is going well. Thank you for all you are doing, for the prayers, for all your time and energy and for caring about what happens to me. You are my brave warriors. Please be careful. I thank you. with love, Cici

Cassandra called me on Sunday at 8:30 PM and was upset. "Do *not* talk in the apartment anymore! The women can hear that you have been talking about this in the apartment!"

I was a bit shocked. "But you told me it was okay on the covered terrace!"

"I thought it was okay but they can hear you so stop."

I said, of course. "Listen, I've written a long letter because I feel it's time I told you some things about my family." I paused. "My brother killed himself," I said and she immediately said, "We knew that."

"But why didn't you say you knew that?"

"We know a lot of things that we can't say to you. It's like coming to your house. You must invite us to enter. Some of these things we can't say to you."

I frowned and didn't respond.

Later I left the laundry closet light on, glowing through the half-open, louvred doors. It was a big step to turn off the kitchen ceiling light but I did it. I decided that I was pathetic.

The next day was Monday and she called and said she couldn't come. I pulled over and parked on Minorca. "I can't talk for long. I am not allowed to go home and right now I'm staying with another woman from the church." I started to speak but she cut me off. "The church does not want Father Gabriel to come here or to work from Canada. He's being sent to another location." It was all starting to sound like the C.I.A. to me. "You know how we thought we had it out of the apartment?" she asked.

"I don't really know that because I feel very uneasy there."

Cassandra said, "That's because something has come back. Your father is standing over you. He's watching you. He can't hurt you but he is there." I heard women's voices talking in the background. They weren't speaking English or Spanish. It was that odd language. "Things are unraveling. Getting this out of your apartment is more difficult that we thought. The church won't let Father Gabriel do anything and they've switched me to another place, too. I'm not supposed to contact anyone. Not my kids, no one."

I always felt I was being given privileged information. If I asked questions, they wouldn't be answered. "We are getting you out of there." Abruptly, she hung up.

Five days went by with no word from her. I had the goat dream again and again. It was a sweet dog with its head in my lap and I was petting it the way I used to pet Silky for hours. Suddenly it was the head of a goat and I would jump awake in disgust. I went numb with fear when I saw the goat man again. He was always going into the kitchen, hunched over horribly. Terror paralyzed me. My heart seemed to stop beating. Impossible, of course.

I constantly told myself not to panic, that Cassandra would not leave me to live forever in my haunted penthouse. Her voicemail was full. There was more happening at night in the apartment. When I closed my eyes, I heard the little rattle noise as if someone were holding a piece of paper a foot away and then giving it a shake. Sometimes it sounded as if someone were turning a page. It was now about every minute. A demon standing there reading? Even worse, when I got used to that and kept my eyes closed, feeling entirely exhausted, something softly touched my face. It was not a spider, it was not fabric. It was the hand from Rome and it wouldn't allow me to fall asleep. My body ached from tiredness. Beside the coffee table, someone or something stood. Sometimes I heard a noise as if weight were being shifted, as if it were standing on one foot and then the other. I didn't have the courage to swipe at the space with my fist but how I wanted to!

One night, actually it was one morning around three, I was reading when I heard a rustle noise, like a fluttering of wings, across the room. It became louder. I looked at my desk and saw dozens of sheets of paper rising and whirling up to the ceiling in a circle like some miniature tornado of pages. I watched the paper go round and round and in about a minute they all seemed to fall back to the desk. I didn't get up, go over to investigate, didn't do anything. I was not afraid so my reaction was more along the lines of 'well, that was interesting.'

The next morning I went over to my desk and sat down and thought that it looked neater than usual. But in a few minutes I realized that I couldn't find that page with certain phone numbers on it, the page with the Philadelphia realtors, this and that. Missing. Two days later I noticed another earring from my jewelry box on an empty shelf beside the television. Then I saw paper behind the bookcase. When I moved it away from the wall I saw dozens of pages, wadded up, crumpled and stuffed behind it. The missing pages.

Chapter Twenty

Jim liked the name I proposed. I checked to find out if it had been taken in Florida and it hadn't so I submitted all the documents to the Florida Secretary of State so we could be an L.L.C. Of course, I was glad to have this project but it wasn't a case, it wasn't work I enjoyed. And it wasn't going to turn a profit for a long time.

Melinda had become my closest confidante. When she called me, I would say, "Everything is fine. Are you at home?" and then rush out or leave wherever I was, park the car, usually on Madeira or Majorca, and call her back or she called me. She listened, she comforted me. Today she insisted that Cassandra would not desert me. "Not when you've come this far."

"This far?" I yelped. "Things are actually worse!"

It was late in the afternoon of the sixth day without communication when Cassandra called. "I haven't forgotten you. I'm working hard for you. We all are." She asked how things were and I told her about the paper rattling becoming pretty much non-stop and the touching and she murmured, "Not good." She would send someone to pick up my latest letter. "You know we have several people in the Grove," she said, and I wondered, witches, psychics, several what kind of people exactly?

My dinner with a friend the next night was cancelled. It occurred to me again and again that I had no friend in Miami in whom I could confide. My cousin Tad was out. It was all long-distance commiseration. When I went out, when I was with anyone, it was entirely superficial, all pretense. I was smiling for that pocket of time and even laughing over this or that. But in the back of my mind, I wondered what was waiting for me at home.

Cassandra called late the next afternoon and asked me to meet her in the Grove at Starbucks at half past seven. I closed the bedroom door, grabbed my letter and dashed out. I tried to make copies of the pages at Kinko's but only one part of the page was printed. It was a three-inch wide swathe in the middle and looked like poetry. A man behind the counter had to do it. Every foray at Kinko's was an adventure. I could not make copies of anything to do with Cassandra!

Traffic in the Grove was a quagmire of cars stopping for jaywalkers in shorts and flip-flops, cars double-parked with blinkers blinking and cars snailing along full of tourists simply gawking at the fauna of South Florida. The Chihuahua crawled but I found a parking place and zipped in. Walking across the street to Starbucks, a nice-looking man smiled at me and said, "Hello." The interest was most unusual.

I sat down across from this woman with long blonde hair and a golden tan, young enough to be my daughter. She held my fate in her hands. "Where are we now?" I asked.

"We've changed plans," she says. "It's too strong. We can't separate it from you so we are separating it from the apartment."

"But does that mean it will be with me? It will come with me?" I felt physically sick.

"No. We are returning your father and his friends to the ground."

"Cassandra, I can't, as a decent person, ever sell this condo to someone knowing that they will suffer the way I have. I can't do it."

"They won't. You will be free to go and whoever moves in will have no problems. It's you, it's the connection to you and not to the apartment but we will separate them from the apartment so that you can leave."

I stared at her. "So you can put all these...these things...the goat man and Daddy...in the ground and I can go? And you are sure they won't come out again when someone else moves in?"

"No. They aren't interested in anybody else."

Well, that's good and that's bad. "How are your kids?" I asked. They were extraordinarily beautiful little children. Rose must have been six and her brother eight and then there was a little baby still being carried around. Usually by the smiling, twenty-something nanny. How reasonable.

"Rose told me this morning that people come to her at night. She says they stand beside her bed and talk to her but she can't quite hear what they are saying."

Not reasonable.

"She is very psychic and is showing it already. She was born with the caul. Just the way I was."

"What is that?" I asked.

"It's a membrane, very thin, over your face. My sister had it, too."

"Is this hereditary then? You said your mother was a psychic…"

"Being a psychic does run in families. My husband's mother is a psychic so Rose gets this from both sides."

"How is he? Your husband?" He was very handsome and looked Latin to me the one time I'd seen him.

"He's fine. The reason he is fine with my crazy hours and not being at home is because of his mother. She was called away for days at a time."

"What does your husband do? Does he work in Miami?"

"He has his own construction company, does very well. And I know why you are asking me this."

I felt very uncomfortable as she said, "You are worried about me asking you for money. But I don't need money. My husband makes a good living. And haven't I told you that God has given me a gift and it would be a sin to take money for it? I will never ask you for money."

Well, never try to skirt an issue with a psychic, I think. "Yes, I am terribly worried about money."

"Of course, I know that! Listen to me! What has happened with your father, what is going on in the apartment has to do with money, with your not being able to make it, not being able to have it. It means things come within reach and then are pulled away. This is not your fault."

I looked down at my hands on the table. "All I want is to work. To work hard, to do what I do best and to be paid for it. I don't care about the lottery. I don't care about money per se but I do care about being allowed to *earn* it."

"This is all going to change," she said earnestly. Then she seemed to switch gears. "We have to be more careful with the phones. The women could hear everything you were saying in the apartment so you must remember to get off the land. Why don't we have some kind of a code? If I say 'ice cream' then you will know I have good news."

I laughed. "How long before *they* will know about 'ice cream' and we have to change the code to 'chocolate cake?'"

She shook her head smiling and her long, straight, blonde hair moved on her bare shoulders in the tank top. "Okay! So when I say 'ice cream' and you are in the apartment, hang up and leave and call me when you get off the land."

"It's a deal," I said lightly. There was loud laughter coming from behind her and we both turned to look and saw it was just teenagers joking around. "I have someone coming to the apartment tomorrow with his fiancée and the mold is growing."

Cassandra looked very alert. "I thought it had gone away."

"It came back this morning. It grows very quickly and it's thick and black. Think of Hitler's moustache. I stood on a chair with a steak knife but even as I scraped it off it was replacing itself immediately." I grimaced. "It's rather disgusting." Her face was serious as she listened. "I blasted it with the hair dryer on 'high' and that seemed to slow it down. Nobody came today but tomorrow…"

A man passed our table, looking at my legs in appreciation. That had not happened in such a long time and now—two times in an hour. Strange.

"Keep track of it and let me know."

"I nearly forgot. Here's the letter."

Cassandra took the white envelope and said she had to leave. She stood up in a swirl of a long blue skirt and sandals. "I have to give the nanny a day off and it might be good to spend some time with my husband." I stood, too, and we both smiled. I wondered what her marriage was really like. How could she possibly have children, a very attractive, probably successful husband, be gone for days at a time and survive on nearly no sleep?

She leaned up and kissed me and then said fervently, "I love you and this is going to be taken care of. Be patient." She was out the door and gone before I could say a word.

Later as I gathered the Bible, the white albacore, the little green flashlight, I thought yeah, yeah, Scarlett. Be patient. Tomorrow is another day. I lay down on the French daybed, arranged the pillows, heard the little rattle of someone invisible turning a page and clicked on the TV. Jay Leno would save me from thinking for an hour and a half and then…tomorrow would be today. Pfffffft!

Chapter Twenty-One

As I lay in the sun after my swim, I thought that all of this had made me terrified of dying. I thought it would be peaceful. I did not think that people who did terrible things to other people stayed to haunt them, to hurt them. I believed that we floated away in the wind and that the good things we did stayed on earth.

For three days I heard nothing from Cassandra. I virtually lived in the Coral Gables Library, I took notes and then I wrote to her.

Cassandra—You asked me to put on paper the Coral Gables connections.

You said (like Father G) that all in my life has led me here. I can't stop thinking of that.

My father had a brother named Angus McNair and from the time I was little I knew that he lived in a place called Coral Gables. Angus was small and unattractive in comparison to my father who was tall and handsome but they were very much the same to their wives and children. Angus had a gentle, nice wife named Margaret Frances. Mother liked her, and so did I. They had three children; I never met the two boys. There was a son whose name I can't remember who supposedly "drank and smoked himself to death" and another son they called Sonny (Angus Jr.) and a daughter everyone called Polly. My first cousins.

The story I heard when I was about fourteen in Mississippi was that Sonny (about twenty years old) was being very secretive in his room and had a two-way radio and was disappearing for days at a time. It was 1961. My aunt and uncle got word that he had been arrested in Cuba and was in a prison on the Isle of Pines. He had been going back and forth with Cuban friends taking guns to overthrow Castro. Uncle Angus called Daddy, who knew senators and people in Washington, for help. Lots of phone calls when long distance calls were an event. Weeks went by. Sonny did send letters to his mother from prison. Then it was on television that he had been executed by firing squad. That was April 20th, 1961, which was just after the Bay of Pigs fiasco which was April 17th. Soon after this my poor aunt, Margaret Frances, was put in a mental hospital.

On Friday, I went to the Coral Gables library and looked up their address which is in Coral Gables. I went there yesterday. The house looked small and sad.

I also tried to find any Miami Herald stories about my cousin. There was no mention of him which is quite odd since he was from here. Stranger still is that he was on the front page of The New York Times. On Monday, I'll make copies of those articles. Daddy had clout and money and kept the story out of the papers in Miami and in Jackson. I remember that he was angry that it was on the national news.

When I was little, I heard about Polly, Uncle Angus's daughter. She fell in love with a Catholic and her father was furious and forbade her to marry him. My father was the same way about Catholics and the night before my brother's wedding to a Catholic with an Irish last name, he screamed that the bride was "the scum of the earth!" That sickened me as the next day he was all smiles and charm in front of everyone. Daddy certainly detested Catholics but he hated the Irish, too, so it's never been clear to me which upset him more.

Anyway, Polly did marry the Catholic and Uncle Angus said he never wanted to see or speak to her again. She went away and the marriage ended. Years later, after Sonny died, after so much had happened, when her father was dying, Polly came to him, literally on his deathbed, and begged her father's forgiveness for marrying a Catholic. He turned his face away, would not look at her and then he died. In Coral Gables.

Yet another tender McNair story. Can you understand why I told Mother I wanted to have a complete blood transfusion the minute I was old enough to be told I had "McNair blood" and then later I wanted to change my name?

Another thing that leaps into my mind is that my father married a woman I'll call Ruth B. She was from Miami. They married in September and I didn't get the pearl necklace that Christmas Eve and I think he was dead right after New Year's. The secretaries in Daddy's office building were always on friendly terms with my mother and one of them told her that there were explosive phone calls between Daddy and the new wife. Daddy had never shown his rage with Mother to any outsider. But with the second wife, he constantly screamed on his office phone.

I met Ruth B for the first and only time at Daddy's funeral. She and Aunt Frances were both wearing red suits and having a contest to see who could cry the loudest. Not maroon, not wine-colored but fire-engine-red suits. At the funeral, they were in each other's arms but within days would fight like alley cats over Daddy's will.

In 2003, when I first moved here, I tried to look for her name under several different spellings but I had no luck. She was actually from Coral Gables. Close to him in age, she would be around 100 if she were alive, since he was born in 1905. My brother Stirling and Mother and I all thought that she killed him and got away with it. It happened in Naples, Florida, where Daddy had bought a condominium. He was in Jackson for Christmas Eve and Christmas, (the Christmas of the pearls) and then he and Ruth flew to Florida.

Her story is that, at about ten o'clock at night, he told her to give him a shot for his asthma and she did and he died. He used to have Mother do that. He was a doctor and could have easily done it himself but because Mother hated doing it, he made her. Okay, so the 2nd wife gave him the shot and he died. Possible. But then it gets strange. She said she was "so upset" that she didn't think to call a doctor or an ambulance. She stayed there in the bedroom with his body until 6 AM and then she still didn't call a doctor but she called her sister-in-law, my aunt, in Jackson. Aunt Frances didn't tell her to call a doctor either but she chartered a private plane and flew to Naples and the two women somehow got him on the plane, back to Jackson and the funeral was the next day and he was buried. This is what Aunt Frances told Mother and me at the time.

No autopsy. I think it is illegal to transport bodies from one state to another without an autopsy. There was a death certificate and Mother was told it said 'heart attack.' Daddy was 62 and he was in amazing shape; Mother was adamant that he had not had a heart attack.

Nothing about the grief-stricken widow's behavior or Aunt Frances's makes sense. Then, of course, there was the will. One written in pencil was supposedly stolen from Daddy's safe in the apartment he kept in Jackson. Of course, the pencil will was in favor of Ruth B. There was yet another missing will that was in favor of my aunt. According to her. My brothers sent armed guards to the apartment but they were too late. The wall safe was open and empty. Rob and Curtis, as executors, paid the second wife something and she drove away in Daddy's Mercedes and disappeared forever.

My sister lived in Coral Gables in perhaps the early 1970s. I came to visit her here. She was a paralegal for a Miami law firm. Then she moved to Texas but I think she came back to Coral Gables in the 1980s when she married. I don't know where she lived in Coral Gables.

Stirling lived in Coral Gables for at least a year and I think he attended Miami-Dade Junior College. Daddy had suddenly refused to pay his tuition at Mississippi State and when my brother applied for a scholarship and the dean found out his father was Dr. McNair in Jackson, he was laughed out of the dean's office. Stirling would graduate from college and later, even with his background of lousy Mississippi public schools, be accepted at Columbia University business school in New York. Amazing. He worked as a busboy at the Waldorf Astoria to pay his tuition but the schedule was too much and he had to drop out of Columbia. I am now taking classes at what is now Miami-Dade College.

It is odd that this little patch of land called Coral Gables could be the setting for so much family history. None of it connected to any fondness for Uncle Angus.

His and Daddy's mother thought money was the most important thing in life. According to Mother, Big Momma was devious and cunning; that was her legacy to her children. I know nothing of her family background.

I remember not ever wanting to be alone with her. When she died, Aunt Frances lifted me up to the coffin (I was about 5 years old) and lowered me down on top of her to "kiss Big Momma goodbye." I did the only sensible thing and screamed my head off until somebody rescued me.

Never having one conversation with my father means I have questions. Mother told me she wondered why Daddy would never tell her how his brother Crawford died. He was a few years younger than Daddy and died as a little boy. This was probably in Vicksburg, where Daddy was born.

In 1994, I lived with Mother in Mississippi and she introduced me to a very attractive thirty-year-old woman whose grandmother was Big Momma's sister. Our fathers were first cousins.

Mother liked her but I met her with some hesitation. However, we got along and she confided in me. She told me how savagely her grandmother had treated her father. Her father had many of Daddy's same traits. The really shocking thing to me was that this attractive young woman HAD NO MEMORY OF ANYTHING BEFORE HER TWELFTH BIRTHDAY.

This can happen, according to psychiatrists, to people who have been traumatized by a situation. The reality is unbearable or literally unthinkable and the mind closes off. She did not seem to think it was the least bit unusual that she had no memory of first grade, of any birthday party, of any pet, of anything, until the age of twelve. She was educated, well-spoken, but obviously something unimaginable went on in her household.

Those two sisters born in the 1880s in Mississippi had sons and the sons—Daddy and her father—had us as daughters. Both these men—first cousins—had terrible tempers. I wonder what happened to those two sisters to have made them so harsh to their sons. And through it all runs this love of money. What this breeds is envy and jealousy, and an all-pervasive misery because there is never enough. Somebody has more.

I am sorry if I am overloading you and Father Gabriel with this but this goes back at least three generations so it is a hundred years.

One last thought: My father's father was a kind and patient person, according to Mother. He died when I was very little but always called me his "little black-eyed Susan." I remember holding onto his hand and liking him. Big Momma made his life hell. Mother saved me from Daddy. My second cousin had a nice mother and that awful father who was Daddy's cousin. Uncle Angus was pretty terrible but he married Margaret Frances and she was a very dear person. One thread that runs through this is that these characters all persuaded decent people to marry them.

When I was little I had no idea of how babies came into the world but I understood that it took two people. I always thought it was so that every child would have one parent to protect them from the other.

Must stop. I am sorry this is so long. Maybe it is helpful to know this background or maybe it means nothing. I am seeing patterns by writing this down.

I think of you both every hour of the day and send you all love and good thoughts.

I printed out the letter and put it in a white envelope. I pushed it under the door of her 'office' in Coconut Grove the next day.

Melinda called. I told her I was now sleeping on a piece of paper with the number 7 written on it. Under the mattress. Very bizarre but I do as I'm told. I am a foreigner in a strange land.

Chapter Twenty-Two

Last night as I reclined on the French daybed, a huge shadow crossed over me. It was near the ceiling and many feet wide. I remember being a little girl, lying in the grass, hearing the clacking of propellers and having the dark shape of a small plane fly over me. But this was more like a giant sting ray. A wave of blackness in total silence. I went cold with fear and then it was gone.

It is the end of August. It feels as if years have passed since Bastille Day.

I called Wright & Ferguson yesterday to get the date that Daddy died. Thought it would be worthwhile to get the obituary and Savannah at the Eudora Welty library needed the definite day because the obituaries were not in one section forty years ago.

A woman called Judy Lee put me on 'hold' and I listened to classical music and then a man's gentle voice saying that Wright & Ferguson would help you make decisions on the worst day of your life. Whether you chose "the grandeur of a family estate, mausoleums or in-ground gardens, we can help you." Then the voice said it had been serving the families of Jackson since 1929, and something about the Wright family and I wondered if I'd gone to school with any of them. I suppose Wright & Ferguson is to Jackson what Frank E. Campbell is to Manhattan. Daddy, Big Momma, Aunt Frances, Mother—if you are going to die in the capital of Mississippi then it's *the* place for a funeral.

Yesterday Judy Lee told me that she had found only one thing in the file and it said date of death, 1-5-68. I said, "Oh, I was wrong. My parents were divorced and so I have really no papers or information about this. I do remember that the funeral was right away." She said she would check for the date of the funeral but the archives were in another building. I told her I would call her back as I wasn't living in Jackson anymore."Where are you calling from?" she asked. I said Miami and Judy Lee breathed, "Wow." I thought that was adorable."The obituary is always about a week before the funeral so that people can make plans to be there," she said.

I called the next day and she was on the phone and so I heard all about my choices again. What if you don't want *any* of them? I thought. No mention of scattered in the wind as an option. In-ground garden? Is this a nice way of saying 'pushing up daisies?'

When I reached Judy Lee she sounded a bit excited. She had a death certificate issued in Florida. Collier County. Naples. I said, "Are you sure? Not Mississippi?" She was sure. It was Florida.

Then she said she also had a page typed on a manual typewriter. She asked where I went to college and I said Briarcliff and she said, "Well, that's what it says here. "Two daughters both attending Briarcliff College in New York.'"

The way she said 'New York' was as if she liked saying it and didn't get to say it often.

She started to read the death certificate aloud. "Died unexpectedly on Thursday night." I interrupted. "What's the date?" "There isn't a date on it," she said. "It just says Thursday." She read on: "Age on last birthday was 62 years. Hospital was La Tour Rivage." She pronounced it Riv-age. "I'm reading from a black page with white letters and it's hard."

"I never knew he was taken to a hospital," I said. "Does it say what he died of?"

She sighed. "Looks like acute myocardial something and death was within five minutes of the onset and occurred at 2 a.m. on 1/5/68."

"He never had heart trouble. He was in very good shape. He played eighteen holes of golf every Wednesday, every Saturday and every Sunday." I stopped. "Was there an autopsy?"

"There's a box here and it's checked 'no.'"

I asked, "Isn't it the law that there has to be an autopsy before you can take a body from one state to another?" She said she didn't know but she didn't think so if the body was embalmed.

"Embalmed?" I was surprised. "You mean that you at Wright & Ferguson embalmed him?"

"No. It wasn't done here."

"So the hospital did it?"

"No. It was, let's see, this is hard to read. George Pittman. George Pittman Funeral Home and the bill was dated 1/6/67." She laughed. "They keep getting that wrong." She paused "The bill was for $ 261.50."

I was stunned. "I didn't think he'd gone to a hospital. I thought he'd been flown from the apartment right to Jackson."

"Oh, no," said Judy Lee. "Here's the bill for Mortuary Air Services from Naples to Jackson. Three hundred and seventy-five dollars."

I was really surprised.

"There's a register book," she said. "That was signed over to Frances Bell. Wonder who that was?"

"That's his sister. That would have been the right thing to do."

I heard Judy Lee turn some pages. "You said he was divorced but it says here that he was married."

"Oh, that's his second wife," I said.

"Oh," she breathed. Judy Lee was obviously intrigued. Finding her, having her on the phone was a stroke of luck.

"They got married in September, fought the whole time and, well, in January, he was gone."

"Oh!" she exhaled.

"That's wicked of me," I said, "but I heard a lot of stories and as I said, it was a long time ago."

"Oh, yes," said Judy Lee. Her imagination was bubbling like a tea kettle on the boil. She said she would mail me a copy of the typed page since a fax might be hard to read. I told her that she had been a wonderful help.

She said, "You have to give me a bed if I ever get myself to Miami!" and we both laughed.

We hung up and I smiled. 'Ever get myself to Miami.' She made it sound like hiking through the Everglades barefooted.

I called Bronwen out on the covered terrace. Even though the horrid goat man came from out there and Daddy wandered all over the apartment, I felt, in daylight anyway, that it was okay to talk on the phone. Bronwen and I got hysterical laughing over something that happened a few years ago. Then I asked her if she knew what a caul was and she did. I had Googled it and knew that only one in 80,000 babies was born with it.

"It's meant to be very good luck," said Bronwen. "The person is also supposed to have prenatural powers, things like second sight."

"Yes, like Charlemagne, Napoleon and Freud," I said. "But Liberace had it, too!"

Bronwen's doorbell rang in London and we hung up.

Savannah called me from the Eudora Welty Library sounding triumphant. "It's the front page of the paper! And there is a photograph of your dad." She would mail me a copy; I thanked her profusely.

It was five o'clock and I was out on the covered terrace, thinking, he died when he was sixty-two. I felt sad. How terrible to be taken to the hospital already dead. Embalmed by George Pittman. Put on a plane for $375 and flown over the Gulf of Mexico for the funeral in Jackson at Wright & Ferguson. In the chapel, said Judy Lee. I started crying. He never appreciated how wonderful Mother was. He missed who she was.

His reputation was that of a very brilliant surgeon. I had a friend in Jackson and Daddy operated on her eye when she was about six. Years later I saw her in New York City and she said she'd been thinking of me because she had been to a New York ophthalmologist who had examined her eyes and seen the scar. He asked her who had performed the operation all those years ago and she said, "It was Dr. McNair in Jackson, Mississippi." This New York City doctor said, "I have heard of him. This is the most beautiful work I have ever seen."

He had everything and he never realized.

It was rather touching that Mr. Wright would save the Rotary Club program saying Daddy was Rotarian of the Month dated 1961—seven years before—and put it in his file with his death certificate. Daddy missed everything. Like turning your back on a beautiful painting. Like talking to someone with the most lively, cleverest sense of humor and you can't laugh because he speaks Portuguese and you don't. Like falling asleep on a train going through the Alps and not seeing hours of breathtaking landscapes.

I remembered that my sister and I were called in to Dean French's office and told that she had bad news for us. How relieved I was that it wasn't Mother. Then the traveling all day to get to Jackson late that night. The next morning in McRae's buying what? A black hat? Pantyhose? Can't remember but I felt that everybody was staring at me.

I stood at the kitchen window facing the big terrace with the wind blowing in and I thought, this is what I felt like on the bow of a boat on Lake Geneva. Or on the dock with the wind coming off the lake late on a summer afternoon. How I wished I were in Europe again. France, Italy, Switzerland. For a few minutes I pretended I was in Geneva having a glass of wine and the sweetest air was wafting me in the face.

Suddenly I remembered sitting on the top step of the staircase after dinner and hearing him say to Mother, "Git rid of those dolls! All uv 'em!

She's too attached!" I loved my dolls. They had first names and, when I could read, even last names picked out of the Jackson phone book. I hid them. Later I would think it was like hiding Jews from the Nazis. I slept with them packed around me under the sheet in summer heat. I kept watch. The scare blew over, his demand was forgotten.

I also remembered sitting on the top step of the staircase after dinner and hearing Daddy command Mother, "Git get rid of that dog! She's too attached to that dog." Mother murmuring something and his insisting that "she" was "too attached to it." I wept. Tears poured out of me, my head on my knees listening, loving Silky, my cocker spaniel, and thinking he *will* get rid of him! Feeling torn inside out with fear and anguish. Silky was going to be given away because I loved him so much!

What kind of person does that to a tiny, two-and-a-half-foot-tall, little girl? Why? It was only a few days later that Daddy called me to talk to him in my parents' bedroom early in the morning. The maid hadn't made the bed yet and I was still in my nightgown and he told me that Silky had been run over and that the driver couldn't see him because he was black. I cried and cried and the pink flowers on my nightgown turned red with tears. And even when he was telling me this, I was wondering, Did you do this? Did you? Because I was "too attached?"

He never knew me. Not a thing about me. There was not one conversation. He never came to one graduation or one school play but I actually dreaded the idea that he might. We never told a joke, a riddle, a funny story; we never laughed together. Not once.

I tied it all up with ribbons that last dinner. It was early summer, after freshman year, and I knew he was leaving the house the next day because of the divorce. The dining room windows were open and I could smell the gardenias. I was just home from Briarcliff where *I* had felt like a flower all year—opening at last, no longer labelled 'Dr. McNair's daughter.' Away from Mississippi, I was now being delighted by people who thought I was funny and pretty, being liked, exhilarated by such good attention. Being away from that grim dining room table but feeling guilty that I had left Mother behind. Calling her on Sunday night and hoping that she wouldn't put Daddy on the phone. Usually he wasn't there.

The Demons of Coral Gables

This dinner, I thought, I will let him have it. I poured it on thick. I talked about going to school with an Engelhard and with a Ford from Grosse Pointe and the daughter of this and that ambassador and I tossed in Park Avenue and Fifth Avenue and I told him about marriage proposals and the maharajah from Columbia who was so handsome in his white suit and how we had a wonderful time at the most amazingly elegant restaurants. I talked about him most because I knew Daddy would think he was "not quite white" but that the money would make that palatable. I wanted him to be vaguely uneasy and I revelled in that. I mentioned that the girl who had fixed me up was from Delhi and how she'd told me his family was so rich that his sister had a "thirty-elephant wedding."

I laid it on with a trowel. Yale and Princeton, weekends in New Canaan and Darien. I saw Daddy smiling, enjoying it and thought, you actually think I'm worthwhile. But this is the last time I ever have to sit at this dining room table with you. You will never shout at me again or tell me I'm stupid. This is the last time I ever have to look at you. And it was.

Until Coral Gables.

Chapter Twenty-Three

I watched the news and poured myself a glass of wine. I seemed to put the goblet on the coffee table more as a ceremony than anything else. At one or two in the morning, I poured it out in the sink. Reminded me of Mother. Sometimes, inexplicably in a good mood, my father would call Mother in to watch the six o'clock news with him. Huntley-Brinkley. He would always have a glass of sherry already poured for her as he sipped his bourbon. Mother would sit perched on the couch until she could make an excuse to "go and check on the fish. I don't want Mary to add salt to it" or to "see what we're having for dessert." She would take the untouched glass with her into the kitchen and Mary would watch her pour the amber liquid down the sink. Neither woman ever said a word about it.

The big news in Miami was on television. Crowds of Calle Ocho were all berserk over Fidel Castro going into the hospital and turning over control to his brother.

Fidel Castro. You executed my cousin. I wanted to go to the library to read the front page of *The New York Times* the next day but I had people coming in the morning and in the afternoon. My cousin believed in something. Maybe he would have preferred not to die for it but he was brave enough to get in a boat in the dark and go over the water with guns. Time after time, always risking capture.

The sky was changing color. I watched a plane take off and disappear sooner than usual. These days it was not only what was in the dark but what was *in the light*. I sensed I was being watched all day long. The clicks in the kitchen stopped when I actually walked in. The sky was suddenly less blue, another day was gone, and the darkness was coming. Time to close the bedroom door. Pffffft.

The next morning David called from London when I was on my way home from the post office. He'd been a close friend since the 1980s, a man I could usually confide in, a voice of reason. "I'm the only person in all of Miami, who walks farther than their parked car," I joked. It was really hot. "But I like seeing the tiny dinosaurs." The two and three-inch long lizards scuttled out of the way ahead of me on the sidewalk. "So how are the tropics? Has Europe lost you forever?" I sat on a bench in the shade a few houses down from my building. We bantered back and forth. I debated whether to tell him what was happening and then I did.

He believed me. "In our old house where I used to live in Suffolk there was a cottage on the edge of the property called St. Crispins. It was actually on St. Crispins Day during the night that the young girl who lived there saw Roman soldiers, in full uniform, marching through the living room. She came running up the lawn screaming. She saw them, clear as could be. About two miles away there exists the remains of a Roman tumulus and an encampment. Apparently, Roman troops had used this path on their way to that encampment more than a thousand years ago..."

I was fascinated. I was also delighted to be believed. Of all the people in my life, I would never have picked a Scottish financier, a commodities trader, to understand.

People came, in ones and twos, and they all loved my apartment. One couple stayed for nearly an hour talking about how they'd arrange the living room. Patrizia called at six with their offer and, of course, we accepted it. I was far too jaded to celebrate.

That night I lay on my back staring up at the ceiling and started to think of what happened in Rome and wondered: what if it *did* relate to me? What if it really were because of me? It had never happened before, according to Eve. A detective would say if it happened with you and never with anyone else then shouldn't you think that it *was* related to you?

There was a specific something standing beside the coffee table. Sometimes I heard it moving. I slept and was awakened by the rattling of the invisible paper. I dozed off and my face was touched. Do they take turns torturing me? The pfffffft person must be taking a break. I looked at the clock. It was one-fifteen and then it was two-fifteen. The apartment seemed to be still except for the little rattle. I did sleep at about four and I woke up at six and thought, another night gone. I put on sneakers, grabbed my bag with my bikini and in a flash I was out the door. A new day.

It was another luminous, bright, Florida morning. My yellow living room seemed to glow with sunlight. I came in from the covered terrace having put my wet bikini over the railing to dry. I glanced at the Haitian screen and on it, somehow on top of it, sat a black and white goat. I stopped, blood frozen, and stared. In a blink it was gone. I walked over to the painted wooden screen and with one hand batted all the straw hats off the top where they perched in colorful profusion and, still chilled, watched them fall to the floor.

When I told Cassandra what I thought I saw, she said, "Oh, yes, we knew he was in the apartment a few days ago. It was the Whole Foods goat." I wanted to scream.

Later, I wondered why, after all that had happened, should I think it was at all unusual that this goat I petted in a parking lot was sitting, with its legs folded, entirely relaxed, same black and white face, horns and all, in my apartment on top of my Haitian screen.

When I was little, I was always the one to see the person standing beside the closet door. The roses wallpaper always had rows of faces and never flowers. Was I imagining it or really *seeing* all this? Were there demons around me even then? I felt like the same little kid all these years later. Did everyone see what I saw at that age? In one of the boxes I was sorting, I found something that first seemed to be the start of a short story and then I realized it was a memory. Typed on paper gone yellow. Hand-written originally but typed in college.

"Jackson, Mississippi, past midnight. I can't sleep. I am lying on my side staring into the room, keeping watch. I have a cap gun under my pillow. I'm afraid of my father. He is one thing but I dread the darkness, too. I see the clothes draped on the rocking chair that look like a man sitting there. The closet door must be closed. My younger sister is bribed with candy cigarettes to keep the bathroom light on but when my parents come upstairs they turn it off anyway. I hate sleeping because I have nightmares and because my father might come.

Tonight I actually *feel* the silence, inhale the darkness. The window is open to the Old Canton Road but there are no cars at this hour and both Mother and Daddy are down the hall asleep. I watch as one white figure after another comes through the open bedroom door and leans down over my sleeping sister. One after another, as tall as I am, they enter, bend down and take a step or two and disappear. I watch, not daring to breathe. My hand is under my pillow on my gun, my finger on the trigger. I stare. There are so many of them. I forget to count. At least forty misty, white forms in the shape of a person. Finally it is over. They are gone. I wait for daylight.

I am seven years old."

I put the paper back in the box. I couldn't have written it at age seven. I remembered the experience clearly though I didn't remember writing it down. Maybe Cassandra was right and all this had been with me for my whole life. I knew my fear of my father had.

I went to the Coral Gables library and whizzing through *The New York Times* microfiche, I landed on April 19th. The year was 1963 and the country was in a panic about Castro and Cuba. There smack in the middle of the front page was the column with my cousin's name all over the place. The headline was "Two U.S. Citizens Executed in Cuba." It said that "A Cuban firing squad executed two Americans early today in Pinar del Rio on charges of counterrevolutionary activity.... Angus McNair, 23, whose parents live in Coral Gables, Fla."

Daddy kept it out of *The Miami Herald*.

On impulse, I asked if there were old telephone books and was directed to a row of shelves. Daddy's second wife had lived just about six minutes from Adriano Avenue. I passed her street all the time in the Chihuahua. My sister had lived on Sidonia where I'd often parked to talk on the phone. It was a rather eventful day at the library.

Dared to sleep in bikini underpants and a white tank top. Woke at three, woke at four but it was actually a deep and dreamless sleep and I felt refreshed. Maybe I was becoming a normal person again if one ignored the fact that I refused to sleep in my bedroom, must sleep in my clothes and must have a light on as I clutched a Bible, a flashlight and a can of tuna fish all night long. Completely normal.

Waiting for dawn. Wondered where Father Gabriel was, had he found out anything about getting rid of the goat once and for all? Cassandra said something about getting Daddy and all his friends back in the ground again and I thought of Franklin and wondered if some kind of lightning rod could be fashioned. If all the abhorrent creatures including Daddy could be attracted to one place and then all of that energy could be shot, exploded into the earth in one enormous spark. Once and forever.

The fan breathed on. It sat on a box, squarely in the middle and couldn't fall over. I had checked and double-checked. It purred a few feet away from me which was perfect because anything I heard I could tell myself was the fan. I refused to get up, to investigate.

I thought of my neighbor, Anna, in the elevator yesterday afternoon saying that she has had one person come to see her apartment since May. One person! It's three bedrooms with two baths priced at 449K which she said was reasonable. She insisted that the market had changed. "If we don't sell this year then forget about it. Next year there will be hundreds of brand-new condos on the market. We're dead." Comforting.

A new day. I went swimming at the Biltmore, came home and called Adam in New York before he left for the law firm. Just to say 'good morning' as he often did to me. It was half past seven. He immediately asked if I had sold the condo and I said that all three couples and Lexie and the professor had all changed their minds. "It's unbelievable!" he exclaimed. "It's such a great apartment!" He actually saw it when he was on vacation last year and considered buying it himself. Suddenly it was prime time and he had to go to work. Poor thing. It was 100 degrees in NYC and he, as always, wore a suit and a tie.

That evening I came back from Books & Books after dinner with a friend and thought how tired I was. I read a bit of Benjamin Franklin but I kept reading the same paragraphs, and at eleven I thought maybe I would *try* to sleep. I dimmed the chandelier and actually slept for a few minutes.

Pfffffft. At midnight the chandelier lights were very bright as if the dimmer had been moved. Pfffffft. I was not in hysterics, but didn't like it much. Found myself staring at the room as if looking at chunks of air. Was anything solid standing there, floating there, invisible, I wondered. Then I saw the enormous goat man, over seven feet tall with the hunched back walk across the hall into the kitchen. My eyes watered with fear. I sat up, eyes wide, staring at the hallway wondering what I would do if he showed himself again or came towards me.

I was very tired. I did dream so I know I slept.

CRASH! I sat up and saw that the huge box fan had fallen over. I got up and righted it. Maybe the vibration had just worked at it until it was off-balance. However, it had not fallen over all the other nights. It was now exactly two in the morning and at precisely midnight the chandelier had awakened me.

I settled down again. Was goat man still in the kitchen? Doing what? More dreams. The hand touched my face and I woke up and looked at the clock and it was only 2:14. I couldn't believe so much had happened in fourteen minutes. I dreamed, something touched my face and I woke up. I dreamed, I was touched, I woke up. On and on until six o'clock. Now it was getting light. Another night gone. I was tired but I would get up and swim and think that maybe today someone would buy the apartment. Maybe today everything would change.

Pfffffft.

Chapter Twenty-Four

"I'll talk fast. I'm on an hour break. Sorry not to have called in awhile. Some of the women have gone back to Tampa so only one other woman and I are working on this."

"How exactly are you working on it?" I asked.

"Don't worry," Cassandra said. "Father Gabriel is still in Paris which is probably a good sign. I am not allowed to be in on the conference calls here because I am not ordained. He calls and talks to Father Peter and then Father Peter talks to Father Ramon who is an old friend of Father Gabriel." I started to ask when Father Gabriel was coming back but Cassandra kept talking. "I know that if it were up to Father Gabriel then he would contact me but he is in another church and the Mother Superior of that church can say that he can or he can't. So I know he can't. But maybe he has found something in the archives that they don't want me to know about. I'm waiting for the call now."

"I worked at the Vatican for two years and I know its rules are unbreakable." I remembered dipping my time card upon arrival like a factory worker. I also remembered being a total of seven minutes late in the span of a month and, on the last day of the month, having to go to the second floor office and sit in a chair for seven minutes!

"Listen, your father is there but we want to keep that other thing away."

"Daddy is back?"

"Yes, but it's okay if it's just your dad there."

Her call waiting beep sounded and we hung up immediately.

I was in the Chihuahua parked on Madeira. My psychic had rushed to take a call from a Puerto Rican exorcist who was studying archives in Paris to find out how to get rid of the goat in my apartment. And she had said, "But it's okay if it's only your dad."

Yes. It's perfectly okay that my dead father is living with me in my penthouse that everyone likes and no one will buy.

My cell rang and it was Patrizia who told me the offer from the Brazilian banker had been withdrawn. I didn't even ask her why. She was more upset than I was. Five minutes later she called again and said a realtor wanted to bring someone from Ft. Lauderdale tomorrow afternoon. I managed a weak laugh and thanked her.

So that's the way it was. People came, people left. Offers were made, offers were unmade. More people came.

One morning after five nights of much less than usual sleep, someone named Julian called. He had seen the ad on the internet and gotten my number bypassing Homes by Owner. I hesitated then thought I could turn it over to Patrizia later if he were really interested. Julian sounded reasonable so I said to come. The doorbell rang and in walked a man in his forties and one little shrimpy boy. Named Julian. The man introduced himself as "I'm the father since he isn't old enough to drive." I hid my disappointment, thought that Julian gave good phone, and showed them through with my usual enthusiasm. They liked it very much. Then the father asked how much was the rent. I walked them to the elevator and was entirely nice, even wished them luck in finding the right place.

I wanted to touch base with Sharon, our website designer, but she was out of town so all I could do was leave a message. I'd hired her on the spot at an art gallery opening but I was regretting it. She had still not finished the new company website which meant we couldn't give out business cards, contact possible clients. Unbelievably slow. Time was going by. It was one excuse after another. She seemed oblivious to any sort of time frame or deadline. I was living in the land of mañana.

I hung up and Raquel called with the news that the couple from Vero Beach who wanted to buy my condo for their college-age daughter had changed their minds about making an offer. She was so sorry that I felt sorry for her having to tell me. I thanked her and snapped the phone closed.

Whenever I felt like grinding my teeth in frustration, things got better. I slept for three whole hours without waking up that night. My cancelled Italian class was on again. I saw a house in Philadelphia on the internet that I really liked, Bronwen called and made me laugh, and I counted a record twenty-nine tiny dinosaurs as I walked to the post office.

It was time to close the bedroom door.

Clarissa McNair

Dear Cassandra,

I have written quite a few letters to you but don't want to use you and Father Gabriel as my psychiatrists so rarely send anything. I write to clarify my thoughts.

I need a bit of news. Or at least communication. I had sudden and very strong feelings of wanting to kill myself this afternoon. It swept over me and I thought, why do I keep trying?

I am now in a downward spiral and can't see daylight. This is unusual for me but the mortgage payment has gone up and I am now living on my credit cards. I should be used to people making a bid on the condo and backing out but every single time we accept a bid I think 'this is it' and I am newly amazed when it falls through. I am such an optimistic person that when I have occasionally bought a lottery ticket I have been amazed *not* to win. But now, I don't feel like that same person.

The darkness still frightens me. The clicks in the kitchen are about every two minutes in the daytime. Several nights the chandelier has gone from dim to very bright or from brightest to nearly off. Last night the area around my desk glowed bright red as if it were about to burst into flames or as if it were the reflection of a tremendous fire. Terrific news is that the sores from the gold cross are entirely gone. I didn't like being reminded of what happened and now I don't have to be.

How much I want to work again! The one project I have going won't bring in any money for many months.

I am not in a safe place spiritually right now. Please tell me what is happening. I remember that you and Father Gabriel have both said you won't desert me. I think of that very often. I need you more than ever.

Words cannot express my gratitude to you but my hope about leaving this apartment is fading. I wonder if I will ever escape this.

Love, Cici

That letter all sounded like whining so I put it in my desk drawer and slammed it closed. Pitiful. Loathsome. I hated the way I sounded. Then I grabbed my keys and took a drive with the windows up, the a.c. on for a change, and the radio blasting. The Beatles didn't help. I parked the car because I had tears in my eyes. I blew my nose, put on lipstick and dark glasses and started the car again. I pulled into a drugstore parking lot and went in and bought a Hershey bar with almonds. As I devoured it in the same parking lot, my throat filled with tears. Dammit. Chocolate didn't help. I drove to the Biltmore and took my third swim of the day. I swam until my shoulders and my legs hurt. My theory is that if you cry in the shower or when you're swimming, you are really not. So much exterior liquid is involved that tears don't count. I drove home, loudly announced, "Hey, everybody, I'm back!" and painted my toenails bubble-gum pink. I went out on the covered terrace and grabbed a book. I read a chapter of *The Confederacy of Dunces* and when I laughed out loud I knew I would be okay. For today, anyway.

On Bastille Day or night, everything I thought I knew was now questioned. We are born, we live, we die. Some of us actually contribute to the world. Some of us have children, others leave behind good works. But most of us eat, sleep, propagate and die. Death is the end. I checked organ donor 'yes' on my driver's license so that maybe someone I will never know can benefit. But death is the end. Dust to dust. "Birth to earth," as the Jets sang in *West Side Story*. "Womb to tomb." "When you're a Jet, you're a Jet all the way from your first cigarette till your last dying day…"

I remembered listening to Bernstein's score again and again. Lifting the arm on the record player and putting it on my favorite songs over and over. With the den doors closed, after school, I danced between the coffee table and Daddy's desk and sang every word as if I were there, in New York City, far, far away from Mississippi. I didn't care about Maria and Tony. I wanted to be a Jet.

Chapter Twenty-Five

I drove to my Italian class that next evening and actually forgot about demons as I listened to all the Spanish-speakers stumble with the Italian accent. On the way home, I ate Pepperidge Farm cookies in the car and sang along with the radio and pretended to be a normal person but when I walked into the apartment, I felt a deep sadness. I thought, what if I gave up? What if I decided that I can't do this anymore? There was a loud, bump! noise on the other side of the closed bedroom door. That snapped me out of it. I was immediately in full survival mode.

I slept very little as the pfffffft noise was every other minute and I found that the silence in between was laden with my wondering when I would hear it again. There was no peace. I closed my eyes and my face was touched. It was not a tap but more like a stroke. The noise and the touch added up to sleep deprivation and was how people are tortured, I thought. I was reminded of Cher in *Moonstruck* slapping Nicholas Gage. "Snap out of it!" she shouted at him. I imagined her slapping me and barking the same command.

This could not last forever. I was exhausted. I closed my eyes, heard the pfffffft and felt the touch and said to myself, whoever you are, whatever you are: I hate you.

The next morning I was swimming and missed Bronwen's call so I called her back on my landline then raced out to the car so she could call me on my cell. She asked how I was and I said I thought I was getting used to things. I welcomed her silly chatter which was a break from my own situation. We talked about how Deirdre's husband, Phillip, called her and talked for twenty minutes and how she shouted at him that he was the most annoying man she had ever known. I told her that he thought she was flirting with him. "Oh, darling! No!" shouted Bronwen. She told me that Deirdre made her promise to go with Phillip and to sprinkle her ashes between England and the Isle of Wight and "so I'm in for that." Deirdre was twenty years older than Phillip. She was in her eighties, and planned to go first.

We both loved Deirdre more than anyone but her fourth husband was a trial for all three of us.

"We will inherit him and have to be nice to him forever because of Deirdre," I stated as Bronwen groaned. We hung up as Bronwen had to get ready for a dinner and I had to go out for a haircut.

How many Florida haircuts were in my future? Could this be the final one?

I watched a bit of the news and then thought I would close the bedroom door before dark. Later I pushed my palm against it gently and then with force to make sure it was closed. All my organs would shut down if that door ever opened after sunset. I watched *Match Point* on the covered terrace and thought Woody had made a good choice with Scarlett.

Then I walked into the living room and saw that there were clouds hanging in the air. The room was filled with them; they were so thick I could not see the other side of the room. Strangest of all was the smell. They were wet to my hands when I touched them and smelled sweet like lake water.

I felt despair sweep over me. I felt like weeping. Like throwing myself off the balcony. I tried to remember laughing with Bronwen, tried to think of something pleasant. Of today's swim. Of tomorrow's swim. I felt as if I were being taken over by something dank and dismal, a palpable gloom.

I tried to call Cassandra but her message box was full so then I called the other number she used when she was with Father Gabriel and she answered. It was ten o'clock and she said she had just walked into the house and was taking a shower and making sure her kids were okay since she had not really been home for two or three weeks. I knew I was being selfish but I told her I felt a deep sorrow and then I described the clouds in the living room. "I feel like giving up."

She said, "That's a spirit in the house. We are getting rid of it tonight. Bathemus is not there but another one is there and it is gaining strength. It can't hurt you but know that the depression and the heaviness you feel is from that. It's been for the last three or four days, hasn't it?" I reluctantly admitted that yes, it had been.

Why did I keep pushing this away? I could not believe it. Wouldn't it have been easier to think, oh, yes, this is all true? But I was resistant to it. I did believe in self-fulfilling prophecies so I rejected the idea that things were going wrong because of a curse. I hated the idea that Daddy was here. *I did not want to believe I was surrounded by monsters.* I saw them, I heard them, they touched me. But no!

Cassandra went on. "You feel very negative, lonely. You are magnifying now." I didn't know what this meant. Before I could ask, she said, "I'm going to call someone next door to the church so that they can tell the church to light candles all night for you."

I felt quite tired. "I saw the horrible goat man, eight feet tall last night. Maybe only seven feet because he's all bent over. I don't know. And I saw the floating goat again in daylight."

"Don't tell me!" she said sharply. "It's not important. It's to distract us."

Yes, I thought. That's the word. It was distracting to see a goat in mid-air, little legs folded under, right here in my apartment. She kept talking. "Now, listen to me. I want you to go through the house and tell it to leave. Tell it that it has no dominion over you, that you want it to leave, it has no authority and you want it to go away."

"I can't go in the bedroom," I said.

"No, I don't want you to go into the bedroom." She sighed. "We have to get the apartment sold. I talked to Father Gabriel and he knows how to get rid of this."

"Good," was all I could manage.

Before she hung up, I told her there was an inspection tomorrow. "This Venezuelan is really interested. The buyer wants the inspection before he makes his bid. My apartment passes all inspections so maybe this is it!"

"Don't worry if it doesn't happen."

"What do you mean? The sale?"

"I mean the inspection will be cancelled. The man is unreliable. But don't worry about it."

"You *know* he is unreliable?"

She laughed. "Yes, we know a lot of things!"

The next morning at five of ten when the apartment was pristine and I thought the doorbell would ring any minute, the phone rang instead. The inspection was cancelled.

Monday came and Cassandra cancelled seeing me in a quick phone call. "It's impossible. I'm sorry." She said 'I love you" and hung up. I felt a thousand miles from anyone. A corner penthouse. High in the sky. I remembered her instructions from the call before and went through the rooms from kitchen to living room to the covered terrace shouting, "Get out!" the way one would shout at an animal. "Get out! I don't want you here! You have no dominion over me so leave now! Get out get out get out!" Then I sat down at my desk to answer emails. Pfffffft.

Chapter Twenty-Six

Another night gone. Another swim. Another couple coming at noon. I tapped my thoughts into the computer. I knew that someday I would have to write about this but first I had to survive it and escape.

I was perpetually tense and rather tired in the daylight and at night the choice was to stare into the semi-darkness knowing that someone was standing over me or to be touched if I tried to sleep. True sleep was on a chaise at the Biltmore. At my last Italian class I was so tired that la professoressa, Anna, commented on it.

I told myself to be detached. This was an adventure. Yes, at once horrifying and bizarre but an adventure. Was it destiny as Father Gabriel said? Was this encounter with the demonic to prepare me for the 'something important' I must do as Cassandra kept saying? I must trust them to lead me through and out the other side of all this darkness.

I made a chart of the McNairs; Big Momma had three children not counting Crawford who never grew up. Daddy had five of us, Aunt Frances had two and Uncle Angus had three. Out of ten children of my generation, six of us I know had spent time in Coral Gables. Three grew up there and three of the five in my family lived there, all for separate reasons spanning decades. I don't know if the other four were ever here. Maybe more than six out of ten.

I received a manila envelope from Judy Lee at Wright & Ferguson with the copy of the black death certificate, the Rotary club program, the typed page which seemed to be notes for the obituary plus the list of pall bearers. Wirt Yerger was one, and men whose names I grew up knowing. Mother was born on the Main Line, outside of Philadelphia, and Daddy went to Jefferson Medical School in Philadelphia. That's where they met but I had no idea they lived there for very long. They lived in Elkins Park. My three brothers were born before the outbreak of World War II, before my father became a Naval officer and ended up in the Pacific.

I had the ominous feeling someone was reading over my shoulder and suddenly my bare arms were covered in goose bumps. The temperature in the room had dropped forty degrees. I put the pages back in the envelope and decided to take it to the pool tomorrow. I was almost getting used to the pfffffft noise. Plus the flutter of a page. Someone was there. Another dimension but only two feet away in earthly distance. Intellectually I rejected it but I heard it and I *felt* it. Even now in daylight. Dead and invisible but *there*.

I often saw my cousin, Tad, and tried to confide in him. He was the only person in Florida I could trust not to talk about this. But he wouldn't talk about it with me; his mind was made up and it was closed. I asked him to come to my apartment, time after time, to see what was happening. He refused.

The days passed, the nights passed. Very slowly. Pfffffft. Every night was hours longer than it should have been. My eyes hurt from staring at air and my very skin ached with weariness. I endured a new fear of being hurt. Hurt by something I couldn't see, something immense that stood beside me hour by hour. Please don't touch me. Please don't let me see you. Pfffffft.

I wrote the Jenkins who kept inviting me to visit them in Maine. It was a delicious idea to get on a plane and never look back but it wasn't the time to go. Trying to sound upbeat, I wrote about the new company, my partner in Chicago, and that I was about to order 250 business cards. I also wrote that my fervent prayer was not to be here long enough to give them all out.

I darted out to the post office and mailed the letter, then went to the bank and put two thousand dollars cash advance on my Visa card to pay for part of the mortgage. In thirty minutes, I was home again. I brushed my hair into a slicked-back ponytail, sat down at my desk and disobeyed the rule. Cassandra answered her phone and said, "I can't talk to you. I'm on my way to the airport to pick up some women from Quebec. I will call you tomorrow."

I said, "No, please. Just tell me if I can go away, if I can leave town for awhile. Yesterday I saw water on the bedroom floor in the shape of a cross. Maybe it means nothing but there was no source for it, no reason for it to be there. It was in the grouting around the square Mexican tiles so, yes, of course, it would be at right angles."

Cassandra said maybe it meant something, maybe not. It was in the place where the portal to hell was. Supposedly Father Gabriel closed that the first time he was here and I had not had any more terrible heat in that room since. Cassandra said I could go away, that she had to hang up, promised to call me tomorrow.

The next morning after my swim, I went into my bedroom with a brand-new, white washcloth and a large, new sandwich bag. The water was still there. I sopped it up and then smelled the washcloth. No smell. I looked up at the ceiling, the walls, trying to find a source for the clear liquid. Yes, it was in the shape of a cross because it was in the right angles of the one-foot square Mexican tiles. I sniffed the washcloth again and then I put it into the plastic bag.

Jim in Chicago was back and forth with emails about our fledgling company. I'd dealt with the Florida documents, gotten all in order.

I wrote Spiesman, a private detective friend, the truth: things were not going very well. He had sent me a photo of adorable baby turtles. Weeks ago. I had been negligent.

Last night the pfffffft stopped for awhile, there was no hand, and I heard no page rattle and dozed off. Was awakened by a crash in the bedroom which sounded like a huge number of books falling from a great height. So what? I sighed. It's just that there weren't a huge number of books in there to fall. They were all packed in boxes. As long as it was not something trying to break the door down I was not going to get hysterical.

Chapter Twenty-Seven

Another day of people trooping through and saying they love it. Another conversation with Patrizia about how *much* people love it. Another night. I looked at the clock and it was 3 AM so I actually slept for about fifteen minutes. I managed to sleep after lunch even with the pfffffft noise and was awakened by the phone. More possible buyers. Yes, twenty minutes is fine, I said as I noticed blue stones in evidence on a bookcase.

People came, they raved, they left. I went swimming again at five and read some of the Ben Franklin book. It was heartbreaking that his son was a Tory against independence. Franklin wrote, "I was welcomed in France." Divine.

I wanted answers from Cassandra. I wondered where Father Gabriel was. In my bleakest moments, I wondered if their promises to help me were sincere. Yes, of course, they were. But *could* they? Everything in my apartment seemed worse. The promise was "to get rid of this for you." I thought this meant getting rid of the spirit that was keeping the condo from being sold and the spirit that was keeping me from making any money. I didn't know anything more than I knew seventeen very long nights ago.

I put this month's mortgage payment on my credit card.

I felt abandoned. I wanted answers. I thought of leaving a message for Cassandra saying that if I didn't hear from her soon that I would find someone else to come and clear the apartment. I stood on the terrace, gazed out over the Coral Gables landscape, and knew I didn't mean it, wouldn't do it. It was like threatening to fire a volunteer. Your *only* volunteer.

I was entirely dependent upon two people to like me enough, to be interested enough to help me. There was no one else so how could I complain? I must remain in their good graces. I had no choice. I wanted to do something but I was in this frozen waiting period. I wanted to take action; the waiting was grinding me down, made me feel weak.

One morning I decided to get the packet for the concealed weapon permit as pushed to do by Kevin, a private detective in New York. Florida was easy compared to other states and yet the Florida license was valid in several other states. "Just get it," he'd said. "This is a good chance to have the permit and you might want it in the future." I thought too many people had guns in the first place and didn't want one. Working undercover with a gun would have been too dangerous as I could never have talked myself out of a bad situation had it been discovered. But, I told Kevin, I'd check on the permit.

The Coral Gables Police Department said call this number and I did and then they said call *this* number and I did and finally somebody said go to any gun shop and pick up the packet and they will tell you what to do. I remembered a little shopping center off Flagler that I used to pass on the way to the printer for my business cards.

It was GUNS and next door was QUICK CASH and next door to that was PAWN SHOP. All this a few blocks past the Illusion Motel with free cable. Then I saw the Extacy Motel with rates by the week. The others looked like by-the-hour places so Extacy must be more upmarket. I parked the car in front of CHARLIE'S ARMORY which was next door to the SPLENDORS UNISEX skin care and waxing salon. I went in and was practically devoured by two friendly males in a flurry of shaking hands and grinning introductions.

Big Latino flashed his Miami PD badge and then I met Charlie who had a strong southern accent that you don't hear much around here. I held the Smith & Wesson and then the Walther PK Luther and was told about safeties and locks and bullets, and all I could think of was being at the bedside of someone saying 'I am so sorry. I am so sorry that you are completely paralyzed or that your entire liver is gone. I am so sorry.' If not at their bedside then at their graveside. Death, more death.

Maybe Charlie saw I lacked the killer instinct. He took the second gun away from me and said that a concealed weapon did not necessarily mean a gun so maybe I would be happy with a taser for only a thousand dollars. I stood there and thought I couldn't do that either. What if the person had a heart attack and I was forced to put down my taser and give him mouth-to-mouth?

There was a cemetery on the way home and I thought how I used to hold my breath when I passed one and now I don't need to anymore. Had I grown up? No. It's just that at least a dozen people who should be lying down under dusty, plastic flower arrangements are in my apartment. I should hold my breath in my apartment.

Half past eight at night. Just back from Books & Books. After putting on a skirt and lipstick I felt sort of pink and white and summery. I walked over there—in a total steam bath of an evening—and the speaker had been cancelled. Walked back. Two men on the corner sitting on a bench stopped me and said "Do you know you look like a movie star ? You are so beautiful." I smiled and thanked them and said that made me feel wonderful and kept walking. It 's getting dark very quickly, I thought. Or maybe they've been quietly drinking all day.

Why the sudden male attention? The man at Starbucks looking at my legs, Thor at the pool. Later the Swede would call and talk for an hour from South Beach. Then Jack at Books & Books on Friday night had suddenly become so flirtatious. I was sitting there on a stool, killing time, waiting for Cassandra to 'clear' the apartment. It wasn't perfume because it was too hot to wear it. I wondered if the disgusting goat had anything to do with all this.

Nice to not be afraid of the dark. Outdoors it seemed reasonable but in my hallway or my bedroom or the living room there was something unnatural about it. I passed the bench in front of the building next door where Father Gabriel and Cassandra and I sat after their second visit. I remembered her saying that my father had to forgive me and I had to forgive him. I immediately asked, "What does he have to forgive me for?" and she said, "You have to reach some kind of understanding." He's dead, I wanted to scream but I had said evenly, "I don't *want* to understand him. I want him out of my apartment."

Oprah had three women on her show today. All with big problems that stemmed from self-hatred, from feeling worthless. "Someone stole this from you as a child," said that psychologist with the heart-shaped face. "Who told you you were worthless?" she demanded. These women were all nodding, couldn't wait to talk. One was anorexic, another gained 100 pounds after being rejected by her husband, another one called herself trash, and all because someone told them they were worthless when they were little. Daddy was really terrible to say I was stupid and that he hated me and I'd never amount to a hill of beans a thousand times ...to me...a little girl and then, over the years, to me, his teenaged daughter. Why was I okay? Or was I? Maybe I was a mess and everyone was being nice and not telling me. But I felt okay and I thought it was because there was some tiny kernel of bravery inside me and because of Mother.

Wonder where Cassandra is, why she doesn't call. Did Father Gabriel find what he needed in Paris? Was he back? How could he be in a church in Quebec and not speak French? Does Cassandra ever sleep? What sort of nuns are these who sew their own clothes and must be cloistered? What kinds of meetings do they have? Voting on whether to help me or not? Why are spirits attracted to me? Does everyone have spirits? If not, why not?

I was on the phone with Bronwen and we got hysterical. She screamed, "I think you're right! Phillip is coming on to me! Every time Deirdre goes out to get her hair done or to do her charity work he calls me and talks for twenty minutes! I can't get him off the phone!" I said, "Deirdre is in her eighties and he's planning ahead. You're a good cook and he wants you. You'll have to take care of him forever."

She shouted, "No! I just shout at him! And he says, you are a wonderful woman. You understand everything. And I just shout at him!" Bronwen is now shouting at me and I am laughing.

Then she asked me what was happening and I told her that I'd tried to talk the manager of a tiny French restaurant into hiring me as a dessert chef one day a week. "It's possible but he has to ask the owner who is out of town. I have to watch out because this plantar fasciitis thing means I shouldn't stand for too long. I also talked to the owner of a bakery who might need me if someone goes on vacation." I could tell Bronwen was mystified. "I was a dessert chef," I told her. "In New York for two restaurants. Long before I met you." She laughed in surprise. "I would love a job doing just about anything but I promised the brokers I'd be available to show the apartment. That's part of the deal. If I could do something in the middle of the night—I'm not sleeping anyway—or super early in the morning, that would be fine. Or something here in the apartment."

We chatted on. I told her about finding all those twenty-pound bales of marijuana hidden way back beyond the dunes with the marine biologist the week before. Twenty-five of them! "Usually we see the tracks and the drag marks of the shell coming up from the water and follow them to where the mother turtle has dug the hole and laid her eggs. Then we build a barricade around it, which is very sweaty work, to protect it from being dug up by animals and to deter humans who steal the eggs and sell them." I paused. It upset me. It was immoral. They were endangered. "We keep meticulous records of all this. Well, last Friday we followed dragging marks in the sand that were obviously not turtle tracks. We left the beach, the dunes, the marsh grass and kept going. It was wild vegetation, like the beginning of a jungle; we could barely walk." Then it was proceeding on the path of flattened marsh grass and then through the broken branches of bushes. Smugglers had dumped the drugs by boat the night before. "We called the police and they came and there were helicopters, sniffer dogs, DEA men with machine guns," I said.

"Your life is beyond exciting," said Bronwen.

"It was my kind of day," I grinned. "My kind of excitement is earthly."

She asked about the apartment and I told her that because the exorcist said that all in my life had led to my being in this apartment right here in Coral Gables, I had done some research. "I'm amazed that Daddy kept the news of my cousin being captured for running guns to Cuba and then put in front of a firing squad out of *The Miami Herald* when it was on the front page of *The New York Times*."

Bronwen said, "I must say, darling, your family is not boring. *My* family on the other hand is *so* boring." We laughed about nothing and about everything and the sun was shining in my beautiful lemon-yellow living room and the world seemed sane. She had mice in her London apartment and we could not decide if it were better or worse than my problem. Bronwen's voice was very serious. "At least your demons are house-broken."

Chapter Twenty-Eight

That night I dozed off during an old movie with Ray Milland, woke later and clicked the TV off then dozed again. I was awakened by the strong smell of tobacco. I expected to see a man standing over me smoking a cigar. It was like three cigars actually. The tobacco smell was overpowering but I saw no cigar, no smoke. I got up and went out the front door. There had to be an explanation. I was sure someone was smoking a cigar on the big terrace but no, it was empty and the air smelled cool and fresh. The big hall chandelier was ablaze, of course. I went back into my apartment. All the windows were open but I was nauseated. I couldn't sleep and I lay on the daybed, thinking, until daylight. Later that morning, I checked my desk for a cigar butt or several. Feeling ridiculous. Celestial cigars? Of course, I found nothing.

I now heard the little pfffffft noise countless times night and day. Could it really be Daddy as Cassandra said? Maybe it was best I hadn't moved to Philadelphia with all this chaos going with me. I'd be shopping for a psychic and an exorcist there. The Yellow Pages?

Another night was slipping into morning very slowly. It was three o'clock and the pfffffft noise was beside me. Tonight, the paper noise was exactly like someone turning a page every two minutes or so and there were crashes in my bedroom. The laundry room light was on and the fan was purring.

I had written Judy Lee a thank-you note and mailed it to Wright & Ferguson. She had sent me photocopies of all in the file and I'd put them away for now. What if Daddy had died ten years sooner? Fifteen years sooner? Would we have all been different? Would Mother have married someone kind and loving?

I was lying there thinking I might be living among boxes in this apartment forever and I started to think about offing myself again. It should not even be a verb. It was a passive act as it was removing oneself from thinking, feeling, worrying, and suffering of all sorts. Then I thought, better do more research before I go ahead. I do NOT want to live behind the wall with demonic spirits like Daddy. Maybe *that is* what they mean by hell. Maybe I'd be in that hellish heat going back and forth through the porthole in my green bedroom. I could barely stand Miami weather so that's no way to live. Or die. Or are we all dead *now*? And I have to remember to call it a portal and not a porthole. Suddenly I started to laugh.

Then I began to think of suicide again and decided not to kill myself here. Why do I want people to say she died in Coral Gables when I don't even want to *live* in Coral Gables? I'd better get myself to a better place, a place that I don't mind being associated with as the last thing anyone ever says about me. Death in Venice is one thing. *The Clarion Ledger* said Daddy died in Venice, Florida, when really Naples is much more upmarket and Daddy would *never* have lived in Venice, Florida.

The clock said quarter to five. I was in my dead flounder state on my back with hands crossed on my chest like a corpse and one eye on the light coming from the laundry room. Carefully avoiding any glass surface so as not to summon faces. No. No suicide in Coral Gables. I remembered my friend Victor in Rome telling a story about his uncle and ending with, "He died in Monte Carlo." Now *that's* more like it.

An hour and a half later, while swimming, I decided how it would work. I would pay the damn $250 condo fee, make out a will leaving the entire contents of this place to someone, make sure there's enough money to take out of the bank for the last mortgage— or no! I would be wildly irresponsible and simply not pay it! Then I'd put a flight to New York on my Visa and go. I'd see people then I'd fly to London and see Deirdre and Bronwen, maybe even go on to Rome. Last step would be checking into a hotel. Do Not Disturb sign on the door. Razor blades. Big fear of waking up or throwing up the pills, did not want to botch this one last act. Try to keep it in the tub. A very nice, entirely sincere note of apology to the maid. Plus a big tip. All the cash I have left. Hope I do not haunt her dreams. Hope I don't haunt anybody. Hope there's nothing afterwards.

Didn't want to be trapped behind a wall or on the other side of the porthole to hell. Didn't want to be trapped anywhere. I mean wasn't that the point of killing myself? Because I was sick of being trapped *here*.

Cassandra called and suggested we meet at Starbucks at five. Larry, her husband, could watch the kids. I spent the afternoon reading about exorcism on the internet. All very sensitive. The poor exorcists are evidently treated like dirt by the Catholic Church. A hundred and fifty of them from five continents were not even allowed to come to the Wednesday audience and, let me tell you, just about anybody can get into that.

I parked on Oak Street just off Virginia and went to Starbucks and picked a table. In three minutes she arrived in her signature long skirt and sandals. She wore a little spaghetti-strap top with long coal-black hair flowing over her shoulders. It had been dyed and it did not suit her. She looked tough and hard and, I reluctantly conceded, like a witch. Her face, her bruises, her eyes had completely healed.

I told her about my new ideas about Daddy, that he missed everything. He married Mother who loved him, at least initially. Then a second wife who probably killed him. I told her that I had not cried when he died but that I had cried, here, all these years later. She said, "You may not remember but I told you that forgiveness had to happen."

"I remember it very well because it annoyed me so much." She grinned and I shrugged. I wasn't sure crying about him was forgiveness. I gave her my new business card and said I was going to do everything I could to get it going. She didn't look at it, didn't read it but put it in her skirt pocket and said, "I know you will."

"Once the website is in order, I have a lot of people to contact. I feel as if I've been here longer than three years. Well, three years come Halloween."

"Well, that will be about the time when we get you out."

I sighed.

She flipped her long hair over her tan shoulders and said, "A lot has changed. It was to be that Father Gabriel and I would be working together to help you but now all communication between me and him has been cut off. I've been told that he is back in France."

"Is he coming back to Miami?"

"He was sent to two other locations. One of the locations was Rome, the other one I don't know. There is a woman named Pamela in the church who places the calls between here and Rome. She told me that Bathemus is tied in with France."

"Does this have anything to do with me and my apartment?"

"Yes, it does. Father Gabriel *did* find the documentation. I wanted him to fax it to me or just tell me but they aren't letting us talk."

"Why not?" I insisted.

"Everything has to go to Quebec, to his church in Quebec."

I leaned back in the chair and sighed.

"It's okay. If they tell him we won't help you, we don't care because he will know what to do and he can come back here and I will work with him. I can work with the church in West Palm Beach."

"What is the name of the church in West Palm Beach?"

"There is no name, it is all just spiritualists."

"The one in Quebec?"

"It's very famous but if you are going to write about this then I don't want to tell you the name." She saw my face. "They know you worked at the Vatican and that's good. You are one of them. But they don't want anything to get out, nothing public. I can't have you make a mistake and write the name anywhere. I know you wouldn't do it on purpose."

"No, I wouldn't. But it's fine. I don't have to know." One of them? Thank goodness I worked at Vatican Radio for those two years. I never imagined that it would help me gain acceptance with spiritualists and exorcists decades and a continent away later.

"I just want to know if Father Gabriel has the information to get rid of the stuff in my apartment."

"He does. And remember that his idea was to gather a group of demonologists of his own around him and that's what he will do. But the idea that they won't let us talk means that he has found something. The information from him goes to Quebec and then to the church here and finally to me but they decide what I know."

I could sense her frustration. "Cassandra, we both know how bureaucratic the church is."

She nodded. "I don't think they are telling him that I want to talk to him..." her voice trailed off. Her face was lined with fatigue.

"I know you have three kids and a husband and a life and that this is exhausting." I thought of all the phone calls unreturned, all the times she had said we would meet and the meeting had been cancelled, all the times of my hearing 'mailbox full.' "If this cannot be done or you can't do any more or you don't want to deal with it, then tell me. Tell me now." I held my breath. Would I be sorry I had dared to ask?

She burst out, "No! I've been beaten up—look, I have new bruises." She held out her arms and I saw them. Why hadn't I seen these before? "I'm not giving up on this! This has become bigger than you but they know that Father

Gabriel went over there *because* of you. Now you are just a small fish in this but it doesn't matter because we are allied together and we are going to finish this no matter what happens." She was adamant.

Of course, I was relieved to know she was still going to help me but 'small fish?' Beaten up again? I was electric with anger. "Where is that cemetery? I'm going there with you. Let me go with you!"

She looked chagrined. "It was in the church. I was trying to do something alone and that was stupid." She took a deep breath. "Don't think I'm going to go through all this and give up!"

I stared into those gold-colored eyes and I believed her. Then I got out my paper with the questions and realized she had anwered most of them. "Is Daddy still there?"

"Yes."

"What does he want?"

"We don't know but once we find out we can take care of everything." She paused as if wondering whether to go on. "Bathemus and your father made a pact a long time ago. But we don't know what the pact was about. Bathemus makes promises but doesn't always keep them. We don't know what it has to do with you. Once we know..."

"Cassandra, what if Daddy was murdered and he wants me to prove it? To find that Ruth person— who is probably dead by now— and prove she killed him?"

She laughed. "Oh, that's only in the movies!"

I stared at her. I hadn't seen her laugh in a long time. Yes, of course. The movies. And whatever insanity is happening to me is *real life*?

She told me her grandmother-in-law was robbed. "They were watching her place. She's a psychic, too, and they saw people coming and going and thought it was a cash business. They hit her in the head with a gun and told her not to move or they would kill her and she was on the floor for four hours! She is in South Miami Hospital."

"That is awful! Is she going to be alright?"

"She is okay but she has broken ribs where they kicked her and a concussion." She started to stand up. "Let's go out together. I'll walk with you to the car," she said. We were outside on the crowded sidewalk. The air was getting cooler, the summer was finally ending. Cassandra suddenly said, "I don't think you get it. You still don't get it. You entered into the pact when you bought the apartment."

"All my friends screamed at me that it was security."

"It's not your fault but it was too easy, wasn't it?"

I nodded. "I never thought the sale would go through. There was always another credit check, another document and I waited for someone to call and say, 'we are so sorry but you don't qualify.'"

"It was the most beautiful apartment you saw, the rent was right and it was too easy from the very first. Too good to be true. Bathemus has been with you for a long time. He was with you and with your father when you were a little girl in the house."

"I wonder about that. I have had the same dream for years. I am little and I come into the house where I grew up and it's dark. It's filled with clouds of gray and black and no one is home and I run from door to door closing doors in the dark and locking them and it's hard to reach the locks but I am very frightened because there is something massive and dangerous outside and I must lock the doors. And then when I get to the last door, the big front door, I push it closed with all my strength and the lock is nearly impossible to turn but I do and I think, it's okay, I'm safe, and suddenly I realize that whatever is most dangerous, most terrible and huge is standing right behind me *in the house*."

"Demons have been with your family for generations."

Crowds were swirling around us. There was noise, shouting, music. She stopped on the sidewalk and said, "I love you," and I repeated it. She kissed me on the cheek and we turned and walked away in different directions.

Chapter Twenty-Nine

That night I dreamed that I reached around to touch a mosquito bite on my leg. The back of my thigh. When my finger touched it torrents of blood poured out. Waves of it, gallons of it. I woke up and thought, okay, only a dream. The laundry room light was on, the apartment in that dim light was silent. No pfffffft noise at the moment. What was that smell? At first it seemed metallic. I got up and walked around the living room. Then I opened the front door. Was it blowing in from outside? What was it? No, it was in the living room. It was the smell of blood. I looked down at my white shorts and thought, the only blood was in my dream. Then the odor changed. It smelled earthy. Was it semen? No, it was a feminine smell. Was that what placenta smelled like? Was there a woman standing before me? I was sure something was standing there and it wasn't the pfffffft character. I sprayed Dune perfume on a clean dishtowel and put it beside my face on the pillow. Finally, I slept again.

On Saturday I had my legs waxed. I turned over on my stomach and Beatriz asked what the mark was. She handed me a mirror to look at a perfectly round black circle about two inches in diameter on the back of my thigh. It resembled a nipple. She took alcohol and tried to wipe it off but I said, "No, I think it's a bruise." She frowned, got out a magnifying glass, peered at it and then nodded. "Eet looks like a neeple."

Cassandra told me on the phone not to go to a doctor until she saw it. "I slept for awhile last night and I think it happened when I was dreaming of a mosquito biting me."

"Do you have any holy water?"

"I have Perrier."

Cassandra said to remind her to bring me holy water. "There is a woman in the apartment and she is angry, vicious. You were attacked. Bathemus is back, too."

"Back?" is all I could manage to say.

"He is in a form that won't frighten you. You won't see anything terrible." I started to speak but she went on, "Be calm. Be strong. God will take care of you." She hung up.

I parked on Majorca and punched in the number. Amazingly, Cassandra answered and said she was on her way to Orlando to pick up some documents. I didn't know if these documents related to my apartment or not. The plan was for her to ask this church in Orlando to speak to the West Palm Beach church and someone there would speak to the Quebec church. She said she must keep pushing to communicate with Father Gabriel; she was going to talk to the Mother Superior about this.

Before she hung up I interjected, "I'm lowering the price and I want to know if it's the right time to have the open house or not. It would be in a few weeks."

"*Why* are you lowering the price?"

"Because I'm desperate to get out of here!"

"What is it now?"

"It was 329 and it's been 327 for the past two weeks but I might lower it to 320."

"No, don't do that! Don't!"

"But everyone says that 327 is a fair price so wouldn't it be sensible to lower it and make it irresistible?"

"Do not change the numbers because you will let Bathemus know that you are desperate to leave and he will enter again."

I sighed. Didn't the entire world know I was desperate to leave?

"Now, listen to me," ordered my psychic acting as real estate consultant for my ghoul-ridden penthouse. "If you ask 327 and they offer 320, you can take it."

I bit my lip. "Okay."

"Everyone is working on this," she said. "Are you going away?"

"Yes, I want to. Is it okay?"

"Definitely. We can work on the house while you're away, while the house is empty."

"I'm leaving next Friday and will be back on Monday."

"Can't talk anymore, traffic is getting nuts. Have a good time. Try to relax."

"Sure thing. And you—get some sleep." She laughed at this ludicrous idea.

She hung up and I snapped my phone closed and reached for the car keys. I never thought Florida real estate could be so complicated.

That Thursday night I felt happy. I would fly into Philadelphia very early Friday morning, see houses, check into a hotel, see more houses on Saturday and Sunday and fly home on Monday. I had picked 27 properties from websites on the internet. The realtor said two were under contract but she had four more possibilities for me. Maybe best of all was that I could sleep for three nights. I couldn't wait to get on the plane.

In the hotel on Friday night, I got ready for bed, to *sleep*. I danced in front of the mirror in my turquoise silk teddy; I gloried in being alone! By Monday I felt recovered, as if I were over an illness. I had slept, I had laughed, I had seen two houses I really liked. I got on the plane for Miami and told myself to sustain all these positive feelings.

I sat at my desk. I'd had my swim, a cheese sandwich and a Diet Coke. I felt good. The yellow living room glowed in the early morning sunlight. The bedroom door was open, the apartment was very still. "Cici." My entire body went cold. "Cici." My name was spoken by someone standing before me. A third time. "Cici." Tears of fear sprang into my eyes. It was flat in tone, not a masculine or a feminine voice but it was very clear.

I stood up, crossed my arms across my chest and rubbed my hands up and down on my bare arms then I grabbed the car keys and my basket bag and left the apartment. I parked on Madeira in the Chihuahua, read every single word of *The New York Times,* and tried to forget what it sounded like.

Chapter Thirty

A psychiatrist might say that Daddy's behavior was learned from his mother and hers from her mother or her father and back it goes. And that his sour view of life was shaped by his mean-spirited, domineering, scheming mother because she overruled his loving, gentle father. Like brown eyes being dominant over blue ones. But blue-eyed babies *are* born to a parent with brown eyes and children don't necessarily take on the stronger parent's world view and behavior patterns. I know that his brother Angus, his mother, his mother's sister all had the same outlook on life and were not kind to their children.

Aunt Frances was highly manipulative and selfish. Conniving was the word Mother used to describe all the McNairs. Small-boned and thin, she had an iron-gray pageboy that never moved, big brown eyes with bags under them, a nicotine-stained, yellow moustache and a hacking cough. She chain-smoked Camels and drank about twenty Coke-Colas a day. That's what we called them. To be fair, they used to come in those little green glass bottles. Aunt Frances always wore a shirtwaist dress with a narrow self-belt and her monogram embroidered in a contrasting color over her small left breast. The shirtwaists were in every color imaginable. She and her daughter, my cousin we called Sister, had lots of clothes. Her shoes were the first shoes I ever knew the name of: spectator pumps. With all the little holes. She always drove a Chevrolet that was some shade of blue. I can remember an Impala, serial Impalas. A turquoise car named after a fleet animal of the Serengetti.

When she came to see Mother, if they sat in the den, she would sit in Daddy's big red leather chair that Mother and I called 'his throne.' No one else would *ever* sit there. Usually they talked in the living room. I know Mother didn't trust her and held back, was careful. The maid would bring her a Coke-Cola or maybe two on a tray with a tall glass of ice cubes. An ashtray would be beside her and she'd be puffing away on her Camels and talking in her deep, husky, Southern-accented voice.

Mother always said she was on 'dope' and had a deal going with the pharmacist at Brent's drugstore. She was a schoolteacher five days a week. On some weekends she would lock herself in her house and get raging drunk and make scary phone calls to me and my sister late on a Saturday night when our parents were away at Mississippi State or Ole Miss football games and Mary the maid was staying with us. She would growl like an animal and spit curse words but we knew who it was. Maybe she was not heartless the way her brothers were but she wasn't balanced or happy either. I am sure she was jealous of Mother and of our living in a big house. Daddy was actually evil-intentioned but if Aunt Frances was, I won't ever know.

David called from London. I told him that all was fine but he'd have to call me on my cell. In five minutes I was in the Chihuahua bringing him an update. I was so pleased he believed me. He said, "Of course, I believe every word. England is full of old houses and the Anglican priest is often invited to bless the house, to rid the building of spirits. It's very typical." He paused. "And don't forget that anyone from the Highlands of Scotland knows about the Brahan Seer." He told me the Scottish clairvoyant was born in the early 17th century. "He's often compared to Nostradamus." David was a reasonable, educated man and hearing him talk about this suffused me with relief.

I heard from both the bakery owner and the little French restaurant manager on the same morning. The same response: no. They couldn't "take on anyone right now" but they would keep my name and phone number.

I thought of my father a lot. Of course. He had moved in and he kept me awake all night. I suddenly saw Daddy as someone only a few years older than I was and wondered, *what* did he have when he died? After his life was over, he had children who feared him, children he'd treated inhumanely, a wife he had treated with malevolence for thirty-three years right up to signing the divorce papers and a second wife who probably married him for his money and then killed him. He thought money was the most important thing, the *only* important thing. For him, for anyone. If they didn't have money, they were worthless.

For me, money is money. It's currency, it's seashells or beads. It's to exchange for what you need—like food—or what you want —like a plane ticket or a book. It's never been anything more to me. A heroine in one of my novels says, "Money is for taxis when it rains and chocolate and new shoes."

Dr. Stirling Sharp McNair was a great success to the outside world. He had everything anyone could ever want but he must have been so miserably unhappy. This made me think of the pact that Cassandra and Father Gabriel kept saying was a big part of this. A deal with the Devil? Wealth and fame in return for your soul? But it couldn't be possible. I couldn't believe this.

People are supposed to live their lives and die. If I could imagine that my father was actually living with me in my condo then everything I ever thought was true had exploded into little pieces.

I went to visit friends in Maine. I began to feel like myself again. That tight feeling in my skin went away. That cringing anticipation of being touched when I closed my eyes at night went away. I was *away* from all the darkness of Coral Gables.

I spent a few days in New York seeing friends before I flew back to Miami. My cell phone rang upon arrival in New York City and this voice said, "This is Richard of Actors Rep. Can you go to an audition tomorrow?"

I said, "Who?" because I had forgotten his name or that I even *had* an agent. Actually I have two—I answered a tiny ad and it was amazingly easy for me to get them a few years ago when detective work was non-existent. I was on *Law & Order* several times. Richard said, "And you speak Italian, right?" and I said, "Oh, sure." "And you have your headshots with you, of course." What? I shrieked mentally. They were at the bottom of some brown box in Coral Gables, I guessed. So I said I didn't and he said you'd better come to the office and pick one up for the auditon and I said "Okay. Where are you?"

He was laughing. I guess it was because everyone must be dying for a call from their agent and I was like a mental patient on the phone. So he told me the address and then I said, "You said it pays 1500 dollars and that's great but I can't remember —how much do you get?" He told me ten percent and hung up laughing. The idea was for me to go to an office on Fifth Avenue after lunch with my friend and do my thing. My cell rang during lunch and it was postponed.

Cancelled, postponed, whatever, I felt elated. *Somebody* wanted me.

The next day on Madison Avenue, five women from New Jersey were very lost and I used my cell phone to find the correct address and explained exactly how to get there. They were *so* grateful and one said, "You are so nice! You didn't have to do this!" Another one gushed, "Are you an actress?"

Of course, I was beyond delighted and I thought, my only audition in two years was cancelled yesterday but I'm being recognized on the streets of Manhattan as an actress!

However, since my name was not in lights quite yet I had to tell them I was only a private detective and all five of them screamed in unison. So I gave them a business card and told them to call me if they got arrested. They were beyond thrilled.

I told this story at dinner that evening and everyone appreciated it with lots of laughing. So Maine and New York revived me. I saw three p.i. colleagues and I probably *do* have detective work in NYC and, of course, there is my acting career.

I looked out the window of the plane as we took off from LaGuardia and thought, life is such a kick!

Chapter Thirty-One

Another sleepless night. I was definitely back.

Dear Cassandra,

First of all, how are you? Sleeping? Once in a while? I really hope so.
I am back from my trip to Maine and New York.
I still haven't heard from Father Gabriel and your phone has been 'message box full' for the last two days. You said that you would work on the apartment while I was away. What stage are we in? Where is Father Gabriel? Is he back? Does he have the information you need?
The realtors want to do an open house. Is this a good idea? Are people still going to go away and have bad dreams? WHAT SHOULD I DO ABOUT THIS?
I left a message for you three days ago saying that I felt good in the apartment and within an hour I saw a big gray form cross the hall from the bathroom into the kitchen. It was pretty scary. About eight feet tall. The shape of a person but not the goat man. I know him. It was somebody else.
I am trying to be creative in dealing with all this. I want to do all I can and if I can help you please tell me how.
I talked to friends about new ideas. One plan was for me to try to line up work in NYC and then fly up for a five-day week and then fly back here. I could stay with one friend after another. I have the most generous friends. The drawback is I can't be here to show people through the apartment! So that plan is out the window.
It's psychologically debilitating to go on not making any money when I want to work, when I have the energy and when I'm good at what I do.
After this trip, I am not allowing any bad thoughts in this apartment. I don't have any complaining conversations on the phone. I am all POSITIVE in thought and word!
PLEASE CALL ME....love, Cici

(Another unsent letter. Maybe I am sorting things out in my mind. Besides, she is psychic and I shouldn't have to tell her anything.)

I had been back from my trip a few days and all seemed pretty much the same as when I'd left. I walked in from Books & Books one evening and felt something in the apartment was very wrong. I was drawn to the outdoor terrace, walked out there, turned on the standing lamp and gasped. All the bookcases were lying on the floor. They were all big, over-my-head tall and it looked like someone in a rage had pushed them over. I ran out of the apartment as if it were on fire. Clutching my car keys, I pounded the elevator button with a clenched fist. In a few minutes I was driving away from Adriano Avenue. I whimpered into the phone, "Cassandra, I'm in the car and this time I don't know if I can go back! Please call me!"

I was shivering with fear as I snapped the phone closed. My watch said half past nine so she was probably on her way to church. I drove for a few minutes taking deep breaths then circled around and parked on the corner of Salzedo and Adriano. The billboard on the empty lot promised luxurious new condos in the coming year. The unobstructed view of my building was of a dark and sinister silhouette.

I called Melinda who told me to concentrate on breathing. She suggested a hotel room at least for tonight, at least until Cassandra could tell me what to do. I told her I didn't dare put it on my credit card but I felt better just hearing Melinda's voice. I called L.A. P.I. who seemed excited about it. "They are showing you in a big way they are there and they are strong. But you are stronger. You are the strong one. You aren't going to be defeated."

He kept talking. That word 'strong' was being madly overused. I didn't feel strong and I didn't feel better but I let him talk. I stretched my legs across the front seat and stared at my condo. It looked like a cardboard cutout of a Spanish castle against the dark sky. It also looked like the setting for a horror movie.

Cassandra did not call me. I played the car radio until midnight and suddenly I felt angry. This apartment was costing me a fortune and I couldn't spend the night there? Was I going to use the ladies room at the Holiday Inn and sleep in the Chihuahua?

I had to go back. I rose in the elevator thinking that no matter what was going on inside that apartment, the space was *mine*. The square footage, those views, the terraces all belonged to me. This was the first property I ever owned. Daddy left land and real estate to my brothers and sister but not to me or

Stirling. Nearly forty years ago my siblings inherited property, had it to sell, and money to buy more. Now, finally, I had managed to buy something. Signing the papers had made me feel like an adult. It was a haunted penthouse but it was *my* haunted penthouse. I turned the key in the lock then pushed the door open and walked in.

The air was strange, not fresh, but I spent a quiet night reading and re-reading the same twelve pages of Benjamin Franklin. I didn't think I'd ever finish that book. Pfffffft.

Even in the bright sunlight of the next morning I resisted going out on the covered terrace but I knew I'd have to if Patrizia or Raquel called. I stood in the doorway. The scene looked ominous. Bookcases toppled, leaning on a fallen one or flat on the floor. Large boxes for the linen and pillows, wardrobes for hanging clothes had been pushed over. I took a deep breath and started to put everything upright and in its proper place again.

Cassandra's take on the bookcases was rage that I had gone on my trip. It was like a child having a tantrum. It waited till I was back to show me how mad it was! "Don't be afraid to stand in the doorway when you come home and say, 'I'm not afraid of you. I'm here.'"

"I'll try," I said.

She said to go ahead with the open house and I started getting ready for it. I put all the boxes in one half of the big covered terrace room so that the living room and bedroom and halls were clear. Then I went to Home Depot and bought lots of geraniums in terracotta pots and put them all over since bookshelves and most surfaces were bare. My idea was to have Anna on the second floor have an open house at the same time. We both used Homes by Owner and we were not in competition since she had a three-bedroom apartment. I wanted people to come in and see hers and then think 'oh, there's a one-bedroom in the penthouse so let's go up and see it for my sister Maria.' It would be great if somebody bought hers and then thought of another family member who could buy mine. These Latin families are very close.

I spent time on the phone begging the management company to fix my part of the roof so that I could close the hole in my living room ceiling. I hung up and swore I would never live in a condo again. They had not yet fixed the roof from Wilma and it had been a *year* since Wilma and they simply couldn't seem to get organized. I really thought it would be easier to live in any banana republic you could name. Rome was a breeze compared to this. A breeze. Rome was run with Swiss efficiency compared to Miami.

I talked to Melinda several times over the next week. "I don't know if Cassandra 'knows' it but I did call the church in Quebec that she mentioned. Well, maybe I did. Once I heard her say the name when she was talking to Father Gabriel. It starts with St. Catherine and the second part I couldn't quite get so I went on the internet and called five churches in Quebec that could have been the one. My French is not good but I asked for a Father Gabriel and thought I might be able to find out if he is a demonologist. No luck." I sighed. "Then again maybe they wouldn't tell me even if they did know him. So I found a list of all the Catholic churches in West Palm Beach. None of them are affiliated with a church in Quebec."

Melinda said, "If there is no way to find his credentials, to check on him, we have to assume he is the real deal. You have to believe him."

"I do. Really I do, Melinda. I simply hate not understanding this. I want to believe what I'm being told because I want to believe he and Cassandra are honest but I can't comprehend what goes on every single night! I keep wanting a rational, earthly explanation."

"That would certainly be easier than the horror story you've been told. Now, think. Is there anyone who would want to gaslight you? You've had quite a past."

I thought for a minute. "There isn't anyone who hates me this much. Besides, how could anyone get into my apartment?"

"If it's the CIA you know they could."

"Well, what about the noises? In my bedroom?" I asked. "The French doors lock from the inside and they were locked the next morning after Bastille Day, are always locked, and no one could have gotten out again without coming through the living room and I was right there. Wide awake and rigid with fear." I thought of the window but it was too small. A dwarf CIA agent?

Melinda said, "I always think of that man in Rome who was rumored to be station chief of the CIA."

I grimaced remembering his obsession with me, his trying to get me fired at la Radio Vaticana when I rejected him. "But he is so old. He would be entirely feeble by now."

"Then there's that maniac Welshman. The MI5 one."

I recalled much charm and how desperately he wanted to marry me. He had been so deliriously enthusiastic about making me his wife that he forgot he already had one.

Melinda asked, "So what do you think?"

"I think I attract atrocious men," I said. "Listen, I keep imagining what my reaction as a detective would be if I came to me and said, I need help."

Melinda said, "Okay. I like that approach. I'm listening."

"I would try to figure out if I—or the client—were the victim of a scam. If somehow Cassandra and Father Gabriel could benefit from all this. How? Let's take fame or reputation. They say I can write a book but don't use their names. Okay. Toss that out. Money. They have never asked me for money. Have they manufactured all these noises and lights so that they can rid my apartment of them, have it sold and then ask for money? Money for the church? A big donation claiming that the place would never have sold without their intervention?"

"It is possible," said Melinda. "But the place has been inspected how many times?"

"About eight, maybe ten. Every inch of it. No weird wires or hidden speakers or microphones. They would have been found." I took a deep breath. "I think of Cassandra saying she saw something terrifying and how we had to rush out. She could just be a pretty good actress. Father Gabriel could have taken a pill to make his face go white and pour with sweat. He could have had it in his pocket and taken it in my apartment knowing the drug would take effect in ten minutes across the street at the Holiday Inn."

"Do you think he did?"

I shook my head. "No, I think he was truly upset. I've discussed all this with L.A. P.I. and he can't figure out a scam either. There has to be something gained." I twisted around to reach the notebook on the back seat. "Melinda, I've made a list. Listen. There are a lot of things that can't be explained." I settled myself in the driver's seat again and started to read. "The noises from my bedroom. Starting with Bastille Day. Crashing. Now the occasional crash. No explanation. The crack noises in the kitchen. I hear them all the time now. Like someone's knees in gym class. The faces in the Beardsley. No explanation. I am not asleep, I am not drunk, I am not insane. The liquid all over my shorts.

Sorry I washed them. No explanation. The strange clear liquid in the shape of a cross on the floor in my bedroom. Could not find a source. Where did it come from? The little turning of the page noise. The pfffffft noise. I've now heard it thousands of times. No explanation. I won't even toss in the definite feeling that someone stands beside the coffee table for hours. The blisters all over my chest from the gold cross. Who on earth is allergic to gold! The incredible heat in my bedroom. The smell of sulphur that I don't even want to think about. No explanation except from Father Gabriel and Cassandra. The portal to hell."

"Oh, oh, oh," cried Melinda. "*Not* the old portal from hell explanation!" We burst out laughing.

"I know, I know, it all sounds ridiculous!" I tossed the notebook into the back again. "But, listen! He said he closed it and it has never been that hot in there again."

"Okay, okay, so you have a portal to hell in your bedroom. Sorry. *Had*."

"What about the black wave like a plane going over me? The huge gray shape about eight feet tall with the big head darting across the hall? I've seen him at least five times. That black nipple mark on the back of my leg? It makes me ill to think of something *dead* biting me. That morning I came back from swimming and heard all these voices on the other side of the bedroom door."

"That gave me chills. The cocktail party for demons."

"But I have to tell you something funny. Yesterday I put a new roll of toilet paper in the guest bathroom, the bathroom outside of my bedroom, and about an hour later I heard this big SNAP! noise and saw the metal holder shoot out of the bathroom and across the hall and into the bedroom."

"Powerful spring?" asked Melinda.

"You don't understand. It wouldn't take a pool shark to see that it wasn't possible for it to do that. With amazing force, even if it zigged and zagged, the trajectory was simply not possible." "What do you mean?"

"I mean Minnesota Fats couldn't've pulled it off. It went right *through* the walls. And through the bedroom door which was closed."

Melinda made an aaaaah! noise. "I don't know if I want to know any more."

I laughed. "Maybe a piece of wood or a wall *is* just a cluster of molecules. That is what L.A. P.I. keeps saying."

"Changing the subject—from something I know nothing about—I have to ask you about the night of the bookcases when you and I talked when you were sitting in the car. I know you called L.A. P.I. and left messages for Cassandra. What I want to know is, why did you go back in there?"

"Melinda, I kept staring at the silhouette like some medieval castle and thinking, I pay a mortgage for that place, a huge mortgage, and I have to go back. I started to think I own this place! It is mine! But it was also like a scene in a movie when the entire audience is screaming 'Don't go in there! Don't open the door! Don't go in there!'"

"So!?" she demanded. "Why did you go back that night?"

I grinned. "I had to go to the bathroom."

We both erupted in giggles and I thought, I am going to get through this. With the help of my friends.

Chapter Thirty-Two

A Chicago couple loved the place. Phone calls by the dozen went back and forth about glass doors being put on the outside terrace and would it be permitted, etcetera. Yes, it would be permitted. Day after day of their calls back and forth for eight days and then they decided to buy another property.

Another couple the same week loved it. Raquel was sure they would make an offer. Calls back and forth and then 'no.'

A call came from a man who saw it months ago, has been out of the country but said he could not stop thinking about it and wanted to see it again.

That night on the way home I went up to seventy miles an hour just to let the Chihuahua run a bit and, as I curved around in the traffic entering the highway from downtown, I realized: I was really tired. It had been almost two months since the Bastille Day noise.

I checked for phone messages as I did every day and heard five of them that were left over a week ago. As if they were snared in the ether and only now had freed themselves. A sixth was only one day old, from Jim. He said he was mailing me a check for his half of the printing expenses. He is a good man, I thought. Then he dropped the bomb that he wanted changes to the brochures. He'd signed off on them only last week and I'd had ten of them done as he had suggested. Now he would email his edits. The booklets were bound and finished and expensive and destined for the wastebasket. I sighed. I supposed this would mean a change to the website. And dealing with Sharon again. I would email him instead of calling him back. I wasn't sure how enthusiastic I could sound on the phone. Making money on this seemed quite far away.

L.A. P.I. called when I was leaving the Biltmore much later than usual. I sat in the parked Chihuahua and listened to him. "They are here with us but most people don't believe it. They can't. It would destroy them. They can't deal with it. When someone says, 'I don't believe it,' they aren't being malicious. They just can't grasp it."

Maybe. My cousin flat-out refused to come to my apartment any night I'd asked him. I kept asking him. He refused to *see* what was happening. No, that wasn't quite correct. He, who would perpetually describe himself as liberal and open-minded, refused to even *look*.

"Both Cassandra and Father Gabriel said that I attracted spirits. I hate that but they said it was a gift."

"It is a gift," came the voice from California. "But lots of people attract spirits. They are involved with traffic and work and hair appointments and aren't open to the idea of it." I heard his desk chair creak. "You are in the world capital of this."

"Then I should be able to get help here of all places."

"Did you know that 90% of voodoo is for good?"

"I don't know any percentages but I do know it's often for healing. They use herbs and ingredients from nature."

"You are in the world capital of voodoo."

"The biologist and I on the beach at Key Biscayne doing turtle duty often find headless animals. I guess they are used for ceremonies. We find the campfires."

John said, "We really know so little." He kept talking. "Meditate," he advised. "What about meditation?"

"I never have, "I said.

"Involve yourself at their level and find out what they want."

"Oh, John, " I sighed in exasperation. "For heaven's sake. Do they even speak English?"

"I don't know. Maybe they speak old English or German. Do you want me to bring someone else in on this?"

I told him I appreciated a second opinion but I felt afraid of having Cassandra drop me, I was afraid of antagonizing her. "She is all I've got!"

He understood. "I won't do anything until I talk to you."

All this as I sat in my wet bikini and pareo in the Chihuahua under a tree in the Biltmore parking lot. I explained that Cassandra says I can't talk on the phone in the apartment but emails are okay. "She is wrong about that, " interjected John. "What is the differeence between hearing on the phone and hearing your thoughts? This is not three dimensions and she is thinking in three dimensions." I heard his desk chair creak again. Detectives always have chairs on castors. It's mandatory.

John said, "I wish I were there to sleep in your bed and to feel the room."

I laughed. "I think I like you too much to let you do it." I looked up at the bright blue sky through the foliage. "John, I don't really mind having spirits around. The little Haitian boy is supposed to be good and won't hurt me. He's my friend but he isn't strong. It's probably okay to live with the spirits. I don't care anymore. They can be in the back seat of the Chihuahua eating popcorn for all I care." I covered my yawn. "But I'd like to be more familiar with something called sleep. And I want this money problem to be solved. I know that no one becomes a detective for the money but I have cases and projects and they proceed right up till the last and then go south."

"It's not a coincidence. Cassandra has told you it's *not*. Things you want are being taken away from you." He seemed to make up his mind. "I'm going to get someone to help you. I'll ask around."

"Oh, no, don't do that! The worst thing would be for anyone you know to have a friend who mentions that someone selling her condo here has these awful problems. That rumor would spread and I would be stuck here forever." We agreed: the world is too small.

Later, when I had given up on Cassandra, she called at 6 o'clock and apologized. " Listen, I'll get straight to the point. I feel pessimistic about the real estate. I know you want to get out of there but it doesn't look good."

"Oh," I said hollowly.

"That property is binded to you. Doing what it wants to do."

I didn't know what binded meant but it sounded rather permanent. "I know I keep saying it but—financially *I have to leave*."

"I understand."

"I'm having the open house on Saturday, the 16th, from two to five in the afternoon. I must keep trying. I must do it."

"I'll have the church make little scented candles for you. Not just to smell good but to keep the bad spirits away."

I'd nearly forgotten to ask her about John. "Listen, I have a very good private detective friend in California who is very sympathetic about what I'm going through. He is more intellectual about it whereas I think you are more spiritual in your approach. He reads, he studies and he said he would use crystals."

"No!"

"He said you would probably kill him for suggesting it."

"Don't you remember when I told you not to stare into the glass or into the mirrors? Crystals will magnify it like a mirror. Crystals are a teleporter and will magnify the spirits." She repeated, "No crystals. We must have an energy to separate you from the apartment. You must be able to walk away. Have you moved the bookcases?"

"Yes, they are upright again. I couldn't have people coming in and seeing them the way they were."

"Do you have any pictures?"

"Yes, I took photographs."

"Can you meet me at Starbucks tomorrow at four? Bring the pictures."

"Okay, but meanwhile, is there anything I can do?"

"No. The noose is getting tighter and the spirit is getting stronger." I felt miserable. She continued, "It doesn't take a rocket scientist to read your last letter and to understand how involved your family is and what it all means."

At that point, I couldn't remember which letter that might be. I kept writing them and not sending them. "What if I tried to communicate? Directly?" I asked.

"I don't think you can break through. This has been with your father such a long time. These other entities."

Entities. I guessed she didn't want to say goat man and the demons. "Is the Haitian boy still with me?"

"Yes. He is fine, he can stay."

We hung up. I drove to Walgreen's to drop off the film.

Watched *Meerkat Manor* and nearly died of sadness when poor little Shakespeare suffered with the hurt leg from the snake bite and was losing weight and getting weak and those big birds were up in the tree watching him limp around. I was nearly crying.

It was a typical night. I sat on the French daybed flipping through *New York* magazine and *Vogue* and *Bazaar* as I watched Jay Leno, then Conan, then an old Bette Davis movie. Something stood beside me, as usual. I wasn't the only one turning pages. Pfffffft.

Chapter Thirty-Three

Two realtors came the next morning. I hurried back from my swim to make sure everything was perfect and it was. Patrizia said that Ivette the realtor had gotten good feedback and had a few questions. We were to talk later.

    I went back to the Biltmore to sit by the pool where I read both yesterday's and today's *New York Times*. Lovely interlude not even knowing where I was. A holiday. All day thinking that I was seeing Cassandra at four o'clock. Photos had been picked up from Walgreen's and I was ready. At two, Cassandra called and cancelled. "I do have news from Father Gabriel and it is good news. He cannot make contact until next week but there is a simple procedure to get you out of this."

"Oh! Finally!"

"He's been fighting a lot of religious politics."

"Wonderful, wonderful!"

She laughed. "Just hold on a little longer!"

    We hung up. She did not call back, we didn't meet and I didn't show her the photographs but it didn't matter. Things were going to be alright.

Bronwen couldn't sleep and called me from Italy. "I'm fine," I told her. I was sitting at my desk so I could say nothing more. "I still sleep with the light on and my talismans around me. Especially the white albacore tuna." We laughed and she told me about Sperlonga and the dinner party that evening. Later, Janice, an old acquaintance, called as we hadn't talked for months. She was full of her divorce news, one injustice after another. I tried to summon sympathy and finally just let her talk.

    I watched *F is for Fake* with Orson Welles and it actually put me to sleep. Pfffffft woke me up. I decided to be uber-brave and turn off the laundry room light in the back of the kitchen and when I did I noticed a light on in my bedroom showing under the closed door.

    Nothing could have persuaded me to open that door so I got down on my hands and knees and saw it shining on the tiles in my bedroom. Finally I went out my front door, across the big terrace to my own terrace expecting to find it bathed in moonlight. No. I peeked in the French doors. The room was dark, nothing I could see was causing that white light under the door. I could even see the crack under the door. No light. Back to the living room. The light was showing until dawn. The second night was Saturday, same thing. I did the same thing. Sunday, the same. Could see nothing as a source of this light but it shone quite clearly on the hall side of the bedroom door. I called out, "I know you're there and I am delighted."

It was Monday, September 11th, 2006. I had been in New York City five years ago on that day.

Bronwen called at noon and said, "Darling, are you alright?" and I hung up and raced out to the Chihuahua, bolted out of the garage and parked off the land. We picked up the conversation in about six minutes flat. "I hung up the phone with you yesterday and thought I'd be absolutely out of my mind with fear. Did it happen again last night?"

"Yes. It came back. I am trying to be calm. Trying to think ...whatever it is...it's positive. I haven't been able to tell Cassandra but L.A. P.I. has been encouraging me to feel that it's good. So I keep making this little speech to the light under the door saying I'm happy it's there."

"My God! You are so terribly brave! I would have run out screaming! Darling, you are so terribly, terribly brave!"

Driving home, I suddenly thought that whatever it was, it was *dead*. Gray and dead. The sun was bright, the sky was azure, the flowers beside the driveway were shocking pink, and my penthouse in Coral Gables was full of death.

That night I turned off all the lights in the apartment at about 10 PM. Immediately, I saw a faint glow which grew bigger and brighter. Within half an hour it was the same light as usual. I went outside around to the French doors and peered in. Again, no source of light in my dark bedroom but I saw a gray form in front of the photographs. Like a person. Not moving. Just standing there. About five feet tall and maybe 100 pounds if it were solid but I could see the table and the TV through it. The door was painted white but it seemed unnaturally white and I wondered if there were another figure standing in front of it. All I could see for sure was the one gray figure.

I stared for about a minute then I went back around to the front door and entered my apartment again. The white light was still under the door so I said, aloud, that I was glad that it was here and was going to keep me safe. It was there all night. I had only one qualm about it: it reminded me of how my father would stand outside my bedroom door in the middle of the night for hours. I could see his feet because the linen closet light would be on behind him. I tried to put this out of my mind.

How could something gray give off a white light? There might have been a second form. There was a fluidity to it, the way one sees reflections of flames on a ceiling or light in a swimming pool. My bedroom was not huge and this figure was standing precisely where I had found the water on two occasions. Exactly where I thought the portal of hell was. It was standing directly in front of the wall of photos of my family—of me, of mother, of grandparents, of family going back to the 1820s. All Mother's family. I was crazy with curiosity. *What* was it? Or *who* was it?

All was gearing up for the open house on Saturday. I borrowed another $2600 on my Visa card which brought the total closer to the limit.

One morning during that same week I came close to being killed. Or in a wheelchair forever if I were lucky. I didn't see the red light on Le Jeune and Miracle Mile—the big intersection—and somehow sped right through it while looking at the next light hundreds of yards away. Reminded me of the awful dream in *From Here to Eternity* in which Prewitt is on a motorcycle and he sees two motorcycles coming at him side by side so he decides to go between the two headlights and it's a car instead.

I thought what it would be like to hurt someone. To ruin their life because of an accident that was my fault. Or to kill myself in an accident, careless and unthinking, in less than a second. And then what would happen to me? Where would I go? What would I be? Would I be one of them, a gray shape of five foot nine standing for hours in the dark beside a closed door? Would I be the shadow seen out of the corner of your eye? That flit of movement when you come into a room just before you turn on the light?

I began to go to bed earlier. Usually I told myself to stay up, to watch a giddy, skimpily-clad movie star tell a silly story to Conan, to watch the film because it will make the night shorter. The hours of darkness would be fewer. I turned on the laundry room light and got onto the daybed and turned out the lamp. The laundry room light had become enough. Then I got up and turned out the laundry room light and stood in the darkened hallway. There it was! Glowing under the door.

Melinda and I talked. "The only thing that has changed in that room since the light has come is that I dug out some more black and white photographs to put up for the open house. It's not a sharp light, it's—"

"The light? You are driving me crazy! *What* are you seeing?"

"It's a gray form in the shape of a small person. It's maybe five feet tall. It's got a head and shoulders and the rest is blurred but it is definitely the shape of a person."

"I can't believe this! I can't believe this!" She was shouting into the phone.

"See what happens when we don't talk for a week?" I laughed.

"So...so...so," she stammered. "It's like this little ghost standing there staring at your pictures?"

"Exactly." I took a deep breath. "And every night I tell it how pleased I am it is there."

"You're losing your mind, you know," Melinda stated quite solemnly.

"Yes, it has occurred to me," I answered. "But look, I've got Daddy, Bathemus, the goat man and who knows who else in the apartment. The Haitian boy means well but is no help at all. If Photo Ghost is not hurting me, not scaring me, I think I'd better make friends with him."

Chapter Thirty-Four

L.A. P.I. called late one afternoon that same week before the open house. I parked in the shade on Alcazar, kicked off my sandals, held a cold Diet Coke to my neck for the coolness. "There is a world of difference between the New Age stuff and what is going on with you there," he said. We agreed that Cassandra was very closely involved with the Catholic Church but we couldn't understand in what capacity. John kept talking. "So many of these movements changed. L.Ron Hubbard was a brilliant man but it's all changed. You have egos involved and what started out as pure is changed." I listened but I knew nothing about this man Hubbard and was not at all interested.

"John, I can't stop thinking about what's in my bedroom. It is so strange to stare at something and not know what it is. Like seeing an animal on safari and not knowing the name or the species. I kept staring and staring, wanting to absorb the details but there are no details. I looked long enough to never doubt what I saw. It is a whitish form."

"Form. Think about it. We live in a three-dimensional world and there are twelve. I keep telling you that a door is not solid. To them, there are no doors. All molecules are moving at different speeds. Nothing matters to them."

I sighed. I wondered, does matter *matter?*

John continued. This wasn't the private detective John but the California John. "If you've ever taken hallucinogenic drugs you know that walls move. I've seen it. The drugs open a portal that shows you that things do move."

I have never taken and have no intention of taking hallucinogenic drugs. I could see toilet paper holders shoot through walls without drugs. The conversation wound back to the form. "Did you confront it?" he demanded.

"No, because it's only about five feet tall and I'm five-nine and I don't want to scare it. I feel protective of anyone shorter."

John actually groaned. "I don't have anything to say to you! Your apartment is crowded with your dead father and a pack of his demonic pals and 'you don't want to scare it.' Hopeless!"

We both started laughing. "I have to hang up and go back to the ghoul-packed penthouse. Raquel is sending people over at three."

"Good luck," said John and then added, "Maybe it's too soon and these aren't the ones. Don't waste your time. You can't leave till the week after Halloween, remember?"

"John!" I said, thoroughly put-out. "If I didn't like you so much I'd tell you to go to hell!"

He was laughing as I hung up.

If Cassandra was right then I should be moving in less than eight weeks. I would go to Philadelphia, find a house, close on the condo, pack up, organize a moving company and *go*. I did a steady breaststroke across the pool, thinking that the Biltmore had given structure to my days and saved me from insanity.

I asked a few people if they wanted to come to the open house to drink wine and lend moral support. We often bumped into each other at Books & Books. Charlie and Faith had plans and Sam really wanted to come but Calista, his father's fifth wife and widow, wanted to have the "scattering" that Saturday around noon. Sam's father died last week and the ashes were to go into the Gulf of Mexico. He said he would try to come at the end of the afternoon but it was quite a long drive and there was always traffic. I suggested they all come on Sunday instead. "I'll fill you in and we can toast the sale."

Yes, of course, I meant that. This open house would be the turning point. I felt as if it had been planned for years. Home Depot was my source of coral and white geraniums. They looked festive, even optimistic. I kept driving back and getting another five or six plants in terra cotta pots.

I looked forward to the darkness. That didn't mean I would sleep but it meant I would see 'him' again. I confirmed that all was in place in the green bedroom. Smoothed the bedspread and straightened a picture or two. I opened the window that abuts the terrace and moved anything on the sill or just inside that might get wet. Now there would not be the glass of the door between me and him when I looked tonight. Just the screen.

IF he comes, IF the white light comes…

Now in daylight, I stood in the doorway of the room talking. "Who are you? Are you someone in Mother's family? Are you the Haitian boy, are you a part of me? What do you want? Are you happy? Are you dead? I think you are. What do you want? Can you help me? I don't think you will hurt me. I'm happy to have you here but show me, show me, show me!" A plume of white smoke appeared against the emerald-green wall. In seconds, it was gone.

I started to leave the room and then noticed dark marks on the floor in the shape of a cross in the same place as the liquid had been. I'd sopped it up ages ago and of course, it was now completely dry. Right where the figure stood last night. I won't say in the shape of a cross; I will say in the center grouting of four tiles and the tiles are square.

Dusk. Wasn't is silly of me to close the door when it can come through? And it was absurd of me to turn on the light when I can't see it in the light. How pathetically three dimensional and primitive I am. I felt sorry for it. I imagined some sense of longing. This figure, translucent, standing alone in a closed, dark room beside a wall of photographs in the middle of the night.

If the white light had been with me in the living room I might have been screaming but on the other side of the door I was not afraid. Even though the door is just moving molecules. L.A. P.I. wrote a long email about molecules and physics and space and I didn't understand a bit of it. How do you get *through* a door? Was it like running so fast, zig and zagging, that the raindrops couldn't hit you?

Bronwen and I talked and she kept saying, "You're so brave!" but I didn't think so. I think I had seen so much, heard so much, felt so much, I was just not frightened by something that I didn't think would hurt me.

Susan, a journalist friend, called. I had made the mistake of confiding in her over lunch in New York the month before. I had known her for twenty years and was surprised that she was not only unsympathetic but that she blamed me. "You are not fighting it! Telling it to go away! Why aren't you acting instead of reacting!" It was an idiotic conversation. Trying to describe something over seven feet tall with an animal head. Telling her that something touched my face, night after night, when I was nearly falling asleep. Telling her that something stood beside me all night long, that doors slammed, that clouds formed in my living room. She was very angry that I was not "being proactive! Stand up to it! Fight it! Picture an angel cutting off its head!"

I said, "But I don't know what it looks like."

She practically screamed at me,"Visualize what it looks like! You're a strong person and you are just reacting and you're not fighting it!" Don't call me strong, I thought. I remembered the scene with all the bookcases turned over, the violent nature of that as she ranted on.

I told her I had faith in Cassandra and was doing all she advised. "But this has gone on for months and months!" she shouted.

I was well aware of how long it had gone on. "Two months." I dated everything from Bastille Day.

Susan seemed so angry at *me*.

So I gave her no details of any new developments but just said that yes, there were still problems in the apartment. I asked about her daughter, we said our goodbyes, and I was sorry she had called.

L.A. P.I's call was welcome after Susan's. His new theory was that it was not me but the apartment and once it was sold I would be free to lead a good life. John also talked about peripherally seeing things. I was very afraid of that. I told him I didn't look in the glass of anything I have framed and barely glanced in the mirror when I brushed my teeth. I used my compact mirror for everything. There were times I had seen something over my shoulder. He had had the same experiences.

I listened to him and thought how tired I was of hearing and seeing things that seemed to have stepped towards me from behind an invisible veil.

Chapter Thirty-Five

I left two phone messages for Cassandra and felt as if I were harassing her. "I know you have an entire life without my insanity and I hate how much I'm leaning on you! Is Father Gabriel back? You told me it was a simple thing to take care of. If it is, then can I do something?" The beep sounded. Time was up.

"Oh, Cassandra, sorry to call again but the open house is my big chance. What can I do so that people do not leave this place and have bad dreams about buying it? Thanks thanks thanks. So much. For everything." Beep.

Cassandra called at close to 9 PM on Thursday and said she was just about to go in with the women. "All okay?" she asked and I told her I hadn't yet checked for the light but it had been there the night before. "Don't confront it and we'll take care of it tonight."

I said, "But I think it's good." She didn't agree or disagree but said, "No candles for the open house. It's been seen as not a good idea but go ahead with the open house." As if I could possibly stop it. Raquel and Patrizia had done publicity, contacted realtors, were keen for me to make a big success of Saturday.

Cassandra told me to call her at half past eleven. "I probably can't pick up but call me." So I did call and left a message.

At midnight, I went outside and looked and saw that the form was definitely smaller. Four feet tall. Was it shrinking like the Wicked Witch of the West? Was it fading like Tinkerbell? Was it suffering in some way? Was it *dying*?

I turned off the laundry room light at half past three and went around and peered in the open window again and there it was. He? Not moving. The head was definitely facing the wall of photos as if standing in an art gallery, entirely absorbed. Appreciative? Curious? It was now the size of a child.

I thought of it later that morning as I swam in the pool. We are alive and in the light and if there are all these undead, unalive people then are we bumping into them and not knowing it? If they are transparent or translucent or invisible, do they take up space? Was it sad to be in that state? Was it what the Catholics called Purgatory? Was Photo Ghost an angel? No— because it frightened me. Not a lot but some and I guessed that an angel would not want to frighten the subject of its protection.

My fizz, my joy, and my emotional nourishment were all from other places. Talked to Deirdre yesterday and she asked how things were going and I confessed, not too well. "Never mind, Poppit. You never give up. You're so good about that. You are like me in that way."

I smiled and said, "No, neither one of us ever gives up and it makes me feel better just to have you remind me. Never surrender!" She laughed her tinkly little laugh in Oxford.

Bronwen was so funny, calling every other day from London or from Italy if she was there. She sustained me. Melinda in New York. John in Los Angeles. David in London. Lucky me.

I played games in my bleaker moments. Usually in the middle of the night. I asked myself if I would rather have breast cancer or live forever with my dead father. Would I rather be married to someone hideous and not worry about money or would I rather be me now: not sleeping, pretending my life is fine, pretending I have free will? Would I rather be in prison for the rest of my life with no chance of parole or would I rather be me right now living with Daddy who is dead and demons who continue to curse me and all my projects?

This or that. All I wanted was to be on even ground with everyone else. I wanted to be rewarded once in a while. I wanted my book to be published. I wanted lots of criminal cases. I wanted the new company to fly. I wanted this place to be sold to someone who would be happy here. I wanted to have a life without demons. A life without Daddy.

If I ever opened the front door at night the chandelier was on. It was supposed to be on all the time. At night I always saw it ablaze and the next morning it would be off. Miguel, the Venezuelan handyman, always came at around noon, dragged his ladder out of the elevator, climbed up, and changed the bulbs. Again. They would be on until about three or four o'clock that afternoon. He couldn't understand it. He must have been buying bulbs by the dozens.

Gabby, the forewoman of the roofers, was German, in her forties, nearly toothless, usually hard-hatted, always no-nonsense, with muscular arms as big as my thighs. If any woman could boss those Latino men around, she was the one. Hard as a hammer. A few weeks ago, I complained to the men about all their lunch papers and soda cans left on my terrace and nothing changed so I had a talk with her. I told her my apartment was for sale and, of course, the ladder and equipment were understandable but possible buyers came nearly every day and I had to have trash picked up. She listened and evidently she decided I was okay. The trash disappeared.

Gabby greeted me in the garage that Friday before the open house and said she'd sweep my terrace for me. Very nice. I thanked her. In the afternoon, I saw her outside on the big common terrace. Her men were on the roof and she was red-faced, beet-red, pouring with sweat looking up, directing them in Spanish. I filled a pitcher with ice water and grabbed a drinking glass and went out. She was surprised and grateful. "I love my job, " she said in her heavy German accent. "I like all the locations but I hate this one. It's taking forever."

I asked, "When are you going to finish?" and she looked disgusted and said, "In about five years."

I blinked in surprise and asked her why.

"There is a bad spirit here. I feel it in the building. I hate it here. This side of the building, up here, fourth floor. Your side. You know we come sometimes in the morning and at 10 o'clock it rains so we must take all the scaffolding down."

I said, "But it doesn't rain at 10 o'clock." "Oh, yes! Here it does!" She was adamant. "On the roof it does!" She waved her arm over my apartment. "Everything bad happens here. There is a bad spirit here. I can feel it."

I told her about the lights in the hall. It worried me to be open with her. I had this feeling that somebody was saying 'what is that awful smell?' and it was *me*.

Miguel put in new bulbs again. The air conditioning man came and said my a.c. was fine for at least six months, maybe a year. It would pass the next inspection for the next potential buyer.

Cassandra and I talked. She said, "We are preparing for the open house. I've been in church and I just walked in the door. I'm heating up soup and changing my clothes to go back."

I wished I had more of an idea of what she does, where she goes, who these women are. And where was Father Gabriel? "If this is so simple according to Father Gabriel then can we do it? On our own? Can I do something?" and she said, "Let's get the open house done first. I'll see you on Sunday."

We hung up.

It was that night, the night before the much-heralded open house, that I saw the light on under the door in my bedroom at about three in the morning. I went out the front door and across the big terrace to my own private one, letting myself in the gate. I was barefoot and the tiles were smooth and cool under my feet. The sky was black velvet and packed with stars. There seemed to be more than I'd ever seen before. Then I stared through the open window. The figure seemed to be fading as I watched. It was now the size of a four-year-old. The glass of the framed photographs reflected the faint glow of this creature in front of them. I stood there for about twenty minutes in the cool night air and inexplicably felt sad. I knew this was the last time I would see him.

Chapter Thirty-Six

All that planning! All those geraniums! The day. The afternoon. The apartment had never looked better. The table on the covered terrace was simply Martha Stewart and every room looked splendid. It was September 16th and I was moving in six or seven weeks. Wasn't I?

I looked at my watch and saw that it was precisely two o'clock. Suddenly the sky turned black and the wind actually made a shrieking noise. Plump raindrops that seemed several ounces each, pounded the roof and the terraces with fury. At three o'clock I poured myself a glass of wine, sank into a wicker chair and stared out at the gale. The heavens had opened in what appeared to be an attempt to drown every living thing in Dade County. Two couples did come, dripping wet, bedraggled but enthusiastic. I gave them towels and wine and the tour and they, all four of them, adored the place. Of course.

One husband said, very quietly, that he and his wife would be making an offer on Monday. I smiled sweetly. Later, I thought, if only the rain had come at three or four then maybe people would have already parked and arrived. Then I could have kept them here, gotten them drunk, been amusing, as Bronwen would say. But if they went home to bad dreams, what difference did anything make?

It was that night that I was up at 1:30 AM getting a drink of water. I was only a few feet away from the bedroom door. The room where all this began. Whatever is in there is hearing me now. I thought of Daddy and spirits watching me take a shower, change my clothes, floss my teeth. I stood in the hall wondering about Photo Ghost when suddenly a white sphere about the size of a tennis ball landed at my feet and disappeared. Seemed like a small warning to not stick around so I raced back to the safety of my sleeping bag on the daybed and actually got in which I never did and then zipped up which was entirely ridiculous on a Miami night. That early morning, before dawn, six more brightly-glowing missiles shot out from the bedroom door towards me, right at my face. These were neon-orange and looked hot as fire. I held my arms up and closed my eyes expecting flames and burns but they somehow disappeared before reaching me.

I didn't bother Cassandra on Sunday. Charlie and Faith arrived and Sam came over and told us about the sprinking of his father's ashes. It was very hot which was typical but the wind kicked up and the widow wasn't crazy about going out on the boat. Calista looked out at the choppy waves then looked down at the box containing her late husband and said, "Oh, let's just throw him in the canal." So that's what they did.

My three guests drank so much wine that everything seemed hilarious. Two glasses were enough for me to forget all about demons and witches and exorcists.

At ten o'clock, after everyone had gone, Cassandra called. "I am with the women so can't talk for long. It's night so don't say anything just listen." I heard the pfffffft noise off to my left. "You must go right now and buy some oil and put it in Tupperware just inside the front door of your apartment."

"I don't have Tupperware. What about a cereal bowl?" I actually had just one, pretty much all else was packed.

"Fine," she said.

"It will be done within the hour," I said and we hung up. I had olive oil but she'd said to buy it so maybe it had to be a brand-new bottle.

I got into the Chihuahua, went to a convenience store and bought some Famous Amos cookies and a small bottle of Crisco. In fifteen minutes, I was putting the bowl of oil beside the front door. Doing it without question.

"It's a little present," I said the following day as we sat down at Starbucks. Cassandra had chosen a table outside. Outside had the heat index of the Congo. "Something little. I made it. I made jewelry for awhile in New York. Took classes from a fabulous man. The buyer at Bendel's wrote me the nicest letter but it didn't go anywhere." I put the amethyst necklace around Cassandra's neck. She was smiling, appreciative. "The ancient Greeks wore this stone as they marched into battle. It's for warriors. For protection."

"I love it," she said. "Thank you."

The styrofoam cup of oil had miraculously not leaked. I'd taped a lid on it. She moved it to her side of the table.

"I have women coming from Virginia to help us."

"Women?"

"They are all psychics. Spiritualists. Seven of them are in a van driving down right now."

I tried to picture a van full of psychics but all I could imagine were those jokes about nuns in a station wagon.

"They are going to separate you from the apartment using holy water. They will light candles and will be able to see what's in your apartment in the form of visions. Oil and water never mix so this should work. They know everything so far. They know all the bad things that have happened, that you worked at the Vatican, that you were a journalist."

"All the way from Virginia?" was all I could manage. *Seven* psychics?

"Yes. They will all be here tomorrow and a few will go back and forth at times but there will always be at least two here working with me." I must have looked a bit stupefied. "They are women like me, with children, with families. They needed special permission from the church to come." She stopped. "The church looks down on them but when they need them they call on them."

"When would they need them?"

"Maybe for an exorcism. But," she added, looking pained, "The church hates needing them."

We talked for longer than we ever had before. She brought up the church in West Palm Beach again. I thought of her saying that the women don't know who the president of the United States is. "It's Catholic?" I said.

"Yes. But there is no name. It's all spiritualists. The women there never cut their hair, they wear it below the waist, usually in a braid. They don't wear clothes from a store, they don't eat processed food. They were given as infants to the church."

What century is this? I wanted to scream.

Cassandra continued. "I only deal with the older women since the ones my age might be confused or even tempted by my ways. They think of me as a prostitute. I wear jewelry, I have children. They don't drive but they have a driver. He is male. They think it is ungodly to drive."

I kept thinking, this is a group of *Catholics?*

She went on. "They resent me and challenge my belief in God. I tell them that I believe that God sent Jesus to suffer and to die for me and for all of us and didn't Jesus have Jezebel weep for him? So it is not for them to judge me because God hasn't judged me yet."

We never ordered anything and everyone left us alone. Of course, we were the only people sitting outside Starbucks in jungle heat. "Bathemus is the Devil but there are troops of devils, legions of them. Like soldiers. Bathemus is what I saw." She looked at me. "You were led here. You were meant to come to

Coral Gables." I let her talk. "What I am doing with the women will take a little over six weeks." I did the math. That would put us in the first week of November. "They are going to work on me, too. You were separated from me. You are like a fighter who has been hit again and again and can barely get up. We can't let you get beaten down this way."

"I can't believe these women are doing this for me. That *you* are doing this for me."

"It's because you are a good person, a beautiful person and you can't go on suffering for the sins of your father. We are trying to show the spirits that you are not like your father. Or your brothers or your sister. We are working very hard but we are not doing animal sacrifices…" She burst out laughing at the look on my face. "The church won't allow it! I won't allow it!"

It flashed through my mind that a year ago I thought life in Coral Gables was rather dull and now I was caught up in the most mysterious, exhilarating adventure of my life, complete with dead roommates and psychics by the vanload.

Cassandra was saying, "As I told you once before—you have to come to terms with him."

Daddy, of course. Always Daddy. "I think I have. He had everything…"

"But don't you see? That is *it*. He made a pact."

We are back to Faust. Could he have been promised everything and gotten it and been disappointed and dissatisfied anyway?

Cassandra moved on. "The Vatican is big and powerful. Father Gabriel found the documents he needed but they are keeping him from me. This is how I know that we are on to something big."

"But why would the Vatican not want to help him, to help you, to help me?" I rolled my eyes.

"Did you see *The Exorcist*?" she asked.

"I've seen part of it on TV."

"Well, after it was all over, it was the person who helped with the exorcism who let out the news. Not the Catholic Church. Then the church had to admit that an exorcism had taken place. That's how it is with me." She frowned. "They don't want to talk about it. And they certainly don't want to talk about spiritualists or psychics working with their priests."

"Cassandra, I know I keep asking the same things but I want to know if the little Haitian boy is still around?"

"He is around but he is not strong so he doesn't matter. That tobacco smell the other night. That's him. When the Haitians call the spirits they puff on tobacco the way the Cubans are always puffing on cigars but they puff to leave the smoke there so that they can find their way home."

I couldn't grasp it. It was another world. I never knew what questions to ask. I said, "People should know that there are demons and spirits."

Even as I said this aloud, I second-guessed myself. If I, a private detective, have five senses and I have seen and heard and felt and smelled something then it *must* exist. How much proof did *I* need?

Cassandra said she had wanted me to write a book about this from the very beginning but reminded me that Father Gabriel was an ordained priest and was part of the church. We talked about changing names, even leaving Miami out of it but then decided that too many changes would erode the veracity of the story.

"When Father Gabriel first said that everything in my life had led me here, I felt very frightened. This led to the research in the Coral Gables Library. And just when I thought there could be no other links between me and my family and this place..." I gazed into space, remembering. "We had a little chihuahua called Tiny. She was bought to be Daddy's dog and to take away his asthma. That's quite a story but I won't go into it now. Tiny was supposed to be with him all the time when he was in the house but she really became my dog and slept with me from the time I was about thirteen or fourteen. That is when I actually began to sleep. When my father would stand on the other side of my bedroom door in the middle of the night with the light showing under the door and his feet making a shadow, Tiny's fur would rise on end. She was so little, but she bared her teeth and was ready to protect me." I took a deep breath. "Tiny lived with my sister for awhile and Tiny died in Coral Gables." Cassandra was astonished; one hand went over her mouth.

I thought of that sweet little dog's body being sent Railway Express to be buried in back of Mother's house at Turtle Creek. Willie, the yard man, was asked to dig the grave under the pine trees. He had only one eye and a weakness for alcohol. Stirling bailed him out of jail in the middle of the night at least a dozen times but, no matter his shortcomings, he was there with

Mother on this sad day. He dug the little grave and buried Tiny and, according to Mother, said a very beautiful prayer.

I wondered at that moment, why I couldn't see that little chihuahua again instead of a disgusting goat. I wished I could choose who of the dead would live with me.

We sat in silence and then Cassandra said, "I want to ask you for a favor."

"Sure. Anything," I said, hoping it was a reasonable request. Would she ask me to bring her the ear of an albino newt only found in Afghanistan at midnight?

"One of the women is coming with her daughter and wants to order a Halloween costume online. Could you do that? And put it on your credit card? It is called Little Dead Riding Hood and, with shipping, it costs $54." She held out a fifty-dollar bill and a five. I objected. "No, let me do this. You are all doing so much for me." Cassandra insisted I take the money and would later tell me that I'd offended her. I would come to know that she had no computer and no credit cards.

It was raining when we got up from the table. I plopped my straw hat on and walked towards the Chihuahua which did not have a ticket. Joyful day.

Two days later I went to Starbucks to meet with Cassandra at three o'clock and she didn't show. I left a message on her cell and then called her other cell and she answered. She said she wanted to come but "the kids are screaming, Larry can't come home, the babysitter is late, and the dog tried to jump off the balcony." Oh, the glamorous life of a stay-at-home psychic.

We talked on the phone. I told her that there had actually been an offer but it was so very low that the realtors had strongly advised against accepting it. But they said that if I did they would drop their entire commission just to give me more money. Patrizia and Raquel. The Argentine women in my life. No one better, no one more kind. I almost cried when I told Cassandra that I felt so many people were on my side. When I was in New York, I did a little job and a private detective, Kevin, insisted on giving me more money than I had earned. When I thought of the women coming all the way from Virginia to help a stranger...

She listened without comment then said, "This deal is going through." I had turned down the deal. Hadn't she heard me? She was talking quickly. "Finally we are doing what I've wanted to do in the beginning which was to focus on *you*. This isn't dark anymore. We are fighting with *good*. These women are like me and we aren't giving up, we are fighting. We are not going with the gloom and doom. No one wants you to live in danger and fear and dread. God is stronger."

"Cassandra, finally you have help. It's been too much for you."

"I believe in what I'm doing. You are a beautiful person or I wouldn't be doing this. Father Gabriel said he was sending someone to help and he did. Seven someones."

I thought, seven women like Cassandra could tip the world off its axis. "I just wrote you a letter and I describe you as relentless."

I could tell this pleased her. She said, "My problem is telling you too much so today is a sign that I am not to see you. I have to go to church tonight; I will try to see you tomorrow."

I left Starbucks and drove home. The deal was unacceptable and had been rejected but she said the deal would go through?

Chapter Thirty-Seven

It was three days later. "Melinda, hi! No, I'm out in the car so we can talk." I clutched the cell phone in one hand, put on my blinker and turned off Ponce de Leon to park on Sidonia. "Oh, how I wish I were there, too!" It had been so good to see her on my trip to New York, to drink wine, to laugh about things. Face to face.

"So what has happened with the oil?" she said.

I moaned. "Cassandra told me there were so many spirits in the oil that they couldn't separate them!"

"What are you going to do? What are all those psychics from Virginia going to do?" she demanded.

"Specific directions. Take notes if you want, if you think you are ever going to have oil and spirit problems."

"Right," was the sarcastic response. I could see Melinda in front of her living room window looking down at Central Park. The leaves would be turning gold and orange by now.

"Yesterday I was told to take a piece of white paper and, as I stood in the front door of my apartment, to fold it in half and then in half again so it's the sign of the cross when opened. Then I had to drag the paper or touch the paper to the walls. Every wall." I laughed. "Sounds simple but it was really hard to get behind the fridge and that would be a great lurking place for demons and there was no way to get within eight feet of the back wall on the covered terrace because of all the boxes piled up."

"Did you confess that you couldn't do it?"

"Absolutely not. I have to do everything to the letter so that I won't ever look back and think if I had done *that* then it would have been over much sooner. So I taped the paper to the end of my yardstick, got on a chair to go behind the Haitian wardrobe, got on top of boxes on my stomach like a turtle and waved the paper around the back wall as high as I could reach. I had to get inside my walk-in closet for those walls but it's basically a slink-in closet with all the boxes. I was supposed to touch as much of every wall as I could."

"That is just not possible even in an entirely empty apartment!"

"I did my best. Then I went into my bedroom and said, 'all lingering spirits go to the paper in the box.' Then I put the paper in a shoebox and put something on it that had come into the apartment when I first arrived."

"What did you pick? An article of clothing?"

"I didn't think of that. My red leather address book was all I was sure about."

"Have you handed it over to Cassandra?"

"Not yet. But while I was sweating and struggling and climbing on chairs, the Virginia psychics were praying. I had to call Cassandra the minute I folded the paper and she had to call the women."

Melinda was amused. "What would psychics do without cell phones?"

We both laughed merrily.

Melinda said, "I feel that this is going to be over soon. Now that you have Cassandra and seven Virginia psychics and Father Gabriel helping you from wherever he is and—"

"Oh, one more," I interrupted. "Did I tell you about ordering the Halloween costume for the daughter of one of the psychics?"

"Yes."

"She decided she wanted to help me! So she is not allowed to celebrate Halloween. Her costume must be returned the way it came which is via FedEx so that the spirits know she is not celebrating Halloween."

Melinda laughed and said, "What is so outrageous about this whole thing is that it is not going on in some little village in Romania in the 1600s but is happening in Coral Gables in the 21st century and we are using cell phones and FedEx." I could hear her smiling. "I know it's been a terrible experience for you but forgive me if I confess that I sort of love it!"

Cassandra called the next afternoon and immediately began to bombard me with a sort of history. "Look, this has been in your family for generations. It was the reason your brother killed himself. It wants you. Body and mind and spirit. It is gaining strength. Do not talk in the apartment about money!"

"I've almost decided on a place in Phila —"

She shouted, "Stop it! When you are using money from the apartment, when it changes hands, it is unclean. We have to find out how to deal with this. How to separate you."

"I thought you were—"

She interrupted. "It already knows where you are going. It knows the house already. It wants to stay with you. We have to separate you." She sighed in exasperation. "Don't talk about money or the new place with realtors anymore."

That *is* a bit tricky, I thought. Trying to sell a condo and buy a house and not allowed to talk to realtors about it.

"Money is evil," she said.

I said, "No, money is not evil. The love of money is evil and I have never been in love with money." Suddenly I had an odd feeling about Cassandra.

"We know that. We know all of that," she said impatiently. "This might require a sacrifice and we'll have to find out what it is." I heard a door slam on her end. "I have to hang up. I'll call you later if I can."

I thought of this sacrifice as I was stripping off my bikini bottoms and stepping in the shower the next morning. Couldn't be money as they know I haven't got any. Surely they wouldn't take the condo sale money? Would it be an arm or a leg? Would they cut it off me and bury it? Would it be disfiguring? Marking my face and making me suffer for the rest of my life? Or would they take my sense of humor? Make me give up writing? I told myself to not be dramatic and reached for the shampoo. At this point, I was a little disappointed that Cassandra had ruled out animal sacrifice. I was thinking of a nice goat.

Chapter Thirty-Eight

I began to make arrangements only on my cell phone. The realtor, the movers, Dean who will deliver boxes and tape. The Chihuahua became my office.

Dear Cassandra and the Virginia Psychics,

    First of all, I feel like crying with gratitude that you would all travel so far and give your precious time and your abilities to help me. Someone you have never met.
    Cassandra has been my guide in this other world I do not understand. She is much more than a trusted friend.
    I know you are aware of what has been happening to me.
    I now hate dusk which used to be a favorite time of day for me. It seems, that with darkness, anything can happen. I still leave one light on all night. Last night I was awake at one o'clock and smelled matches. My first thought was that the building would burn down and I wouldn't have to worry about selling the apartment. I could see nothing amiss but turned on a second light. Sulphur. I walked out to the covered terrace hoping it was coming from outside but no, it was strongest in the living room. It went away in half an hour and was replaced by the smell of tobacco. At first, it was faint and then stronger and stronger. Something was moving around me where I sat reading. I read until dawn.
    I love the day, I love the light because it means I am one day closer to escaping this.
    I thank you for helping me. There are not enough words to thank you. I embrace you and treasure the kind of love you are showing to me—a stranger in unbelievable trouble. Cassandra, all of this goes double for you. You are valiant, resolute, and brave.
    I would always like to be described as relentless. As a detective, I never give up. I keep trying. I keep imagining that there are other ways to find what I need to know. Cassandra, you are relentless.
    So I hope that we can all prove to be relentless in fighting or stopping whatever is out there, whatever has been haunting me for such a long time. I want it banished from my life.
    I send you all love, Cici

I drove to Coconut Grove and put the letter under the locked glass door of Cassandra's office. Even if she didn't come home today or tomorrow, the nanny or someone would find it.

Cassandra called and again talked about finding out what the sacrifice would be. "What sacrifice?" I asked. "I am not making any sacrifice. I feel I've endured enough."

She said, "Oh, you have misunderstood."

"What sacrifice?" I asked. "To cut off my arm?"

"No, of course not. God would not want you to go around with one arm. You have misinterpreted. You won't be asked to burn the money. That would be stupid. At least not all of it. Maybe some of it. It's dirty. It can't go from one thing to another without a break, without it being cleaned."

Burning money? Being cleaned? I would have to call Intriago, my favorite Ecuadorian money-laundering expert. I didn't respond to what she was saying but her words rang in my ears long after we hung up.

There were calls from my accountant in New York, from the mortgage company in Philadelphia, from the Philadelphia realtor. Yes, yes, I told everyone. My condo was sold, the closing date was not fixed at the moment but would be very soon. I would have the 20 percent down payment. I told myself this was no different than kiting a check. I'd never done that before but this was in the same spirit and didn't people kite checks all the time? I made my voice firm. It was like being undercover. On some level, wearing a wire, on the bad guys' turf, I always believed my story and I did the same here. Yes, the condo was sold.

There were calls from the movers. My offer for the house on East Columbia Avenue was being considered. My realtor insisted on it being contingent on the condo sale in Coral Gables. We went back and forth. All calls were relayed to my cell phone so that Daddy and all the horrors in my apartment wouldn't know about it. Or did they already?

Tried calling Cassandra at noon and then at one and finally left a message. She called me at two and said she just woke up and would call me in forty-five minutes so I did errands. Melinda called and wanted to know what was happening. I parked on Minorca and filled her in. I wasn't the only one counting the days. "It's the middle of October. Three weeks to go," she said. We joked about the hall chandelier being off all day and on all night and the demon timer. We laughed, said goodbye, I started the car and I drove home.

    I missed Cassandra's call. There was one of those much-hated Florida leaf-blowers going outside and I guess I never heard the ring. So we didn't talk but her message said, "Ice cream. We looked at it today and selling the place looks favorable. It will happen." I played the message about six times, felt my face actually flush with excitement. Should I dance? Should I scream? I did neither. I grabbed the car keys, jumped into the Chihuahua, parked on Salzedo and called Melinda and then John. As if she could sense my happiness thousands of miles away, Bronwen called from Italy to ask how I was and said, "Oh, darling" about twelve times with relief in her voice.

Chapter Thirty-Nine

The next morning Bernardo called and asked if the condo had been sold. He wanted to come back and see it again. He had really loved it, I thought, but so had about seven hundred and fifty-seven other people. "Yes, come. Any time you want. Today is fine." I added, "I'd like to hear your news, how you are."

There was a loud sigh. "I'll tell you everything." I heard him turning a page. "I am tied up today but—actually not until one so why don't I come now? Is that okay?"

Bernardo arrived in fifteen minutes. When I opened the door to him, I had just taken chocolate chip cookies out of the oven. The scent was all-pervasive. "I think we've come full circle. I didn't plan this. I was nervous and baking always helps and I had these in the oven when you called." He grinned. I told him to walk through, to make himself at home as I put hot cookies on a plate and returned to the living room.

"I really like being here again." He sat down smiling, put one hand on his belly and said, "I really shouldn't," as he reached for a cookie with his other hand.

"The only reason I didn't make an offer all those months ago was because I had just bought the old Spanish house." I remembered his story very well. Bad timing. "It had always been a dream to buy something old and completely renovate it but keep the romantic, original style. I've been saving magazine articles and books on South Florida architecture for years." He shook his head. "From the start, that house was a misery. The elderly man who owned it didn't want to leave. I didn't want to throw him out. I really didn't want to fight about it, didn't want any legal situation." He frowned. "That was just one thing."

Poor Bernardo. The house was a money pit as so many basic repairs had been neglected over the years. "All I want now is to move into a place that is new and fresh, that is ready to live in. I want to unpack and open a bottle of wine and relax."

I really liked him and I fervently hoped Cassandra and Father Gabriel were right and that nothing bad would linger here after I left. I would never want what happened to me to happen to anyone else. But especially not to this man. "I did love this apartment," I said. "I finally had all my stuff out of storage, all my paintings hung, all my books out of boxes. But I just haven't made enough friends here to want to stay. My work was good, then not good. More than ever it's clear to me that I belong in New York City or near it. I am moving to Philadelphia."

I said it definitely. I knew it would happen now. Yes. Halloween was two weeks away and I would be gone the week after.

Bernardo walked through again. I watched him go into my bedroom and stand beside the portal to hell. Closed, I thought. Yes, of course it was. Bernardo stood right where Photo Ghost used to stand. He was smiling, looked very pleased. "This is just perfect for me." He waved his arm. "In the best part of Coral Gables. A penthouse with three terraces." He was exuberant. "It's nearly unbelievable! It's too good to be true!"

I mentally winced. Cassandra had said that. Father Gabriel had said that. I gave him the Homes by Owner business card, a dozen cookies on a paper plate, and we said 'goodbye.'

I was so restless, so nervous that I baked another batch of cookies. Then I went swimming for the second time that day. On my way home, my cell rang. Patrizia's voice told me everything. She was nearly singing. "Bernardo called and offered the full price. I know this is it. I am a little bit psychic and I know!"

I put on the blinker to turn onto Adriano Avenue and laughed and laughed and laughed.

Chapter Forty

In Philadelphia, my offer for the house on East Columbia Avenue was accepted. I was actually afraid to be happy. That night I dreamt I was there, in bed, in the large room with the fireplace at the top of the stairs on the second floor. Someone was quietly coming up those stairs and then I saw, rising step by step, a skeleton with a head of bones. It walked through the dark and stood over me. A tremendous head, not a skull, but much bigger, of shining white curved bones. They were like tusks, vertical and overlapping, and there was no face. It was horror, it was death.

I reached Cassandra the next afternoon and before I could tell her about the dream, she said, "They know where you are going. We have to work harder. We must separate them from the apartment so that they can't follow." That nightmare, the head of bones shining white in the darkness, and her words echoed in my mind for days.

It was October 20th and Bernardo called to tell me he was having problems with paperwork, his house, the bank. It sounded bleak and I felt taut as a wire with tension. Cassandra told me not to worry. "We know that the sale will go through. We have taken care of it."

The day after Halloween I spoke to Gabby and she told me she thought the bad spirit on my terrace was still there. Her stomach hurt and she felt sick when she was near my apartment. I stared into her blue eyes, her face tomato red from the heat, and thought, she really means it.

Every day I swam and doing a slow breaststroke thought, please, please, let Bernardo buy the condo. The closing was November 6th. This time it had to happen. Cassandra said this would go through. All those months ago she told me I would not be leaving until the week after Halloween. And here it *was*.

MONDAY, NOVEMBER 6, 2006

I was on the daybed in the living room, wide awake, and there was my father standing in front of me in the early morning light. He was wearing a gray suit with a white handkerchief in the breast pocket, a white shirt and a silk tie, his glasses; his hair was perfectly combed. He looked directly at me, was staring for quite a long time. Forty seconds at least. I thought, so now you show yourself! Then he became transparent and I could see my desk and the Haitian screen and he was gone. What did he want from me? Was he still angry? Had Cassandra and Father Gabriel returned him and all the spirits to the ground under the building as they promised?

I swam as usual, showered, dressed. Even when I walked into the conference room of the bank I was afraid that they would say Bernardo had had an accident, that the sale was off. But papers were pushed back and forth and signed and it was over. Bernardo was beaming.

The movers came the next day, on Tuesday, and I was in and out of the elevator and then up again to sweep. When I went into the big covered terrace room I saw that there was a square of colored paper right in the middle of the tile floor. Not one piece of furniture, not one box, nothing but that and it was Cassandra's business card. So that card with her name on it was the last thing in my apartment. I left a few pretty blue stones in the living room and in the kitchen and locked the door for the last time.

I said what she told me to say at the bottom of the front steps as the taxi waited for me on that last afternoon. Actually I read the page aloud six times telling the spirits they could not come with me. I was interrupted by a mover asking me to confirm the number of boxes. Then another mover pushed a clipboard at me and asked me to sign at the bottom. I started over each time to make sure I had said the words enough, had made it clear that I was leaving, and leaving them behind. The cab driver leaned against the hood of his cab with folded arms, staring at me and listening. After one complete reading without interruption, I stepped directly from the condo property on Adriano Avenue, with one big step, into the taxi and he slammed the door and we drove away.

I spent the night with my cousin, telling him nothing of what I had endured and the next morning, on Wednesday, I flew to Philadelphia. I spent two nights with new friends and on Friday, November 10th, went downtown for the closing on my house. All the documents were in order, I signed, and became the owner of a three-story, twelve-room house.

I did not pick that room in the dream as my bedroom. When I moved in I worried but I was really alone. I was no longer afraid of the dark though I did lock my bedroom door every night for several years. The absurdity of it made me smile but I turned the key anyway.

I wrote Cassandra and Father Gabriel a long letter. I told them that I felt changed from the person I was when I came to them for help. There were no words for how grateful I felt. In closing, I promised to write a book about Coral Gables.

I still have many unanswered questions. After I touched the walls with the paper Cassandra told me that the women heard all sorts of things—that they were getting information and learning so much. I wanted to know who was talking to them. I wanted to know what they discovered. Cassandra never told me.

I never found out who or what was touching my face and keeping me awake all night. The same hand as the hand in Rome? Who would rattle the paper just as I was falling asleep? Cassandra had said the pfffffft person was Daddy standing over me but there was so much more I wanted to know. I never found out anything about Photo Ghost but yes, she said, the Haitian boy was still with me.

Chapter Forty-One

PHILADELPHIA, NOVEMBER, 2007

I stood in the doorway of my house and gazed down the street. What could be worse than trying to parallel park a hearse? I guess that being in the back of it at the time would be worse. The old guy with the white hair and the piano keys false teeth was at the wheel, having walked around to Eyre Street and gotten the massive, sleek, polished Black Maria out of the big garage in one of the old carriage houses. Burns Funeral Home had the front door open. A man in a black suit a bit shiny from too many trips to the dry cleaners stood there ready to greet another gunshot victim. Philadelphia was past 400 homicides for the year which was the most for any big city in the country. Burns did a good business.

    Death is all around us. You come and you go. There was a sparrow on the roof outside the library on my second floor. Just too far for me to lean out the window with a broom. Poor little thing expired in the spring and was still there wasting away under the onslaught of sun and rain. I thought I understood death. You were born, you gulped for air, you lived, you grew taller, and then your cells began to die and, at some point, you had an accident, became ill or you just wore out. You died and it is hoped that your friends were a bit sad. Your physical self was buried or cremated and you disintegrated like the sparrow.

    Maybe you left behind a book you had written or children or students who admired you or friends who missed you. Maybe a building you designed or an invention or just a phrase that a lover could never get out of his mind. My point is that you were gone from earth. Or rather, you were in it and you became earth from ashes or flesh and bone. Finito. I doubted that you arrived somewhere else.

    Hell was the somewhere else I heard a lot about at the First Presbyterian Church in Jackson, Mississippi. Hell was dwelled upon in Sunday school and made me feel guilty for taking a peppermint from my aunt's candy jar without permission. But I didn't want to believe what all those Presbyterians were saying and, at age sixteen, risked the rage of my father and joined the Episcopal Church. I'd secretly gone to communicants class after school for weeks but when the Sunday came for me to be confirmed and to actually join St. James,

Mother said I had to tell Daddy. I did. He was furious. We walked in the garden and he told me I was going to Hell.

I didn't believe him. I didn't trust him. I didn't like him. I was elated to be escaping the Presbyterians. The Episcopalians were definitely a happier bunch.

There can be hell on earth. Watch the news tonight. But I could not fathom a place with devils, pitchforks and red-hot furnaces. How could anyone over the age of twelve believe in that?

I respect the finality of death. I used to believe in reincarnation but I don't want to be little and helpless one more time so I don't want to imagine returning and starting over. And I certainly don't want to take algebra again.

You will die, I will die. The elements of fire, earth or water will have their way. Our bodies will decompose like a flower that has bloomed or that banana you forgot to eat.

We will no longer walk the earth. We will not have voices. We will not make noise. We will never be seen again. We will disappear from this dimension. I was sure I understood all this.

Until Coral Gables.

THE END

There will be a sequel called
THE DEVIL WENT TO PARIS

A note from the author:

Paris is a splendid city of baguettes, bicycles, scarves and ballet slippers. I am quite happy here. That first year there were dinners, and lunches, my French tutor came twice a week, I went to the Cannes Film Festival, I started working for a radio station, and I finished a novel.

I had a birthday celebration for my hero and patron saint, Casanova, on April 2nd, 2012, never realizing it was Daddy's birthday, too. Masses of people came and my first party here was a tremendous success.

A few days later I opened the box of notes and photographs from Coral Gables to write the book that you have just read. Within hours, my life changed. That night I reached for my big alarm clock. The hands on the face were gone and the numbers looked like teeth. I put it down immediately and tried to go back to sleep.

That was only the beginning.

I called Cassandra who seemed to blame me. She said my father had made a deal and had not paid his debts and now the debts were mine. "You must make sacrifices," she insisted.

The word had a bad ring to it. This time, I turned to the church. Several churches. I contacted the chief exorcist at the Vatican, the top Episcopal bishop in Europe, Anglican and Catholic priests of several nationalities. I sought the experts. I needed help and I wanted the truth. The truth about Daddy and the truth about my brother, Stirling.

As I write this, I am living the story. I escaped *THE DEMONS OF CORAL GABLES* but unfortunately *THE DEVIL WENT TO PARIS* and he is now living with me. When this is over, the book will be finished. I hope, more than anyone, to type "The End" very soon.

www.ingramcontent.com/pod-product-compliance
Lightning Source LLC
Chambersburg PA
CBHW031626160426
43196CB00006B/301